THE STANLEY CUP STORY

OTHER BOOKS
BY HENRY ROXBOROUGH

Canada at the Olympics
One Hundred . . . Not Out

Lord Stanley of Preston, G.C.B.

THE STANLEY CUP STORY

HENRY ROXBOROUGH

McGraw-Hill Ryerson Limited
Toronto Montreal New York London
Sydney Johannesburg Mexico Panama
Düsseldorf Singapore Rio de Janeiro
Kuala Lumpur New Delhi

The Stanley Cup Story

Revised Edition, 1971

ISBN 0-07-092956-4

ACKNOWLEDGMENT

Many hockey authorities have recalled personal incidents or have led me to good sources of information. I am grateful to all of them.

I am especially indebted to Clarence S. Campbell, President of the National Hockey League, and to his staff; to the curator of the Hockey Hall of Fame; to the library staff of the Province of Ontario; to Dr. Stewart Davidson of McGill University; to old friends long associated with early hockey; to "King" Clancy, hockey's outstanding *raconteur;* and to Foster Hewitt, the voice of hockey for nearly fifty years. I have also had access to the scrapbooks of Dr. Jack Gibson of Berlin and Houghton, and to those of Fred "Cyclone" Taylor. Without the advice and co-operation of these gentlemen, this book could not have been written. I am personally indebted to them.

2 3 4 5 6 7 8 9 AP-71 9 8 7 6 5 4 3

PRINTED AND BOUND IN CANADA

FOREWORD

by

Clarence S. Campbell
PRESIDENT, NATIONAL HOCKEY LEAGUE

Walt Whitman, the American poet, wrote: "Think of the past I warn you; in a little while others will find their past in you and in your time."

That thought is especially appropriate for Canadians who love the game of hockey. We are all aware of its present popularity. It is played by over three hundred thousand boys and adults in Canada; attendances at professional hockey games in Montreal, Toronto, and Vancouver reach full capacity; its national interest is so great that the listening and viewing audiences on radio and television exceed those of any other program. Furthermore, hockey is now played and enjoyed in twenty countries, and it has become the principal attraction and the big revenue-producer at all Winter Olympic Games.

Because of the national and world-wide appreciation of ice hockey, it is fitting that Canadians should record for posterity our right to be recognized as the birthplace and traditional home of the World's Fastest Game.

A form of hockey-on-ice was played in the city of Montreal a century and a quarter ago and achieved great popularity in the garrison cities and towns immediately after Confederation. The first formal codification of recognized playing rules occurred in the 1870s, and regularly organized leagues were operating in the 1880s.

Hockey so aroused the interest of Lord Stanley of Preston, Canada's sixth Governor General, that he sponsored a team from the vice-regal staff which was known as the Rideau Hall Rebels, and in 1892 he donated a challenge trophy to be competed for and held by the best hockey team in Canada. The original trophy was the modest rose bowl which today surmounts the much larger and often-remodelled Stanley Cup.

This Stanley Cup has been, throughout the eighty years of its existence, the focal point of major hockey activity and interest throughout all Canada. The desire for hockey supremacy, symbolized by this trophy, has brought challenging teams from such widely dispersed areas as Dawson City in the Northwest and Halifax in the East.

Fortunes have been spent in quest of the Stanley Cup—many times unsuccessfully. The story of the competition constitutes the major portion of the history of the game. The records of the powerful clubs, and the legends concerning the exploits of the hundreds of outstanding players who played for it, testify to the ever-increasing enthusiasm generated by the game throughout four score years. For the participants there were moments of high drama, of exultation in victory and bitter disappointment in defeat. In the unfolding of this story there is adventure, courage, some humour and the constant ebb and flow of hockey fortunes. For the spectators, there has been the ever-increasing interest and excitement known as the Stanley Cup fever.

It is fitting and proper that we should rejoice in our heritage and in the prospect for its improvement. But it also requires that we should recognize and pay tribute to those who, through our century of progress, pioneered and laid the foundations of the heritage we now enjoy.

It is singularly appropriate that Henry Roxborough has come forward at this time—through the medium of his book *The Stanley Cup Story*—to chronicle the activities of the "Greats" of Hockey. He has done it in a scholarly, interesting and thoroughly entertaining manner. In so doing, he has preserved for future authors, historians and posterity many of the records, much of the lore and the legend associated with the game of Hockey.

It is a book which should be read by all hockey enthusiasts—players and spectators alike.

PREFACE

The Stanley Cup Story will not be the last word to be written about the Stanley Cup; it was certainly not the first. Since the Cup presentation eighty years ago, through word of mouth, press, radio and television, a constant flow of fact and fantasy has been channelled into the eyes and ears of succeeding generations.

Through eight decades, the Stanley Cup has been the axis around which most of hockey's history has revolved. First as an amateur symbol of hockey supremacy, and later as the sign of professional superiority, the sterling silver bowl has lured great teams, starry-eyed players and superb recorders.

The research and preparation involved in this book has been fairly thorough, but it has only tapped the wealth of possible material. Others have prospected in the same fields, and I have gleaned much from their labours.

The Stanley Cup Story is a never-ending story, and the final chapter will not be written—as long as the love of sport and the thrills of competition are enjoyed.

CHAPTER

CONTENTS

Foreword by Clarence S. Campbell v

Preface vii

1 In the Beginning 1

2 I Am Willing to Give a Cup 9

3 Early Fan Fever 18

4 Ottawa Silver Seven 26

5 Trying Times for Trustees 36

6 Money Talks 45

7 Stanley Cup Goes West 53

8 The American Invasion 61

9 Stanley Cup High-Jinks 72

10 Series to Remember 81

11 Individual Histrionics 91

12 Some Were Super-Stars 100

13 Toronto Maple Leafs 116

14 Montreal Canadiens 129

15 Early American Clubs 138

16 The Expansion Years 155

17 In the Days of the "King" 165

18 Hello Canada and Hockey Fans! 176

19 The Road Ahead 183

20 Hockey Hall of Fame 190

21 Records 192

ILLUSTRATIONS

	FACING PAGE
Lord Stanley of Preston, G.C.B.	*Frontispiece*
Victoria Rink, Montreal	24
Montreal Victorias	25
Montreal Shamrocks	25
Ottawa's famous Silver Seven team	56
Some were super-stars	57
New York Americans	88
Manager Conn Smythe discusses strategy	88
Stanley Cup action, 1941 Boston-Toronto series	88
Art Ross and Lester Patrick attend Hockey Hall of Fame opening	89
"Hap" Day—Coach of five Stanley Cup champions	89
Montreal Canadiens' famous Punch Line	89
"Gordie" Howe and Johnny Bower	89
Honoured Members, Hockey Hall of Fame opening day	120
Jean Beliveau, captain Montreal Canadiens, displays the Stanley Cup	121
"Cyclone" Taylor and Foster Hewitt at Hockey Hall of Fame sod-turning ceremony	152
Clarence S. Campbell presents Hall of Fame plaque to "Jack" Adams	152
First Night—Maple Leaf Gardens—1945	153
Montreal Canadiens, Stanley Cup Champions, 1970/71	153

CHAPTER ONE IN THE BEGINNING

Today, with ice hockey a truly international game, fans are developing a world-wide interest in its origin. It is conjectured that the real ancestors of hockey might have been either Greeks, Hollanders, Englishmen, Scandinavians or early Americans. Therefore, while records are available, Canadians should stake their claim to be the founding fathers of the world's fastest game. Unless we do so, our priority might be challenged by foreign pretenders.

In the beginning, let us admit that few games are entirely modern in origin. For instance, three thousand years ago, Egyptians caught and threw a ball and practised something with the features of baseball; they also, as disclosed in tombs, enjoyed shooting an ivory ball with a long cue. Twenty-seven hundred years ago, Greeks ran races, threw javelins, leaped with poles, boxed and wrestled. Around the same era, barefooted Spartans kicked an inflated sheep's bladder in football fashion. Early Phoenicians raced sailing-ships, while Romans matched galloping horses.

Ancient shepherds have been credited with swinging their crooks and banging stones over Palestinian hills and giving birth to a species of golf. Many centuries ago, North American Indians played two-handed crosse and tossed a leather ball filled with horse-hair across a plain which permitted goal-posts five hundred yards apart. Perhaps basketball, which was planned by

Dr. George Naismith, a Canadian, is the only true original of a modern game. Even basketball is seventy years old.

What about hockey? Is it a completely Canadian product? Or is it a melding of sports that originated with ancient peoples?

When we dig into sport's catacombs, we soon learn that hockey has many ancestors. In 478 B.C., the Greek warrior Themistocles built a wall in Athens. At its base clearly portrayed was a sculptured scene showing two athletes holding clubs curved at one end with sticks crossed above a ball as though engaged in a face-off. The sticks resembled those later used in field hockey. So it is probable that some form of the game was played twenty-five hundred years ago.

However, the lads who played in the Themistocles League were not the founders of ice hockey, since the ancients performed in their bare feet. Indeed, it wasn't until A.D. 1000 that European youths living in a colder clime tied sharpened bones to their boots with leather thongs and went scooting across fjords, lochs or fens. A writer in A.D. 1190 described the skaters in picturesque terms:

When the great fenne or moore (which watereth the walls of the citie on the North Side) is frozen, many young men play on the yce—some, striding as wide as they may do, slide swiftly; asome tye bones to their feet and under their heeles, and shoving themselves with a little picked staffe, do slide as swiftlie as a birde flyeth in the air or an arrow out of a cross-bow.

Ever since, for nearly a thousand years, skating has been a popular pastime. But who was the inventor who first combined skating with hockey-in-the-field, and thus founded a new game? This is the point where historians differ.

Hollanders may contend they founded ice-hockey. Around the year 1700, a noted Amsterdam artist painted a portrait of a tall, strong Viking type wearing a woollen, visored cap, with his body swathed in a heavy cloak above the knickers which extended below his knees. He was standing on bone skates which had a curled nose, and the skates were fastened to boots by strips of leather. His leather-encased arms and hands rested on a wooden stick which had a cloth-covered handle and a tapered blade. So perhaps Hollanders were familiar with a game played on ice by men who wore skates and carried clubs. Or, again, the model may only have posed, for other Dutch painters of that era often portrayed flocks of skaters on large ponds with not even one urchin playing shinny.

It is certain that in the eighteenth century, in England, Ireland and Scotland, there were games termed bandy, shinny or hurtling which were early forms of field-hockey. It is not improbable that these mainly summer games were diverted from grass to ice during winters. Indeed, a London writer in 1862 confirmed this had happened, for he condemned hockey on ice in this fashion:

> The various games that are played on the ice are most unworthy of a true skater's attention, and have the further drawback of seriously annoying those who use the skate for its legitimate purposes.
>
> Hockey, for example, ought to be sternly forbidden, as it is not only annoying, but dangerous. In its right place, hockey is a noble game, and deserving of every encouragement; but on the ice it is in its wrong place and should be prohibited. Any weak spot on the ice is sure to give way if the ball should happen to pass near it or over it; for the concourse of fifty or a hundred persons all converging on the same point is a test which no ice, save the strongest, is able to bear. Even the "express trains," so popular on the Serpentine on a frosty night, are not nearly so dangerous as hockey, because they distribute the weight over a large surface with tolerable equality.
>
> Moreover, when a mass of human beings precipitates itself recklessly in any direction, accidents are certain to follow; and if the ice should give way, a fatal result is a natural consequence. The unfortunate man, whose sad death I recall, was knocked down during one of those hockey matches.
>
> The game, moreover, is by no means what it ought to be, as it is impossible to enforce the rules in such a miscellaneous assembly. No one keeps to any particular side or aims at any particular goal; and any one who happens to have a stick hits the ball in any way that seems easiest.
>
> It is more than annoying to have the graceful evolutions of a charming quadrille broken up by the interruptions of a disorderly mob, armed with sticks and charging through the circle of skaters and spectators to the imminent danger of all. I should be truly glad to see the police interfere whenever hockey is commenced.

To summarize, it appears that the Greeks had, in 500 B.C., a game that required a face-off and a hockey stick. During the eleventh century, skating on ice was popular in Scandinavian countries and in England. More than three centuries ago, Dutch artists were portraying uniformed youths with skates and sticks. A century ago, hockey on ice was upsetting London figure-skaters both mentally and bodily.

On occasion some of the early claims for hockey are facetious. An Irishman once professed:

I am sure the game of hockey was invented in Ireland; but after they had played it a few years, they did away with the puck and used only the sticks. Later, some of the descendants of the early Irish players came to Canada. There they revived the game, but for the sake of making it a milder sport, they brought the puck back into prominence.

However, there is enough truth in the early associations of ice and hockey to make Canadians ask whether we were discoverers or copiers. What then can be said in defence of our often-quoted belief that ice hockey is a Canadian production?

Let us frankly recognize that the tools of hockey—the sticks, the skates, the ball-type puck and certainly ice itself—didn't originate in Canada. However, there is ample justification for our boast that hockey on ice, as it is now generally played is an original Canadian creation.

The Canadian Amateur Hockey Association once appointed a committee to determine when hockey began in this country. They reported that Mr. Horsey, an early Kingston historian, had written in his diary:

In 1847, most of the soldier boys were quite at home on skates. They could cut the figure eight and other fancy figures, but shinny was their first delight. Groups would be placed at the Shoal Tower and Point Frederick, and fifty or more players on each side would be in the game.

The committee also reported:

The first hockey was played by Royal Canadian Rifles, an Imperial unit, stationed at Halifax and Kingston in 1855. It is quite possible that English troops stationed in Kingston from 1783 to 1855 played hockey, as there is evidence in old papers, letters and legends that the men and officers located with the Imperial troops were proficient skaters and participated in field hockey. The playing of hockey games in Kingston as early as 1855 is certain.

There is definite evidence that hockey in Canada had still earlier origins, and in other places. It may be only a coincidence and nothing more that hockey had a beginning in 1837. For in 1837 there were rebellions in Upper and Lower Canada.

Mr. John T. Knox, when he was eighty-four years old in 1941, gave some interesting hockey lore to a *Montreal Star* correspondent. Mr. Knox, a charming and reliable gentleman whom I also had the pleasure of knowing, related that, from records passed on to him by his father, Michael Knox, he was certain the first game of hurtling or hockey in Canada had been played in Montreal on the last Saturday in February of 1837, between the Dorchester Club and the Uptown Club. After Dorchester scored the first goal, the crowd flocked onto the ice. When they refused to leave, Dorchester claimed the championship from Montreal.

Mr. Knox also recalled from the records of his father, who was one of the participants, that on the second Saturday in March of 1837, another match was played on a Montreal rink which was situated just below the intersection of Bleury and Dorchester Streets. The defenders were from the Dorchester Club, while the challengers were mostly French Canadian youths playing under the name Canadians. As the date of the game approached, there was considerable excitement. The match was talked about in every home and schoolyard, and the military garrison on St. Helen's Island was invited to attend.

It was agreed that play was to start at 2:00 P.M. on Saturday, with the understanding that the first team to score three goals would become the winner. Another agreement was that no matter what the score, the game would end at 4:00 P.M. The clubs decided that each side would ice eight players—goal, point, cover-point, centre, rover, home, right side and left side. Michael Knox himself was Dorchester's left side. Thus there is historical evidence that—although 1837 is recognized as the year of the uprisings—it is famous as the year when ice-hockey as a team sport was first introduced in Canada.

In the decades following the Montreal beginnings, and through 1867, the year of Confederation, into the 1870's, hockey was growing up on ponds, rivers, lakes and even indoor rinks. J. J. Rowan, in his book *The Emigrant and Sportsman in Canada* (1876), had this to say about skating and hockey:

Canada is *par excellence* the country for the skater. Every Canadian can skate more or less. The rink is the great winter amusement and is to be found in every city. In these enormous wooden tents, well-lighted by day and by night, and fitted with every convenience for the skater, the bands play and young people meet to skate, to dance on skates and to amuse themselves. Many of the girls are good and graceful skaters.

The boy of the country however is addicted to hockey and is, I am compelled to say, a nuisance to the non-hockey playing public. Happily, he is excluded from the rink. His chief victim in the open is a timid elderly skater or a beginner; and such a one on glare ice, surrounded by his tormentors, is indeed a pitiable object. I see him now. He has in an unlucky moment shuffled into the centre of the hockey strife; or more probably, with lightning-like rapidity it has closed around him. There he stands, beating the air with his hands, his body bent to an angle of forty-five degrees with the ice, with no power in his legs nor bones in his ankles, while the hockey urchins swoop and dart around him like so many martins round a sparrow hawk.

Early hockey, which was mainly glorified shinny, was thus often a sin against society. At the time, rules varied in different areas; the number of players on each side was indefinite; uniforms were whatever sweaters and other garments the players happened to be wearing that day; the puck was usually a rubber ball which bounced crazily, especially indoors on an enclosed rink.

Like the world before the creation, hockey in the '60s and early '70s was without form and void, and this discouraged the extension of the game. Then to bring uniformity into the game, so a Halifax club might play a Montreal club, certain Montreal sportsmen, mainly associates at McGill University, drafted some rules. They limited the number of players to nine a side, and proposed a flat and round wooden puck instead of a solid ball. They defined the size of goals, suggested uniforms, gave names to positions and organized leagues. These ideas and customs were not entirely original with the Montreal sponsors, however, for some had earlier been tried in Halifax, where they were known as the Halifax rules. It is also of some significance that many sticks used in Montreal games had been imported from Halifax.

It seems evident that while Kingston and Halifax shared in Canada's early hockey planning, most of it must be attributed to Montreal. Certainly many hockey missionaries graduated from McGill and carried the so-called McGill Rules into new areas.

Thus ice hockey, as distinguished from forms of field-hockey on ice, is definitely Canadian in origin and design. With the advent of common rules, the game spread rapidly to all parts of settled Canada. Leagues were soon organized in Montreal, Ottawa and Kingston. Small boys were playing hockey on the streets; adults were forming teams; Indians on reserves were busily employed making sticks; and spectators crowded rinks to watch contests. In 1883, hockey was sufficiently popular for the Montreal Ice Carnival Committee to conduct a world-championship tournament and to award the winning club a trophy valued at $750. It was appropriately won by a McGill University team which topped five others.

Kingston, too, was an early hockey "hot spot," if the term can be applied to a game played on ice in zero weather. Captain James T. Sutherland, a pioneer Kingston player and hockey executive, recalled that some of the matches in the 1880s were played on a rink just off Brock Street near the Martello Tower. The rink had one peculiar feature that set it apart from all others. Smack in its centre was a sizeable band-stand. This obstacle invited the most surprising plays, for the defence never knew whether the attack would come from the left or the right. All they were sure of was that there would be no attack straight down the ice. Whether the band played while the sorties ensued, Captain Sutherland never revealed, but surely a rendering of "Marching Through Georgia" or "John Brown's Body" would have affected the tempo of the play.

Later, the owner of the rink, Captain Dix, either because his musicians failed to dodge high shots or because the players were tripped up by the wooden stand, removed his hockey rink to a more suitable site. The new rink was lighted by two large arc lights, high up on telegraph poles and suspended above the goals.

Here, in 1886, the first organized league played its final games, while the spectators perched on snowbanks above and around the eighteen-inch boarding. Captain Sutherland attended these matches and recalled that the referee frequently stopped play to permit a goalkeeper to recover his spring-skates when, by shots from the Queen's players, his skates had been knocked from his boots and made to scoot across the ice.

From the town of Kingston, the tide of hockey swept through much of Ontario. In 1890, at a public meeting held in Toronto's Queens Hotel, representatives from the following groups attended: Osgoode Hall, Queen's University, Royal Military College, Athletic (Lacrosse) Club, C Company Royal School of Infantry, Bowmanville, together with St. George's Club, Victoria Club and Granite Clubs of Toronto. They met and talked, but they also formed the Ontario Hockey Association, the first of its kind and size.

One of the prime movers in the founding of the O.H.A. was the Honourable Arthur Stanley, son of the Governor General of Canada who, three years later, gave his name and prestige to hockey's most important symbol: The Stanley Cup.

CHAPTER TWO I AM WILLING TO GIVE A CUP

Canada has been fortunate that her long line of Governors General has included many gentlemen keenly interested in sport. The Marquis of Lansdowne encouraged rifle-shooting. The Earl of Minto donated the Minto Cup for national lacrosse competition. Earl Grey perpetuated his name by offering the Grey Cup for supremacy in rugby football. Lady Byng is remembered for the trophy bearing her name which annually honours the player in the National Hockey League who best combines skill and sportsmanship. Viscount Willingdon's name is associated with team supremacy in golf.

While most Governors General have paid tribute to the influence of sport in Canada's national life, none has been more richly remembered through the years than Lord Stanley of Preston, the sixth in the long vice-regal line. His Excellency's complete title was: Right Honourable Sir Frederick Arthur Stanley, Baron Stanley of Preston, in the County of Lancaster, in the Peerage of Great Britain, Knight Grand Cross of the Most Honourable Order of the Bath. All those distinctions and titles are just the long form for Lord Stanley. Although eminently fitted from birth and by education for his high office, his name has come down through more than seventy years because he was interested enough in hockey to spend ten guineas for a silver bowl.

Prior to his arrival in Canada in 1888, Lord Stanley was

famous as an English sportsman, with a voice of authority in horse-racing, cricket and soccer. But hockey played on ice was a new sport in his life and, at Ottawa, he soon became a loyal fan of the big Ottawa club. Even more, the Governor General sponsored the erection of a large outdoor rink at Rideau Hall and gave his blessing to the formation of a Government House hockey team.

That team was much more than a social group, banded together for tea and crumpets with hockey as a diversion. Instead, the team members were a hardy, well-conditioned lot who wore bright red jerseys and called themselves the Rideau Rebels. At first they preferred pick-up games on their home ice, but they were soon sufficiently skilled to play on any rink.

In late March of 1890, the Government House team played a match of major importance on Dey's Rink against a team of Parliamentarians. The members group included Senator Power and Barron, Fisher, Ward, Creighton and St. D. Lemoine, all Members of Parliament. The Government House sextette comprised Hon. Algernon Stanley and Hon. Arthur Stanley (both sons of the Governor General), Captain McMahon and Messrs. Hawker, Scott and Wingfield (of Coldstream Guards).

The red-shirted Rideau Rebels outlasted and out-scored their opponents by three goals to one. Then inspired by their own performances, the two teams grew very ambitious and formed a composite team for the purpose of invading Toronto.

Hockey had long been popular in Ottawa, Montreal, Quebec, Halifax and Kingston, but its arrival in Toronto was dilatory. In 1887, however, when Mr. T. L. Patton, who had been a capable Montreal goalkeeper, visited his Toronto friend Mr. Massey, he talked so enthusiastically about hockey's possibilities that the host telegraphed to Montreal for eighteen sticks, a puck and a set of rules. When the equipment arrived at a Toronto rink, ten good skaters were invited to take a crack at the new pastime. Instantly the game found acceptance, and before long members of St. George's, Granites and Toronto Athletic Club were seriously practising on indoor rinks. So in February of 1890, the Toronto teams were prepared to accept a challenge from the Ottawa Rebels.

Apparently the first game of the invasion, which was played

on the Granite Club Rink on a Saturday afternoon, was not exactly a sportsman's delight. An observer later lamented:

It is greatly to be regretted that, in a match between amateur teams, some players should so forget themselves before such a number of spectators, a good proportion of whom were ladies, as to indulge in fisticuffs. The action of some of the spectators in rushing onto the ice is also to be condemned, as they had nothing whatever to do in the case.

Despite the rough going, the Rideau Hall players were able to take good care of themselves. With Hon. Arthur Stanley at cover-point, and P. D. Ross (later a Stanley Cup trustee) starring on the forward line, they defeated Toronto Granites by five goals to four.

In the evening, the invading Rebels were probably weary as a result of their afternoon revolution, for they were beaten by the nattily attired members of St. George's team, who wore new dark blue-and-white uniforms. The style of play in vogue in the late 1880s is indicated by a portion of a newspaper account:

Kearns, St. Georges, secured the puck from the face-off and made a pretty rush up the north side, and playing the puck across the rink, McGee secured it and made a hot shot on goal, which however was skilfully stopped by Ward, who by a beautiful lift sent the puck humming down into St. George's territory. Ross and Stanley followed it up, and from a scrimmage Ross made a straight shot on the St. George's flags, which was stopped by Hurst.

While the Ottawa team lost the game, they had apparently won the hearts of Toronto fans, for: "When the visitors scored their only goal, the applause was deafening with the fair sex enthusiastically joining in."

The Rebels not only played games away from home, they also proved to be very good hosts. Late in February of 1890, a team from Lindsay, Ontario, visited Ottawa and played some interesting games on the outdoor Rideau Hall Rink. The home team was ungracious enough to defeat their guests by scores of two goals to one in both the afternoon and evening games. But the hospitality was lavish and generous. The visitors were entertained by Lord Stanley at a Government House lunch. Between games there was a program of tobogganing, skating and dancing. Lord Stanley personally attended the evening game and arranged for supper at the Rideau Club.

The Stanleys of Ottawa did much more for hockey than play and watch, for they promoted hockey. In the autumn of 1890, Hon. Arthur Stanley, the Governor General's son, became so enthusiastic over hockey's possibilities that he discussed its growth with J. A. Barron of Stratford (who later became a judge) and Harry Ward, Member of Parliament for East Durham. The three of them arranged for a conference in Toronto, and the present Ontario Hockey Association, now seventy years old, was founded.

It is interesting to note that the younger Stanleys were so keen about ice hockey, that, in 1895, after Lord Stanley's term had expired and the family had returned to England, they introduced the Canadian brand of ice hockey to Britons. One day, on the frozen lake in the grounds of Buckingham Palace, the five Stanley brothers, plus Lord Annally, played the Palace team. The latter group included the Prince of Wales (later King Edward the Seventh) and the Duke of York (who became King George the Fifth).

Lord Stanley, in his more elderly way, was as enthusiastic about hockey as his sons. He was a devoted fan of the Ottawa club, and he thought no team in the world could beat them. Therefore more as a close friend than as a distant patron he decided something should be done to commemorate the greatness of his favourite club and sport.

So, on March 18, 1892, at a banquet given to the Ottawa Club, Lord Kilcoursie responded to the toast of the Governor General. Lord Kilcoursie was more than an aide to His Excellency, for he was also a forward on the Rideau Rebels team that had earlier lost the hockey championship of Canada to the Ottawa team.

In his reply to the toast, Kilcoursie read a personal letter from the Governor General. It stated:

I have for some time been thinking it would be a good thing if there were a challenge cup, which could be held from year to year by the leading hockey club in Canada. There does not appear to be any outward or visible sign of the championship at present, and considering the interest that hockey matches now elicit, and the importance of having the games fairly played under generally recognized rules, I am willing to give a cup that shall be annually held by the winning club.

I am not quite certain that the present regulations governing the arrangement of matches gives entire satisfaction. It would be worth considering whether they could not be arranged so that each team would play once at home and once at the place where their opponents hail from.

Naturally the proposal was hailed with cheers, and the good Lord soon arranged for Captain Colville, another aide, then in England, to expend ten guineas on a gold-lined silver bowl, standing on an ebony base. The first Stanley Cup trustees were two Ottawa sportsmen, Sheriff Sweetland and Mr. P. D. Ross. The latter, who was an excellent athlete in his youth and a noted newspaper publisher later, remained a trustee for fifty-six years until his death at the age of ninety-one.

Before leaving for England, Lord Stanley had proposed some conditions to the Cup trustees. His Excellency suggested:

(1) The winners shall give bond for the return of the cup in good order, when required by the trustees for the purpose of being handed over to any other team that may in turn win.

(2) Each winning team shall have at their own charge, engraved on a silver ring fitted on the cup for that purpose, the name of the team and the year won.

(3) The cup shall remain a challenge cup, and should not become the property of any team, even if won more than once.

(4) In case of any doubt as to the title of any club to claim the position of champions, the cup shall be held or awarded by the trustees as they may think right, their decision being absolute.

(5) Shall either trustee resign or otherwise drop out, the remaining trustee should nominate a substitute.

Lord Stanley also asked the trustees to suggest some means of making the cup open to all, rather than to any one association.

The trophy, which was promptly and appropriately named The Lord Stanley Cup, was available for presentation during the 1892/93 winter. It had been the fond hope of its donor that the first holder of the sterling silver bowl would be his favourite Ottawa Club. However this wish was not to be fulfilled.

The disappointment was triggered by the loose terms of the presentation. It was Lord Stanley's intention that the trophy would be held by "the leading hockey club in Canada," and in His Excellency's mind, its first holder was to be Ottawa. The Ottawa club had been 1892/93 champions, and they believed they had inherited the honour of becoming the defenders.

However the trustees decided that no one, not even the Ottawa team had been given squatter's rights, so they ordered the Capital club to play Toronto's Osgoode Hall team for the privilege of becoming the first to have its name engraved on the trophy. Indeed, the trustees were even harsher, for they instructed the Ottawa club to play that game in Toronto.

The Ottawa officers replied that they would not have any of that nonsense. They were not going to travel to Toronto to play anyone for the right to become the first Stanley Cup holder. Indeed, they would even resign from membership in the Ontario Hockey Association. The trustees were just as adamant, and it required some courage on their part, for both were Ottawa residents. There was no softening in the attitude of either party, but the trustees had the last word.

One year later, on February 23, 1894, the trustees announced:

> Arrangements have been completed whereby the Lord Stanley Hockey Cup will now pass into the hands of the Montreal Amateur Athletic Association. Some trouble arose last year about the acceptance, and the M.A.A.A. have had it in their possession ever since. The Montreal team will now officially take it over.

So the historic Montreal club, and not Ottawa, was the first to have its name and those of its players engraved on the silver bowl.

In May of 1893, Lord Stanley, then in England, was succeeded by the Earl of Aberdeen. The Earl was more of a curling enthusiast than a hockey fan, but he did occasionally drop the puck when the centre-men crossed sticks. His Excellency and Lady Aberdeen did attend games in Ottawa, Quebec and Toronto. Unfortunately Lord Stanley never watched a match contested for his trophy, yet his donation gave him fame far exceeding that of any of his vice-regal successors.

The first Stanley Cup game was played in Montreal's Victoria Rink on March 22, 1894. The participants were the defending Montreal A.A.A. and the challenging Ottawa Capitals. A newspaper despatch from Montreal read:

The hockey championship was decided tonight, and never before in the history of the game was there such a large crowd or so much enthusiasm. There were fully five thousand persons present at the match; and tin horns, strong lungs and a general rabble predominated. The match resulted in favor of Montreal by three goals to one. The referee forgot to see many things. The ice was fairly good.

THE TEAMS

MONTREAL		OTTAWA
Collins	Goal	Morell
Cameron	Point	Pulford
James	Cover-Point	Young
Routh	Forward	Kirby
Mussen	Forward	J. McDougall
Hodgson	Forward	S. McDougall
Barlow	Forward	Russell

Referee—W. Scott, Toronto; Umpires—Messrs. Anderson and Irwin.

In the first half, the play was of the rushing order, with Montreal getting slightly the best of it. The Ottawas, however, found an opening after about ten minutes play, and Russell scored. As soon as the puck was sent off again, Hodgson carried it to the Ottawa end and undertook to score; but the Ottawa defence were on the alert and saved the goal. A hard struggle ensued, and after ten minutes of rushing and hard hockey, Montreal scored. No other goal was taken in this half, and when the second half commenced, everyone settled down to see a great contest and they were not disappointed. The Ottawas played with much more vim and made it lively for their opponents. The Montrealers were more fortunate, and through the offices of Hodgson and Barlow, two more goals were taken. The match concluded in a victory for the local team by three goals to one. After the match the winners were carried off the rink.

All through the 1890s, hockey was suffering from the pangs of sudden growth. Some of the pioneer occurrences seem humorous when reviewed seventy years later.

In 1890, Montreal A.A.A. were playing Quebec for the championship of the Canadian Amateur Hockey Association. The game was to have started at 8:00 P.M., but when the Quebec team arrived, two of their best players were absent. Undaunted, two friends of the visiting team volunteered to replace them, and without practice, they played in a national final game in ordinary street clothes.

The Montreal team also had trouble. One of its players was bedded-down with *la grippe*. His replacement was so inexperienced that he first enquired from the referee: "Can I cross-check?" Before the official could discourage such conduct, a team-mate nudged the questioner to one side and confidentially advised: "If you have to, it will be all right for you to lay your man out." In a rough game, Montreal won by five to one.

Eastern Canada might have been hockey's cradle, but the game was fast adopted in Western Canada. An early Manitoban once described how hockey came to Winnipeg:

> In the early part of the winter of 1890, while a schoolboy, I was skating with companions in the old Winnipeg open-air rink, which was run by the street railway company. Unexpectedly, I saw something which claimed my interest and caused me to stop my practice of skatorial art and rivet my attention on a scene in the corner of the enclosure. In that area a couple of young men, both strangers to me, were armed with curved sticks, which were much smoother and better shaped than my improvised shinny club. The pair were engaged in a good-natured contest for possession of a dark, round object on the ice. After a few boyish questions, I discovered that the two men were members of one of the new athletic clubs which had just been formed and that they were playing a new game called hockey.

The new game soon had many friends. On November 3, 1890, the Victoria Hockey Club, the first in Manitoba, was formed. It was closely followed by the Winnipeg club. During the winter of 1890/91, matches were played on an outdoor rink. Interest continued, and the next winter an entirely military team from Osborne Barracks began playing. The rivalry became so intense that, on November 11, 1892, a Manitoba hockey association came into being.

Before too long the western teams began boasting about their skills. They proposed to combine the best Winnipeg and Victoria players and invade the east. At first the longer established clubs in Ontario and Quebec were as cold to the idea as winter itself. They believed that the western players were so new to the game that they would offer little opposition. But the Manitobans were so strongly sold on themselves, that the eastern clubs finally yielded and consented to the tour.

The host teams were shockingly surprised. Eleven games were played against good teams at Toronto, Kingston, Peterborough, Niagara Falls, Ottawa and Montreal. What happened? The Winnipeggers won eight of the eleven matches and outscored their opponents by seventy goals to thirty-seven.

The success of the expedition into a far part of the country convinced the westerners they were as good as the best, and they determined to again risk their reputation. In late January of 1894, the Victoria club, seven-men strong, cheered by a host of supporters, pulled out from Winnipeg's Northern Pacific station, destined for Ottawa and other eastern points. On the trip they defeated Ottawa and Montreal, lost an exhibition game in Quebec, then won two more at Ottawa. They crossed into United States and defeated Minneapolis, and returned home to be hailed world champions.

As early as 1895, there was hardly a prairie village where hockey was not already thriving. By 1896, one year later, Winnipeg Victorias were good enough to challenge for the Stanley Cup.

CHAPTER THREE EARLY FAN FEVER

Right from its origin, there was a strange fascination about the Stanley Cup. Perhaps the fact it was donated by a popular Governor General gave it social prestige. Possibly the refusal of the Ottawa club to play for the honour of becoming the first holder aroused public curiosity and interest. Undoubtedly the speed and skill of the players inspired club loyalty. Whatever the causes, there was positive proof that Cup contests whipped up fan enthusiasm so much that it bordered almost on the unreasonable.

Even prior to the first Stanley Cup game in March 1894, the sold-out sign was in effect. The doors of Montreal's historic Victoria Rink were opened for reserved ticket-holders at 7:00 P.M., and at game time there were five thousand spectators in attendance.

The eagerness of fans was not restricted to Montreal and Ottawa; it was in evidence wherever the Stanley Cup was defended. More than sixty years ago, in January of 1902 to be exact, Toronto Wellingtons, who were the Ontario champions, challenged Winnipeg Victorias, who were then Stanley Cup holders. Even though the Toronto team and its supporters did not arrive in the Manitoba capital until the awkward hour of 5:30 P.M., they were welcomed at the station by a big crowd and escorted in carriages in a long procession to the Clarendon Hotel.

This was one of the most hospitable and enthusiastic of all

early series. Because the Iron Dukes were late in arriving, the host club generously gave them their own practice hour at the Winnipeg Auditorium. Later, when it became known that the jerseys of both teams were red in colour, the Victorias not only arranged for Wellingtons to borrow the uniforms of another Winnipeg club for the first game, but also agreed to exchange jerseys for the second match. Because there were differences in eastern and western rules, it was decided to play the first match under Ontario regulations and the other under Manitoba rules. Nothing could have been more amicable than these arrangements.

The fans, too, shared the desire to make it a great series. Prior to the first match, doors for reserved ticket-holders opened at 7:00 P.M. But long before this time, the rush crowd began lining up in front of the Auditorium entrance. The numbers steadily swelled, and when all the doors were opened, there was an hilarious scramble for admission.

It was generally expected that the Toronto club would be outclassed, and bets were made they would not even score a goal. However, Wellingtons played surprisingly well, and while they lost both games by scores of five to three, it was evident that not all the better players of the day resided in Winnipeg, Ottawa and Montreal. The games were so well contested that a newspaper correspondent was inspired to write: "The way the teams played fanned the pent-up enthusiasm into a flame of delirious excitement that affected the most apathetic." Those games must have been good, for few sportswriters have since come close to matching that flowery prose.

When the series ended, the goodwill continued, for the wife of the Toronto Wellington's president was given a handsome bouquet of pink and white carnations. On one off-night the visitors were guests at a theatre party, and on another they were honoured with an impressive banquet.

While all Winnipeg citizens were keen about the series, there was an equal concern back in Toronto. In those years early to bed and early to rise was a custom rather than a proverb. Besides, there was a one-hour difference in the two time zones. Even so, the *Globe* newspaper office in Toronto was crowded for three hours with hockey enthusiasts who hovered around and even above the telegraph desk and almost snatched the messages from the hands of the operator. Maybe the 1902 reporting wasn't as detailed as modern radio and television recording, but the C.P.R. telegraph did provide a bulletin service, over direct wire from Winnipeg, that covered almost every movement of the puck.

Additionally, there was another means of conveying the news to Toronto. Now the device seems strange, even primitive, yet it was effective. With kindly concern for the interests of its customers, the management of the Toronto Street Railway powerhouse had arranged that as soon as the morning newspaper sports department gave them the final score of the game in Winnipeg, they would blow their big whistle. If Wellingtons won, there would be two loud blasts; if they lost, there would be three. Throughout the city, many families already in bed had previously arranged for some member to stay awake, with windows opened and ears cocked. Nervously they awaited the tidings. They heard the first blast, and the second; then they held their breaths, hoping they would hear no more. But alas! On both nights, they were forced to retire with the sad news that they had heard three blasts and that the Iron Dukes had fallen.

A few weeks after that Winnipeg Victoria-Toronto Wellington series, the Winnipeg club was again host to a challenging Montreal Amateur Athletic Association club. It was a keen, hard-fought series, with each team winning one game. In the third and decisive contest, Montreal won by two to one. Again even in defeat, Victorias were perfect hosts. After the final match, they entertained the new cup-holders at a sumptuous dinner.

It was customary for the referee to donate his services for the glory of the occasion rather than for monetary reward. It was therefore a just and reasonable courtesy for both clubs, from their personal funds, to present Referee McFarlane with a magnificent gold watch.

Despite large crowds, there was little financial gain to the clubs participating in Stanley Cup play; but there was prestige and recognition. When the happy Montreal champions returned home, they were welcomed at Windsor Station by over three thousand cheering supporters. The Acting Mayor delivered what a reporter was moved to call "a very beautiful address." Later the victors were banquetted, and each player received a fourteen carat gold watch, suitably engraved.

Even by 1902, the Stanley Cup had become much more than a $50 rose-bowl. It was rapidly acquiring a glamour that had no relation to money, and everywhere sportsmen were flocking to see Stanley Cup contests. In 1903, when Winnipeg Victorias journeyed to Montreal in a vain attempt to recapture the emblem of supremacy, the four-game series attracted eighteen thousand spectators.

That enthusiasm of early 1900s was manifested in varying ways. Sometimes the fans showed their interest in numbers, at other times by extreme ill-will and yet again by kindly deeds.

In 1909, when Ottawa played their old rivals, Montreal Wanderers, in a match that had a bearing on which team would eventually defend the Stanley Cup, there were seven thousand spectators squeezing into the new Ottawa Arena. It was the largest crowd that, until then, had ever attended an Ottawa sports event conducted indoors. Everybody who was prominent was present and the who's who group was augmented by the thousands of so whats. Every reserved seat had been booked twenty-four hours before the game. On the day of the match over five hundred Montreal supporters arrived by trains. Only one hundred seats had been set aside for them, and those without tickets rushed to the rink to see if they could buy standing room back of the upper seats.

Everyone anticipated a titanic struggle. Fortunately in that pre-game tension an unrehearsed incident gave them some relief. When the Ottawa team came to the ice, they were greeted with volleys of explosive cheers. However, one player after another reached the ice, stumbled and fell on his back, as though axed. There was naturally much consternation until it became apparent that all three players, in their eagerness to begin the fray, had neglected to remove the leather scabbards, normally intended to protect the sharp edges of their skates while walking from the dressing room. When the players took that first stroke, they were skating on leather and so they flopped.

At times, fans were not only numerically strong, but they were also exceedingly bitter. One season "Cyclone" Taylor was an Ottawa idol; the next winter he was a deep-dyed villain. At the end of the 1909 season, he was a Stanley Cup hero. Hundreds of Ottawa fans fought their way to shake the hand of the truly great player, even to touch his back, while admirers carried him on their shoulders from the ice to the dressing-room.

That was in 1909. But in 1910, Taylor was wearing the uniform of the Renfrew Millionaires. When he skated on the Ottawa ice to play cover-point for the rival club, two thousand megaphoned men and boys screamed, "Go home, Taylor!" "Back to the Bush League, Taylor!" and much more provocative insults. When the play started, he was pelted with lemons and other contributions not so fruity. Coppers were hurled at his feet, not as a monetary offering but in hope he would stumble over them. Even a whisky flask (empty of course) was flung in his direction and crashed on the ice. At every opportunity Ottawa players slammed him, while crowds roared approval much as the Roman mobs did in the Colosseum. The unruly spectators were enthusiastic enough but for the wrong reason. They were endeavouring to impress Mr. Taylor that who a man may be isn't nearly as important as whom he represents.

Hockey fans more than fifty years ago were not always vitriolic. Sometimes they were as busy as bees and sweet as honey. Renfrew folks had those qualities. In 1910 the Millionaires, who assembled from across Canada and comprised a team of all the talents, had surprisingly finished only third in their league. Then, at the end of the season, they had dashed to New York to play a series with a big monetary reward awaiting the winners. Even so, the Renfrew Council had intended giving the team a bang-up banquet. But when they received advice that the players would likely be going direct to their own home-towns from New York, they were compelled to cancel the affair.

However, the plans of the players were later changed. Without prior warning, word reached Renfrew on a Tuesday noon-hour that the players were returning for one Tuesday evening. It was then too late to reconvene Council, so a group of citizens was hurriedly formed, and the group agreed: "There just has to be a banquet." It was three o'clock before the committee got into action. Invitations were issued, a hall was commissioned, a caterer was hired, and a program was even printed. During the evening, while the food was still in preparation and the tables were still being set, the guests began to arrive. All the while, an orchestra assisting, Lester Patrick led a choir composed of the players and a few friends. They sang patriotic, comic and sentimental songs with a harmony that matched their team-work on the ice. At ten o'clock, some seventy citizens sat down to eat. The menu was adequate:

Soup

Clear Soup

Fish

Steak Salmon Trout   Saratogas

Roast

Roast Turkey   Cranberry Sauce

Relishes

Spanish Queen Olives   Small Pickles

Lea and Perrin's Sauce

Tomato Chutney   California Celery

Desserts

Charlotte Russe   Trifle   Finger Cakes

Cream Cake   Raspberry Tarts

Mixed Cakes

Tea   Coffee

At midnight the speeching and toasting began. Lester Patrick entertained by reciting some of Henry Drummond's poems. The party broke up about 2:30 A.M. That was an example of early fandom at its best.

Sometimes public interest during the early years of hockey was whetted by unusual happenings on or around the ice. One memorable incident occurred on February 19, 1899, when eight thousand shouting fans packed into Montreal Arena to watch a Stanley Cup game between Winnipeg Victorias and Montreal Victorias. What they saw and heard and thought has since been recognized as an interesting event in Cup history. In the first match, with total scores in two games to decide, Winnipeg was leading with only a minute remaining. Then Montreal scored twice in the final sixty seconds to earn a one-goal margin on the round.

It was the second match in the series that sparked one of hockey's most notable schmozzles. It began rather innocently. With thirteen minutes remaining, Montreal were leading by three goals to two in a well-played game, when Gingras, Winnipeg's right wing, was heavily slashed across the knee by Montreal's McDougall. When Gingras fell to the ice, Referee Findlay stopped play and ruled-off McDougall for only two minutes. Instantly, Winnipeg players and officials sizzled with rage. They contended that the foul had been deliberate and that, according to the rules, the attacker should have been removed for the rest of the game. The referee, however, refused to extend the penalty, and the Winnipeg players left the ice and stomped to their dressing-room.

The official, suspecting there was some chicanery, also went to the dressing-room and asked Gingras to show him his knee. It was evident there was no faking. Across the outer side of the knee there was a long abrasion, the right leg was completely helpless, and a doctor advised that it would be impossible for the player to continue. After the referee left the room, McDougall himself came in and admitted that he had lost his temper and made a vicious swipe. His apology was appreciated and accepted; but still it did not restore Gingras, nor did it enable him to continue the play.

In the arena the huge crowd, unaware of all the controversy, waited impatiently. Again the referee entered the visitors' dressing-room, and even when informed of McDougall's confession, he refused to yield. He explained politely enough: "Gentlemen, I have made a mistake. I am sorry for it but cannot change my decision. If you are not satisfied with me, I will retire at once from the ice and have no more to do with the game."

Officers of both clubs asked him to continue, but he firmly refused. As Findlay departed, the Montreal club pleaded with the Winnipeggers to continue with another official. But they, too, were stubborn, and insisted that only the Stanley Cup trustees could appoint a new referee.

Victoria Rink, Montreal. Hockey match being played in 1893.

Montreal Victorias
Stanley Cup Champions 1896. (Note Stanley Cup on pedestal at left)

Montreal Shamrocks
Stanley Cup Champions 1900.

All the while the spectators were unaware of the game-within-a-game that was being played in the dressing-rooms and corridors. A messenger was despatched to the home of the referee. He had softened sufficiently to consent to return to the rink, but his return visit, instead of solving the problem, only added to the confusion.

Again the official ordered the Winnipeg team to return to the ice within fifteen minutes or he would refer the dispute to the trustees for decision. The visitors must have had a good club-house lawyer on their team, for they reminded the referee that when he departed from the arena his authority ceased. The official threat only irritated the challengers, and the Winnipeg players removed their hockey uniforms and changed into street clothes. Some had already left the rink when Mr. Findlay, a conscientious but rather sensitive referee, finally awarded the game to Montreal Victorias. At that moment, the latter club was leading on the round by five goals to three. That result went into Stanley Cup records when trustees Ross and Sweetland refused to upset Referee Findlay's decision.

Such incidents, unrehearsed and without script, instead of alienating the fans of long ago, only served to intrigue them and provide debating material until the next Stanley Cup series could begin.

CHAPTER FOUR OTTAWA SILVER SEVEN

During the first decade of the Twentieth Century, while hockey was undergoing many changes, one club, the Ottawa Silver Seven, over a three-year span, seemed capable of adjusting to every condition. Regardless of new rules, even though ice was keen one night and slush the next, despite player-raiding by promoters in the United States, this club always had the men to match the job. Not on the basis of sentiment but rather on the basis of merit they were voted, many years later, Canada's outstanding hockey team during the first half-century.

In its early sporting years, the city of Ottawa was famed for its achievements in three sports. In the same year the best in the land were the Capitals in lacrosse, the Rough Riders in rugby football and the Silver Seven in hockey. Some of this success was due to the fact that Ottawa, being the national capital, had an opportunity to provide civil-service positions for its athletes. It was also true that, because Ottawa teams excelled in winter, summer and autumn sports, the players moved from one into the next and were thus well-conditioned through all the seasons.

Personal pride in local teams was always strong in Ottawa. It was local loyalty that encouraged Lord Stanley to present his Cup, especially when he believed the first holders of the Cup would be his favourite hockey team. His excellency also named two Ottawa friends to be the first trustees for the award. However, because of the unexpected, the Ottawa club's name was not engraved on the gold-lined silver bowl for almost 10 years after its presentation.

In that interval, Ottawa fans experienced some disappointing times, especially in hockey. In 1897, Ottawa Capitals challenged the current Stanley Cup holders, Montreal Victorias. It was intended as a two-game series with total scores to decide. However the Montreal team won the first match by fifteen goals to two, and it was evident that the losers could never overcome such a strong lead. So the series ended abruptly when the Ottawa management concluded: "It would not be in the interest of hockey generally to continue the present contest."

On another gloomy night in the winter of 1900, Ottawa was scheduled to play against Montreal Shamrocks, but Ottawa was unable to ice even seven players and had to default and pay a hundred-dollar fine. But those discouragements were over in 1903, when the Ottawa team won the championship of the Canadian Amateur Hockey Association.

It was then the custom that whenever a club won league honours from the club holding the Stanley Cup, the new champions automatically became Stanley Cup defenders. Thus, in 1903, the Ottawa Silver Seven (so named because their manager as a token of victory had given each player a silver nugget) inherited the Stanley Cup and began climbing to a fame that is still recognized sixty years later.

The Ottawa team of that year included "Bouse" Hutton, goal; Harvey Pulford, point; Art Moore, cover-point; Frank McGee, centre; and three Gilmour brothers—Bill, Dave and "Sudie" at rover, left wing and right wing. All had grown up on local ponds and canals, and were loaded with civic pride. They were also versatile athletes.

Harvey Pulford, for instance, who was a solid, hard-hitting defenceman in hockey, was also nationally famed in rugby football, rowing, paddling, squash and boxing. All the hockey players were strong skaters, good scorers, rugged checkers with an adaptability that permitted them to play more than one position. They could play rough or clean, depending on the intention of their opponents; and they could alter their style of play from long lifts on soft ice to short accurate passing on hard surfaces.

The Silver Seven made their first defence of the Stanley Cup on March 12, 1903, at Dey's Arena, in a series against Rat Portage Thistles. The Ottawa team won both games by scores of six-two and four-two. The series was not too well attended, and the visitors received a share of only five hundred dollars from a venture that had cost them $1,300. However, all was not lost, for the Thistle players had a nice outing. They enjoyed a couple of games of their favourite sport, and they were guests at a lavish post-series banquet at the Russell House.

The next Stanley Cup series was altogether different, for it teemed with drama, changes of fortune and bitterness. In the first game, played on December 30, 1903, the visiting Winnipeg Rowing Club team was so keen to recapture the trophy that the over-anxious players often over-skated the puck, bunched frequently and occasionally collided with each other. They also suffered injuries to Bawlf, who fell and hurt his back, and to Bennest, who crashed in the fence and broke his thumb. Because of these accidents, together with delays while broken skates were replaced, the game lasted nearly three hours. Before it ended, many spectators had begun to wearily plod their homeward way.

Ottawa Silver Seven won that first game by nine goals to one, and to many observers the series had come and gone. Yet only two nights later, the Winnipeg Club rang in the New Year with a thumping six-two victory over a team that had previously seemed unbeatable.

This sensational reversal was not a fluke. Three nights later the teams met in the decisive third game, and a correspondent wrote: "It was the hardest and most brilliant game ever played in Ottawa. From the time Referee Trihey first started the puck on its checkered career, it was nip and tuck and the rubber knew no rest." The first forty-four minutes were scoreless. But by that time the challengers had been battered into exhaustion, and Ottawa won by a score of two-nothing.

While the game was brilliantly played, it was also the bloodiest match up to that point in Stanley Cup history. The *Winnipeg Free Press'* casualty list read like the aftermath of a rebellion:

Hospital cases of Rowing Club: P. Brown, lame; C. Richards, face swollen, leg hurt; C. Bennest, thumb broken, badly bruised; W. Breen, bruised and broken-up; J. Hall, cut on head; D.

Kirby, cut on head; W. Bawlf, cut and bruised. Seven out of nine injured; two forced to retire from game; three forced to remain in bed after game; one out of hockey for season.

Then the Winnipeg writer added: "It is an open secret that if any team is to beat Ottawa at home in any sport, they must be at least a third stronger."

While the lengthy list of Winnipeg's wounded does not refer to the aches and pains also suffered by the Ottawa players, the western summary was not an exaggeration. A Toronto team could have confirmed these sad tidings.

A few weeks after the western "hospital train" left Ottawa with the wounded on board, the Ontario Hockey Association champions, Toronto Marlboroughs, invaded the capital for a clash against the Silver Seven. It was then the custom for challenges to be accepted at any time. In 1904, Ottawa, in addition to participating in its regular schedule, played three Stanley Cup series in three months.

The Ottawa-Marlborough series was played at Aberdeen Pavilion in Ottawa's Exhibition Grounds. At the end of the first half, the Toronto team was leading by three to one, but in the second half, Ottawa scored five goals and won by six to three. That sudden and acute reversal of form during the two halves was a mystery to many sportsmen; but Marlboroughs had an explanation. They contended their players were faster skaters who played best on the smooth surface during the first half. They also said the Ottawa management was so aware of this truth that, during the interval between the halves, they deliberately salted the ice and thereby slowed-down the Toronto attack. The allegation was never proven, but for many years it was felt that the charge was true. However the Silver Seven won the second match of the Stanley Cup series by eleven to two, so whether or not the home team had resorted to deceit on an earlier occasion really hadn't "cut much ice."

The famed Ottawa team practised the strange custom of maiming opponents with roughness then killing them with kindness. The Marlborough series illustrates this contrast. After the first game, Toronto's Tom Phillips could hardly walk. Winchester finished with an arm so battered he could scarcely hold his stick, while MacLaren was hospitalized with a broken rib.

A Toronto *Globe* observer wrote:

Ottawa players slash, trip and practise the severest kind of cross-checking with a systematic hammering of hands and wrists. They hit a man on the head when the referee isn't looking, and they body a man into the boards after he has passed the puck. The rubber is not the objective, but the man must be stopped at all costs; if he is put out altogether, so much the better.

A Marlborough player gave a more intimate impression of what happened on Ottawa ice. "It was a case of shoot and duck. The Ottawa defence didn't care whether or not a goal was scored; they just walloped to teach you better manners during the next attack."

And yet when the series ended and the wounds as well as the challengers were licked, the Ottawa club entertained their erstwhile foes at a sumptuous dinner, where the servings of praise were as lavish as those of victuals. Still, it must have been difficult for some of the guests to lift their loaded forks up to mouth-level.

Another irony of the Stanley Cup series during the Silver Seven's supremacy was that while the challengers were not only out-scored and out-hit, they also took a beating in their purses. Toronto Marlboroughs, in addition to absorbing the shocks of bumps and bruises, also lost two hundred dollars in the venture.

After the Marlboroughs were socked and dined, the Ottawa team was challenged by Brandon Wheat Kings. Again the defenders proved they were no respecters of either challengers or vice-regal personages. Even though His Excellency the Governor General and the Countess of Minto attended, the home players did not soften their rollicking ways. While they made little effort to make friends on the ice, they certainly could win hockey games.

In January of 1905, they swamped a Dawson City team which, in geological terms, might well have called themselves the Golden Seven, for they had been financed by Colonel Boyle, who had moiled for the precious metal in the Yukon. In this instance however, silver proved more valuable than gold. On the hockey market, Ottawa defeated the voyageurs by two lop-sided scores.

Less than two months later, the Silver Seven met a team that really tested their ability to give and to take. The Rat Portage Thistles had now become the Kenora Thistles, and they were as tough and thorny as the Scottish name they bore. In the first game of the series they humbled the Ottawa defenders by nine goals to three. "Tom" Phillips, a really great player who managed to see Canada from "club to club," scored four of the Thistles' goals.

That defeat both irked and perked the Ottawa fans. To them a rout like this was almost a national calamity, and thousands resolved to see that it didn't happen again. For the second game the crowd was a record-smasher. Some seats sold for three times their regular prices, and the doors of the rink were closed at 7:30 to save the walls from bulging outward. This time the Ottawa management strengthened their team by the additions of Frank McGee and Billy Gilmour, both of whom had not played in the first match. The Silver Seven won the second contest by only four-two, and the stage was set for the all-important final game.

Even though this was the third match in five nights, every seat was sold, and many hundreds of disappointed fans milled around on the streets outside the arena. Again there was a pre-game conflict as to whether eastern or western rules would govern. This dispute was resolved by a compromise: a judge of play would assist the referee in the first half, but in the second half referee "Mike" Grant would work alone.

Like many games of that era, the start was delayed until almost nine o'clock. But once play began, it was so brilliant that one observer called it the most scientific game ever played. It was also one of the most crashing, for bodies on both teams took a terrific hammering. One Kenora player was so exhausted that, when he tumbled in front of his own goal, he had difficulty in rising from the horizontal to the vertical. The referee observed him, but instead of lending a helping hand, he cruelly handed the down-trodden player a five-minute penalty for, of all things, obstructing the Kenora goal.

At half-time, Thistles were leading by two goals to one. Through the second half, the teams were never separated by more than a single goal. With only two minutes remaining, the score was still tied. While the huge crowd rose and cheered, the overhead viewers clutched their rafter perches a little tighter. Then, with only ninety seconds remaining, the ever-dependable McGee triggered his third Ottawa goal to ensure victory for the Silver Seven. When the final gong clanged, "Old fans and young, wild with the joys of victory, leaped from bleachers, boxes and beams, and jammed the ice surface."

By this time it was late in the season, and the Stanley Cup defenders were tired of play and weary from contacts. Yet the trustees, in a desire to please all challengers, ordered the Silver Seven to play Montreal Victorias within a week. Fortunately the Victorias and P. D. Ross, the cup trustee, could not agree whether the series would be a sudden-death game, or two games with total goals on the round to decide, or the best two games in three. While the trustees and the club debated, weather warmed, ice softened, interest lagged, and finally it was too late in the season for further play.

But the winter of 1906 was another season. With their three-year-old winning streak unbroken, the Silver Seven anticipated another good winter. It began very favourably. In late February, Queen's University, the Ontario champions, visited Ottawa in their quest for the Stanley Cup. But the students were no match for the old masters, who won by successive scores of sixteen-seven and twelve-seven. The superiority was so pronounced that the spectators yawned. One week later the Silver Seven continued their Stanley Cup domination by defeating Smith's Falls in two games.

They were riding high on the crest of a wave called success. They had defended the Stanley Cup through eight consecutive series and won them all. They had outscored the best teams in Canada by 151 goals to seventy-four, and they had lost only three Stanley Cup games in twenty played. Even though personnel had changed through the years, there always remained a solid core of dependable stars, quite willing and able to break in the new candidates.

Some of the scoring achievements of the Silver Seven players had been sensational. In one game Frank McGee scored fourteen goals, with five of them coming in a little more than three minutes. In another match, the team scored seven successive goals in four minutes and thirty-nine seconds. Naturally everything that goes up has to come down at one time or another. But even when the reign of the Ottawa club ended, it succumbed in a series that brought glory in defeat.

It happened in March of 1906. At the time, Ottawa Silver Seven and Montreal Wanderers were engaged in a series of two games with total goals on round to count. Upon the result depended both the championship of the Eastern Canadian Hockey Association and possession of the Stanley Cup.

The first game was allocated to Montreal, and prices had been advanced to standing room seventy-five cents; reserved seats one dollar; promenade seats $1.50; and boxes to ten dollars a box. The fans objected to the increased rates, but interest was so strong that by 9:30 A.M. on the day of the game, all tickets were sold and the speculators were re-selling them at prices as high as ten dollars a ticket.

The opening line-ups were almost a who's who of hockey greats. They were so all-time-renowned that six of the participants, many decades later, were honoured in Canada's Hockey Hall of Fame. The starting players were:

MONTREAL		OTTAWA
Menard	Goal	Hague
Strachan	Point	Pulford
Kennedy	Cover Point	Moore
L. Patrick	Rover	Westwick
Glass	Centre	McGee
Russell	Right Wing	A. Smith
Johnston	Left Wing	H. Smith

With a huge crowd in attendance and ice in excellent condition, the two contenders began rather defensively, with each sizing-up the other. After eight minutes of close-checking and hard-hitting, "Pud" Glass scored for Wanderers. Five minutes later he added another, and when the teams left the ice at half-time, Montreal was leading by four to nothing. This score shocked Ottawa supporters, for never had their favourites been that far down at half-time; but there were few loyalists who expected the rout would continue. With hope that springs eternal, they anticipated a complete reversal of form in the second half.

However, when the play resumed, the same trend persisted. Within eleven minutes, Glass scored his third goal, while Russell added two more to make the score Montreal Wanderers seven to Ottawa Silver Seven's nothing. Three minutes later, however, Harry Smith scored for Ottawa, and there was a feeling that more might quickly follow. But this occurrence was a flash rather than a spark, for within six minutes, Wanderers scored twice. The game ended in a nine to one licking for a team that hitherto seemed unbeatable.

True, there was a second game to be played at Dey's Arena in Ottawa, but most hockey observers concluded it would be just a routine joust, with the Silver Seven battling bravely but still dying in a worthy cause. However, the Ottawa management and players were not prepared to give up without presenting an attack to match their proud record. They did not intend scuttling their ship—world hockey champions—without first firing their best volleys at the foe. To improve their chances, they replaced goalkeeper Hague, who had faltered in the first game, with Percy Le Sueur, a stand-up net-minder, who earlier starred for Smith's Falls in a Stanley Cup series.

Right from the face-off in the second game, the tide of play was reversed. The Silver Seven attacked fiercely, while Wanderers' strategy was to play defensively—to lift the puck far down the ice rather than carry it; to build a wall around their own goal and not venture far beyond it. For a while the tactics succeeded. Indeed, during an Ottawa lapse, after twelve scoreless minutes, it was Montreal's Lester Patrick who scored the first goal and gave the Stanley Cup challengers a ten-goal lead on the round. It had been a tough break for the defenders, for they needed all the luck in the world.

Then, with unexpected fury, the winds of fortune changed, and Ottawa began scoring. Frank McGee, the ace scorer of his day, got his first goal in the series; Harry Smith added two more to make the half-time score Ottawa three-Montreal one.

In the dressing-room during the intermission, the Silver Seven players must have listened to some very impressive speeches, for they came out on the ice and began a devastating attack. It earned them three goals in eighty-five seconds. It was then ten-seven on the round; eight minutes later Harry Smith scored to make it ten-eight; ten minutes later Harry fired another, and the margin was only ten to nine. Then ten seconds later, just about as quickly as the same Mr. Smith could get within scoring range, he whipped-in his third successive goal—and the round was tied at ten-ten.

It was one of hockey's most impressive comebacks. At that moment there were about ten minutes remaining, and during five of them "thousands of throats sent-up an air-rending yell of delight." Victory for the home team seemed assured, as Ottawa continued attacking. Harry Smith, who had already scored six goals in the game, fired still another, which would have given the Silver Seven the lead for the first time in the series. But Referee Bob Meldrum disallowed it because the scoring play was offside.

Throughout the early portion of the contest, Wanderers had played conservatively, carefully nursing their huge lead. They had forgotten that old maxim, applicable to both war and sport, that the best defence is a strong attack. Only when Ottawa tied the score did the Montrealers admit that their strategy had failed miserably. Then, with defeat imminent, Lester Patrick, an inspirational rabble-rouser, huddled with his team-mates. Instantly the Montreal tactics reversed, and they sallied bravely into Ottawa territory. They were soon aided by a penalty to Harry Smith, the Silver Seven's high-scoring right-winger. With that threat removed, with Ottawa players tiring from their strenuous uphill struggle, and with Montreal playing seven men to six, Lester Patrick dashed the hopes of the home-team fans when he rifled the puck into the net behind Ottawa's Le Sueur. A minute later, and appropriately because it was St. Patrick's Day, Wanderer's Patrick scored his third goal of the game and the only goals earned by his team.

These two final goals sealed the fate of Ottawa's Silver Seven. At long last, the most celebrated team of its era—and very likely the most esteemed in all hockey history—passed down the road of Stanley Cup champions with heads high and banners flying.

CHAPTER FIVE TRYING TIMES FOR TRUSTEES

Along with the swash-buckling success of the Silver Seven, the early 1900s were fraught with constant feuding among rival teams and explosive argument between the clubs and the Stanley Cup trustees. At times, the contention was so bitter that the prestige of the Cup itself became badly tarnished.

Francis Nelson, the competent sports editor of the *Toronto Globe,* sensed this lack of reverence. In the year the Ottawa reign ended, Mr. Nelson observed: "The Stanley Cup provides a fine spectacle and makes money for the teams and the rink proprietors; but the competition does not advance the interests of the national sport." At the same time, an Ottawa sportsman added his bitter comment: "The Stanley Cup is a detriment to hockey. It would have been better if its well-intentioned donor had taken some other way to show his appreciation."

Some of the early bickering was prompted by the rules of hockey and their interpretation. Originally the referee had powers even a dictator could have envied. He was often the sole official on the ice—yet he also had the responsibility of appointing the goal umpires, keeping score and controlling timekeepers. During play, there were fourteen men on a comparatively small area, and the referee required a hundred eyes and a revolving head to detect offsides, for the puck could not be passed ahead to a team-mate. To compound these problems, there was no definite time-limit on penalties, for the penalty could vary from two minutes to the rest of the game, subject only to the referee's judgment. It was his responsibility to make the penalty fit the crime.

Generally even in Stanley Cup games the position of the referee was an unpaid honour. Any reward was dependent upon the whims of the clubs. After one series played in 1900, between Montreal Shamrocks and Winnipeg Victorias, Referee Baird was not only presented with a valuable signet ring, but he was also "cheered when he replied." Following another Stanley Cup series, Referee McFarlane was so esteemed that the two teams jointly gave him a suitably engraved gold watch. Frequently, however, both clubs would have preferred to contribute a piece of Manila rope, with noose to match.

Some of the early feuding between clubs and officials was prompted by doubts whether or not a goal really had been scored. Mr. W. A. Hewitt, a player, referee or executive through more than sixty years, told me that until 1899 goals were just two uprights, with no net between, often without even a bar across the top. Goal umpires stood on the ice and waved a flag if they thought the puck had been fired between the posts. Usually the umpires were partisans so infernally loyal to their own club that it was difficult for them to distinguish between fact and fantasy. Consequently disputes were numerous, but for many years the decision of the umpire was final. The only relief was to replace the offender with a successor who was often even more attached to one club. Mr. Hewitt and his friend Francis Nelson often gnawed at this bone of contention. They discussed the need for equipment to snare the fast-flying puck and retain it until proof of a score was confirmed. The solution came from an unexpected source.

In 1899, while on a visit to Australia, Mr. Nelson observed the huge nets used by fishermen. He detected their puck-catching possibilities and brought two of them back to Canada. There did not appear to be a suitable opportunity to give them a good test in Toronto, so Mr. Nelson shipped them to Mr. Hewitt, who was then sports editor for the *Montreal Herald.* Prior to a game between Shamrocks and Victorias, he received permission to drape them around and behind the goal posts and secure them on the ice. The equipment would now seem crude, but that night the nets caught the puck and held it long enough for the officials to be assured a goal had been scored. The idea was soon approved, and nets became accepted equipment in Stanley Cup and league matches. Thus the lives of umpires were prolonged, and the dignity of referees was maintained.

During the early Stanley Cup years, there were other innovations to cause controversy at the time, but now they are of little interest. How best to face-off the puck was one contention. Originally face-offs were patterned after lacrosse, and the referee carefully placed the puck between two centre-men's sticks, then hollered 'Play!' Often, before he could leap to safety, the swinging sticks would slash his legs from ankle to hip!

One night Fred Waghorne, who refereed more than two thousand hockey games in his lifetime, decided he had absorbed enough punishment, and he proceeded to do something about it. So "Wag" said to the players: "That's it. Rules or no rules, I'm not going to take any more of that punishment. From now on I'm going to stand and drop the puck between your sticks. Get ready." They did. The referee dropped the puck and jumped clear. The players did not object. There were no more barked shins, and soon the hockey executives accepted Wag's idea and drafted a rule to legalize it.

These early rule-changes improved the game, but they gave some concern to Stanley Cup trustees, for they had to assure them that playing conditions were uniform for both challengers and defenders. They also had to make their own laws as they went along, and they had to use common sense when rules and customs seemed out-dated. Whenever a referee's decision was protested, the trustees generally adopted the policy of supporting the official.

Mr. Ross and Sheriff Sweetland were frequently making decisions not covered by their original instructions. In 1901, for instance, the problem arose: If a club holding the Stanley Cup failed to retain its league championship, did it still have the right to defend the Stanley Cup? "No!" said the trustees. "If Montreal Shamrocks won the Stanley Cup early one winter and later in the season lost the league title to Montreal Wanderers, the cup holders would then become Wanderers and not Shamrocks."

Another controversy arose over the right to challenge for the Stanley Cup. Some defenders felt the trophy belonged to them, by some form of divine right, and that they could accept or reject challengers as they saw fit. The trustees soon discouraged this attitude when they decreed that the champion team of any recognized association could challenge. They also ordered the resulting games to be played in the middle of the season, at any time between December and March.

Sometimes this edict invited revolt. One year there were as many as six challengers, and the trustees were forced to sort them out. They had to allow the holders some time to play their own league games, and permit the club a chance to look after its wounded players before engaging in the next battle against a fresh foe. Despite this, one winter an Ottawa team defended against Winnipeg, Toronto and Brandon, all in a space of two months.

Occasionally the authority of the trustees was scorned. In 1904, Ottawa Silver Seven played a game with the challenging Montreal Wanderers. The contest was so extended that it lasted four hours, and it was so rough there were thirty-six penalties. With only five minutes remaining, Ottawa was leading by five to three. But Wanderers scored two quick goals and tied the game. When it ended, Wanderers refused to play overtime if Dr. Kearns continued as referee. They later appealed to the Cup trustees to declare the first game a draw and then start a new three-game series. The officials refused and promptly ordered the Montreal club to play a deciding game in Ottawa. The Wanderers rejected the command; the series ended in one tied game, and the Silver Seven retained the Stanley Cup.

Resistance to authority again reared its aggravating head in 1905. Trustee Ross ordered Ottawa to accept the challenge of Montreal Victorias five days after the Rat Portage series ended. Even though weary of play, Ottawa agreed. Hoping to meet the tired cup holders before they could catch their wind, Victorias demanded a quick, sudden-death game. "No," insisted the trustees, "that's not fair to the defenders. It has to be a 'two games in three' series, or there will not be any series at all." There was no series.

Sometimes in haste and without precedent to guide them, the

trustees made decisions that they later had to revoke. In 1903, Montreal Amateur Athletic Association had beaten Winnipeg Victorias rather easily in the first game of a two-in-three series. The second game was tied at two-all at the end of regulation time. Thus Montreal, the defenders, claimed a Stanley Cup victory because they had earned a win and a tie and thus could not lose in a three-game series. However, Referee Quinn did not accept their reasoning and ordered the teams to continue into overtime. The clubs struggled through another thirty minutes. As it was then almost Sunday morning, the teams left the ice.

The situation was involved, so the next morning the referee travelled to Ottawa to consult the trustees. The latter hastily decided that the Saturday game would continue on Monday night, and that the winner would be the one scoring the first goal. Thus, if Montreal scored first, they would have won two games and would retain the Stanley Cup. But if Winnipeg should score first, then a third and decisive game would immediately begin.

It was not exactly a wise verdict. It could happen that Winnipeg might not score the first goal until after an hour of overtime. In this event, it would be unfair to the players to promptly start another game, which might also be prolonged until the next morning.

There was still another objection to the trustees' proposal. Thousands of tickets might be sold for the Monday night contest, on the presumption that the Winnipeg team would be the first to score and that another game would follow. However, there was no assurance of this, and if Montreal scored in, say, the first five minutes, the match and the series would automatically be concluded. The fans might, indeed, have paid in full to see a game that ended before they were comfortably seated.

When the trustees were informed of these complications, they huddled some more. This time they rescinded their former decision and ordered the two teams to play a full game on Monday night. If Montreal won, they would retain the Stanley Cup; if Winnipeg won, a fourth game would be necessary at a later date.

That solution seemed logical and practical, but it nettled Montreal's Captain Boon. Because his club was the cup defender, he said it was forced to play so many games that it might not be healthy enough to win their own league championship. He was so incensed that, in the event his team won the fourth game, he promised to recommend that the cup be returned to the trustees. In Boon's opinion, "The cup has proven to be a detriment to the game."

When the trustees finally straightened the series out, they thought their troubles had ended, but they still were not "home free." This time Referee Quinn decided to resign. He stressed that when he earlier agreed to officiate, he had anticipated working no more than three games. Now, on the eve of a fourth game, he was tired, and even more important, both clubs had referred to his officiating in disparaging words. So Mr. Quinn told the trustees to look for another man, and he would enjoy the game as a spectator.

Still the fourth game was played as ordered. Mr. Quinn was the referee, and Montreal won by a score of four goals to one. Following the victory, just to prove that deeds speak louder than words, the Winnipeg club presented Mr. Quinn with a valuable diamond locket. The Montreal team, not quite so approvingly, graciously donated a gold ring.

It seems that long ago some inciter was constantly provoking the trustees into new and embarrassing situations. In 1904 every hockey team in the land wanted to challenge Ottawa's Silver Seven. At one time the champions of the Western Ontario Hockey Association, the Manitoba and Northwest League, the Federal Amateur Hockey League and the Intercollegiate League wanted a crack at the defenders. Some of them unwittingly invited manslaughter-on-skates, for the Ottawa team really gloried in mayhem.

While the trustees were making plans and separating the wheat from the chaff, they courteously asked the Quebec team of the Canadian Amateur Hockey League if they too intended to challenge. The trustees were shaken when Quebec telegraphed back that they had no intention of challenging anyone. But, as winners of their League, they were ready to defend the Stanley Cup against any claimants to the honour. They were considered too cheeky, and their name was not even in the hat.

The two series that probably proved most irritating to the trustees occurred in January and March of 1907. The series were related in that the same two teams—Kenora Thistles and Montreal Wanderers—were the rabble-rousers.

In January, Kenora Thistles had imported so many good players that they challenged Montreal Wanderers, the Stanley Cup holders. The two games were played in Montreal, with the surprising result that Kenora won both games and captured the emblem of hockey supremacy. Equally amazing was the sensational play of Tom Phillips, who scored all four Kenora goals in the first game and three more in the second.

The defeat naturally rankled the proud Wanderers. So at their first opportunity, which happened to be two months later, they challenged Kenora Thistles, which had barely the time to admire their own reflections in Lord Stanley's gleaming bowl. In the meantime, both clubs searched the arenas of the country, hoping to uncover outstanding players who were not unwilling to sell their services for pieces of silver.

Kenora, only a small railroad centre, with no royal road to riches, rather unexpectedly tapped some source of hidden wealth. With these funds available, they signed Fred Whitcroft, who had a Peterborough reputation, and also Right Wing Alf Smith and Rover Harry Westwick, both of whom had been members of Ottawa's Silver Seven and were experienced in Stanley Cup play. The Kenora team's earlier name had been Rat Portage, and Westwick's nickname was "Rat." But these sentimental ties were not nearly as important as the fact that player "Rat" was a good scorer.

When Wanderers heard that their rivals were bolstering themselves with imports, they screamed to Ottawa and demanded justice. The Stanley Cup trustees heard their pleas and quickly proclaimed throughout the country that Kenora had grievously erred and would not be permitted to use Smith and Westwick.

The Thistles' management retorted that the Montreal challengers were also sinners, for they had brought in "Hod" Stuart, a repatriate from professional hockey in Houghton, Michigan. Then, officially, the Kenora officials telegraphed this laconic message to the trustees: "NO WESTWICK. NO SMITH. NO GAME."

They still had space to include in their telegram the words: "WE STILL LOVE YOU." But at that moment they were in no mood for love.

Trustee Foran, who had replaced Sheriff Sweetland, was an old hand in the game of steering his way through controversy. He again warned Kenora that unless they instantly agreed in writing to refrain from using Smith and Westwick, the trustees would take the cup from them and award it by default to Montreal Wanderers.

For a few days the series was on, off and on again. Telegraph wires were blazing with hot messages from Kenora to Ottawa and back. In substance, the messages were orders that the two players involved were not to be used by the defenders. The challengers were not to ice a team if Kenora used them.

All the while, wire by wire, the trustees were being eased out of the picture, and the two clubs were becoming solid friends. Eventually, when Mr. Foran was convinced that the managements were defying his rulings and were intent on playing a series with all players, good or bad, participating, he issued this warning:

> If the two clubs ignore instructions of trustees by mutually agreeing to play Westwick and Smith, when both are ineligible for present cup matches, the series will be treated as void, and the trustees will take charge of the Cup.

It was later emphasized that the trustees would retain the Stanley Cup until various hockey leagues can educate themselves up to a standard where decent sport will be the order of the day.

It was at this stage in the proceedings that one Kenora Thistle officer became so angry that he threatened to hurl Lord Stanley's gift into the wilds of Lake of the Woods. Indeed, he was reportedly in the process of so doing when cooler minds soothed his fevered brow and restrained his throwing arm.

But even with the threat of excommunication hanging over their collective heads, the two clubs did play their series, not in Kenora, but in Winnipeg. Whitcroft, Westwick and Smith were garbed in the uniforms of Kenora Thistles. Fittingly the good guys, the Montreal Wanderers, won the series by a margin of four goals. Then, in true story-book fashion, Trustee Foran concluded that after all the sinners had been conquered, justice had triumphed and that the Montreal Wanderers should have their names engraved on the bowl and would become its natural holders. And all that came to pass in the year 1907.

CHAPTER SIX MONEY TALKS

Rough play, frequent feuding, disrespect for officialdom, together with constant controversy concerning eligibility of challengers—all these contributed to a lessening of the lofty purpose for which Lord Stanley had presented his trophy. However, it was money that finally completed the separation between purpose and practice.

Early in Stanley Cup history, rivalry among Ottawa, Winnipeg, Montreal and Rat Portage (later Kenora) clubs was especially fierce. For a few years, even though fans were eager and crowds large, profits were meagre. Travel costs were high, while prices for admissions to games were low. At first it was customary for arena owners to retain two-thirds of the gross income, leaving only one-third to be divided between the two clubs. This split seemed so unfair that in 1901 the teams rebelled and refused to play until their combined share was raised to fifty per cent.

Even then, Stanley Cup games were not a short-cut to riches. In 1903, when Rat Portage Thistles played in Ottawa, their expenses exceeded their portion of the gate by eight hundred dollars—which was a heck of a way to make money. Toronto Marlboroughs lost two hundred dollars in their Stanley Cup quest. However the prospects were becoming brighter for, in a series between Montreal Shamrocks and Winnipeg Victorias, each club received around three thousand dollars. By 1906, an all-time high of five thousand dollars was derived from a single game in Montreal.

Of course, even this total is comparatively small, especially when compared with today's gates of forty-thousand dollars and more. Even so, it did impress rink-owners and teams that, with enlarged arenas, hockey could be profitable.

The players, too, were soon aware that clubs were willing to pay for their services. More cities were interested in the publicity and prestige of being "the home of the champions." The number of leagues was increasing, and schedules were enlarged. It was quite apparent that the social advantages of being a good player were lessening. It was also becoming necessary for a successful participant to make hockey a career rather than a pastime.

Canadian teams in the larger cities were making undercover payments to their stars, but it was an American club that openly broke the barrier between amateurs and professionals. In the winter of 1903/04, in Houghton, a small Michigan mining-town of thirty-five hundred persons, a team of "all the talents" was assembled. The team was known as the Portage Lake Hockey Club.

The players were gathered by Dr. J. L. Gibson who, some years earlier, had been a member of an intermediate hockey team in Berlin (later Kitchener), Ontario. "Doc" was a dentist, but he was not unacquainted with professional hockey, for in 1897 his Berlin team had won the provincial title. The next year the club was expelled from the Association for harbouring players who were paid for hockey services.

When Dr. Gibson, who was personally a star in many sports, went to Houghton, he was more interested in his dental practice than in playing hockey. However, he made the fatal mistake of taking along his scrapbook, and as he nostalgically thumbed the pages, the urge to again play became overpowering. There were no players of any stature in the copper county. So Gibson and a couple of associates planned to not only bring players from Canada but also form a four-team league.

It was a formidable challenge, but apparently it was no problem to raise money. The founders of the enterprise quickly sent scouts into the hinterlands of Eastern Canada. What they brought back were not just ordinary players, but a group of all-stars who would have been considered great in any age of hockey.

In their first year, not content with playing in their own league, they played a total of twenty-six games in St. Paul, St. Louis, Canadian Soo, American Soo, Pittsburgh and Montreal. They scored 273 goals to their opponents' forty-eight; they lost only twice, and later they decisively defeated their earlier victors.

The teams they played against were not set-ups, for they included the famed Montreal Wanderers, whom they whipped by scores of eight-four and nine-two.

The Portage Lake team of 1905/6 was even superior to the first club. It included such renowned players as Riley Hern, goal; Grindy Forrester, point; Barney Holden, cover-point; Fred "Cyclone" Taylor, rover; Bruce Stuart, centre; Joe Hall, right wing; Fred Lake, left wing. They were truly "iron men," in both the source of their earnings and their physical durability. They played at a time when there were thirty-two minute halves, with no substitutes allowed. Six of the Portage Lake team later played with champion Stanley Cup clubs, while Stuart and Taylor are honoured in the Hockey Hall of Fame.

Strangely, mining played an important role in early hockey. It was iron and copper that enabled Houghton to finance its costly teams. It was Klondike gold that made it possible for Colonel Boyle to provide funds for the Dawson City trek to Ottawa. And it was profits from cobalt and silver that later outbid all other mining areas and lured hockey players to Haileybury, Cobalt and New Liskeard.

In the background of all these promotions lurked the hope that sometime a sponsored team might be good enough to win the Stanley Cup and thus bring fame to the community and the club owner. Some of the episodes associated with these ambitions are part of Stanley Cup history, and no one was better acquainted with the ventures than "Mike" Rodden. "Mike" was a noted athlete, coach, manager, referee and sports editor who had been especially familiar with hockey life in northern Ontario in the years of the cobalt rush. There was a game in Haileybury that Mr. Rodden once recalled with much glee.

During the battle, Cobalt's Harry Smith, a notorious stick man, cut down so many opponents that the locals sent for the gendarmes, and Police Chief Paddy Collins came running with his guns. The chief wasn't very big, but he had the strength of a lion and the speed of a tiger. In no time at all he was piling the warring hockeyists one on top of the other. He gently led Harry Smith away to the jail up on the hill. But when all Smith's victims, including Art Ross, eventually recovered, he was released.

On his arrival home at Cobalt, Smith was welcomed by the town band, led by promoter Tommy Hare, and there wasn't any favour too great for "Battling Harry." Not to be outdone by Cobalt's generosity, Haileybury retaliated by presenting all its players with a mine in the Elk Lake District.

As that season advanced it became a question of not who might win but rather who would survive and why. Finally came the game to end all games, and it was played in the Cobalt Arena, which had the general appearance of an aeroplane hangar. It was supposed to accommodate about twelve hundred fans. But that night even the rafters were black with people, and at least two thousand spectators poured into the rink.

The financial success of the game didn't depend on the gate receipts, for the real money was the staggering sums wagered on the result. A local lawyer put up forty-five thousand dollars, but he became so excited that he couldn't even watch the contest and left the arena quite early for a long walk in the bitter cold. A couple of well-known Cobalt "chance takers" mortgaged all their possessions to cover a bet of fifty thousand dollars wagered by wealthy Noah Timmins, the Haileybury sponsor.

During the first half, the home-town Cobalt team scored five times, and the visiting backers appeared "ready for the cleaners." In the intermission, the disappointed Mr. Timmins dashed into the Haileybury dressing-room roaring murder and deploring that he was being taken for a ride.

And then in great majesty, Billy Nicholson, the biggest goal-keeper in the history of the game, arose and demanded, "Why all the excitement? Why criticize me? I never get properly warmed-up until the other fellows get five goals. After that I'm invincible. This game isn't over. Be of good cheer."

That explanation didn't exactly brighten Noah Timmins, for as he left the dressing-room, he thundered, "If you don't get warmed-up during the last half, you'll feel a lot warmer when this battle is over."

After hearing Nicholson's oration and the Timmins' warning, the Haileybury players, led by "Master Mind" Arthur Ross, tied-up Cobalt's Harry Smith into pretzel knots and nearly body-checked him into the next county.

There never was a money-player like Art Ross, when he wasn't fooling. Again and again he stick-handled through Cobalt players, and he was such an inspirational leader that his mates rallied around him. They came from far behind to tie the count before full-time.

The intermission that followed before the overtime will never be forgotten by the participants. The place had gone mad and those who had wagered their last dollars were frantically excited. Agreement had been made that the first goal scored would decide the match. Noah Timmins again went into the Haileybury dressing-room and announced, "I will give one thousand dollars to the man who scores the first goal."

Both teams trooped out again. Each had its own scoring chances, but goalkeepers Jones for Cobalt and three-hundred-pound Nicholson for Haileybury blocked all shots. One time Ross went through so fast that even the snow was flying behind him as he flashed around the opposing defence. "It's all over," groaned Cobalt fans. But in some mysterious way, Jones made the save. Ross shook his head and dashed back to protect the loquacious Nicholson. Then, at long last, Horace Gaul, an Ottawa import, took a pass from Ross and fired on Jones; the goal umpire's white flag was lofted and Haileybury were victors.

From the galleries crowded with Cobalt supporters, there came cries of despair. Suddenly, from the weight of humanity, the railing collapsed; many fans tumbled fifteen feet to the ice, and some were so seriously injured they had to be taken to the hospital on sleighs.

The hysteria continued. Winning fans showered pennies, dimes, quarters and even dollars on the ice. The air was filled with greenbacks, and the players were trying to catch their floating fortune on the fly.

But Billy Nicholson somehow obtained a tub, and any money iced in his vicinity was quickly snared and "tubbed." When he could find no more loot, and the sweat was pouring from his brow, he calmly turned the tub and its contents upside down and sat on it, so that no one could dislodge him or the money. How much money he collected, "Nick" never admitted, but there were guesses that he wouldn't have to work for a long time.

"Mike" Rodden believed that particular hockey night to be the wildest in the history of northern Ontario. A couple of well-known Cobalt businessmen were forced into bankruptcy. But hockey fanatics never give up, and the next winter Cobalt again entered a team in the National Hockey Association.

In 1909, the N.H.A. included Haileybury, Cobalt, Renfrew, Montreal Wanderers and Montreal Canadiens. At the same time, there existed a rival Canadian Hockey Association, which included Ottawa, Quebec and three Montreal clubs. The competition for players was so keen that it was soon apparent neither group could continue paying the big salaries and survive. So, with financial disaster imminent, the two associations combined into a seven-team league under the name of the National Hockey Association.

While the union of the two associations resulted in the existence of only a single group, the scramble for players and the intense club rivalry still prevailed. The Renfrew team, for instance, was called The Millionaires, and not without reason, for it was financed not by gate receipts but by the wealth of mine-owner Ambrose J. O'Brien and industrialist J. G. Barnett. The Millionaires' team included such high-priced imports as Lester Patrick, Frank Patrick, "Cyclone" Taylor, "Newsy" Lalonde, "Bobby" Rowe, Larry Gilmour, Fred Whitcroft, Nell Kimpton and Bert Lindsay. They were so famous that five of them, together with Mr. O'Brien, are honoured in the Hockey Hall of Fame.

The club pay-roll was high. Taylor, for instance, received twenty-eight hundred dollars and a position; the Patrick brothers got three thousand dollars each. When Frank Patrick was ill and unable to play one game, the Renfrew sponsors offered Edmonton's Hay Millar a thousand dollars if he would play a single game. Millar refused because his Edmonton club was already in Ottawa, waiting to play for the Stanley Cup, and he didn't want to hurt its chances of victory.

Even with all that money and with all that talent, Renfrew still didn't win its league. The principal contributor to their downfall was the Haileybury club financed by the equally wealthy Timmins brothers.

Toward the end of the season, Renfrew visited the Haileybury Arena. In the words of an observer: "They went in intact but came out on stretchers." In the hope of slowing the speedy Millionaires, the home team staged the roughest game of the season. "Cyclone" Taylor was body-checked so forcibly that he was partially projected through the wire-screen surrounding the ice. "Newsy" Lalonde, a rugged competitor in his own right, was crashed into the boards. While one Haileybury player held goalkeeper Bert Lindsay (father of the later famed Detroit star Ted Lindsay), another forward fired a puck that struck the Renfrew goalkeeper in the face. Then, to compound the offence, Haileybury refused to allow a replacement for the injured goalkeeper and compelled him to finish the game. Despite all attempts to mow them down, Renfrew did win the contest. But in the process they were so bady mauled that they were no match for the fresh Montreal Wanderers whom they had to meet in the final game.

All this upsurge of roughness and splurge of dollars had not been foreseen by Lord Stanley of Preston. When His Excellency bestowed his name and ten guineas for a trophy to be awarded the best team in Canada, he never imagined that his gift would become a symbol of professionalism. In his day, hockey was mainly the sport of society. It was played as a diversion by gentlemen who had the time and means to enjoy it as a pastime. But within a few years of the Cup's presentation, the rivalries of clubs and cities, the availability of mining money, the jealous pride of individual sponsors to prove their dollars could buy the best players—all this soon turned the Stanley Cup from its original lofty purpose into the arena of bitter controversy.

All this frantic striving for possession of the bowl irritated sportsmen, confused sports editors and baffled the cup trustees. The latter were deeply involved because amateurs contended that the donor had never intended paying tribute to professional sport. Indeed, at the time Lord Stanley made his gift, all hockey teams were amateur, and the first name engraved on the Cup was that of the Montreal *Amateur* Athletic Association.

However, from 1900 on, professional hockey spread across the country. It soon became rooted in Montreal, Quebec, Ottawa, Toronto, Winnipeg, Rat Portage, not to mention such American centres at Pittsburgh and Houghton. Stanley Cup trustees constantly tried to restrain its influence. But the first big break in the dike came in 1907, when the Eastern Canadian Amateur Hockey Association deleted "Amateur" from its title. Even though it was openly professional, the trustees permitted Montreal Wanderers, its champion team, to retain and defend the Stanley Cup.

One year the packed and stacked league in Northern Ontario sought the right to challenge for the trophy. The trustees had to be consistent and could not deny them the opportunity. But they did frustrate the challengers by stipulating that only players signed by early January would be eligible for Stanley Cup play that year. This decision, as intended, made it impossible for Cobalt and Haileybury to compete for the trophy, as their players had been signed after the deadline. The refusal so nettled the president of the Temiskaming League that he offered seventy-five pounds of pure silver, then valued at seven hundred dollars, for the purpose of making a new trophy to replace the Stanley Cup. Only professionals would contest for the new cup.

In the midst of such defiance of authority, the promoters of amateur sport rose up in wrath and demanded that the Stanley Cup be confirmed as their sole property. They suggested that the professionals might well accept as their award the more costly one offered in Temiskaming.

The cagey professionals, however, were not to be diverted by the offer of even a seven-hundred-dollar trophy instead of a fifty-dollar one. They were quite aware of the prestige behind Lord Stanley's name and Cup. They also recalled that when the Governor General donated his trophy he said: "I have for some time been thinking it would be a good thing if there were a challenge cup, which could be held from year to year by the leading hockey club in Canada." The professionals added that their best team was Canada's leading club, and if the amateurs did not agree, they could challenge for the Stanley Cup and see who would win.

There was no doubt that the professionals would have an easy victory, so no challenge was forthcoming. Moreover, the professionals were prepared to defend their right to the Stanley Cup in the courts. This prompted the amateur hockey leaders to say good-bye forever to the Stanley Cup. Thus, in 1908, Mr. W. M. Northey, a respected sportsman, contacted his friend Sir H. Montagu Allan, C.V.O., a prominent Montreal industrialist and financier. Mr. Northey later recalled:

I induced Sir Montagu to offer a trophy for the encouragement of amateurs and, by regulations, to so safeguard its purpose that it would never become a menace to the ideals it was intended to promote. It was agreed it would be a Challenge trophy eligible to any current league champions; and the surplus funds, after paying the legitimate expenses of the competitors, were to be distributed among charities.

The first Allan cup holder was the Victoria Hockey Club of Montreal. With this presentation, the Stanley Cup, in 1908, became the undisputed symbol of supremacy in professional hockey.

CHAPTER SEVEN STANLEY CUP GOES WEST

With official assurance that the Stanley Cup had become the sole possession of professional hockey, there was a spreading of moneyed leagues throughout the country. In 1910 alone, in the weeks between January 15 and March 12, there were four Stanley Cup series played. Even naming the contestants—Ottawa and Galt, Ottawa and Edmonton, Ottawa and Montreal Wanderers, Montreal Wanderers against Berlin (later Kitchener)—indicates the extent of the expansion. More than fifty years ago there were twenty-five professional hockey clubs in Canada. With all these teams, it was almost impossible to obtain enough good players. Consequently some Stanley Cup series were played between "the haves and the have nots." Even with the scarcity of supply, there was soon to emerge on the Pacific Coast a truly great league that would eventually match the strongest in the East. This western uprising was inspired by two brothers, Frank and Lester Patrick.

When the Renfrew Millionaires failed, in 1910, to win the National Hockey Association championship, the hopes of "Amby" O'Brien to produce a Stanley Cup holder were dashed to the ice. The team had excellent material, but most of the players were individual cogs that just did not mesh. When the club disbanded at the end of the season, most of the players were signed by other Eastern teams. The two Patricks returned to Victoria, British Columbia, where their father Joseph Patrick was a highly respected timber king. Originally the athletic sons intended to settle into business. However, hockey was in their blood, and before long they were surveying the possibilities of not only forming a team but actually founding an entire league.

The young promoters, who were still in their twenties, discovered there was coastal interest in hockey. But the obstacles to its development were many and large. There were very few high-class players in the area. There was little assurance that natural ice would be available for a long schedule of games. The cost of gathering suitable players and building artificial-ice arenas would require some hundreds of thousands of dollars. In other words, they had good reasons for chucking the whole idea. But when their father assured them he would financially guarantee the project, the two youthful promoters attacked the job with vigour and enthusiasm.

Still it was one thing to have the vision and another to bring it into being. The construction of the first artificial-ice rink in Canada was, in itself, a major achievement. But the gathering of suitable players to man the teams, to attract the fans, to fill the arenas, was even more demanding. This was a major-league venture, and the better players were already under contract to Eastern clubs.

At first through friendly contacts the Patricks endeavoured to induce distant sponsors to part with enough good players to give the new league a solid foundation. But they soon learned the Easterners were not going to lend a helping hand to their Western rivals. Then began a battle of dollars and wits. Frank and Lester informed prospective players the climate on the coast was so pleasant that the players should play for almost nothing, just to enjoy the nice sunshine and ocean breezes. When that lure failed, they offered high salaries. In 1912, Jack McDonald, a good player, earned seven hundred dollar for his season at Quebec. When the Patricks offered him twenty-two hundred dollars to play fourteen games for Vancouver, he joined the Westward trek.

In the process of raiding the east, long friendships were broken, sometimes with much bitterness. One day newspaper readers were pleasantly excited by the publication of a letter from

Frank Patrick addressed to the president of the Montreal Wanderers. A portion of it read:

> Your amusing and incoherent letter to hand, it would take a Philadelphia lawyer to decipher just what your words are meant to convey, from the way you have juggled the past, present and future.
>
> I do not care to enter into any controversy with you re hockey conditions in Canada. Your viewpoint is so warped that you allow your personal feelings to run riot with your pen. You are a well-known notoriety seeker, and your epistle will no doubt cause a ripple of laughter from the Atlantic to the Pacific.

While the battle of words continued, the raiding persisted. When the hockey season opened, the West had captured many of the East's hockey heroes. Headed by Frank Patrick, Lester Patrick and "Newsy" Lalonde, the Pacific Coast League, comprising Victoria Aristocrats, Vancouver Maroons (later Millionaires) and New Westminster Royals, played its opening game at Victoria on January 5, 1912. The league was so well-balanced that the pennant race was not decided until the final game of the season.

The Patricks had done a commendable job, and West Coast hockey blossomed quickly. At the end of the second year, the Quebec club, then National Hockey Association champions, travelled to Victoria and played a three-game series with the Pacific Coast winners. The games did not receive the blessing of the Stanley Cup trustees, but they were billed as a series to decide the world's hockey championship. In the engagement, the Victoria Aristocrats defeated Quebec Bulldogs by two games to one.

This achievement rocked Eastern promoters, for they appreciated the fact that the Western group was not a second-class league. They also realized that the Patricks and their associates were running a prosperous organization, and that they knew what good players looked like and had the money to pay them good salaries. Rather than continue a raiding that would harm all professional hockey, the East and West agreed to meet.

In the late summer of 1913, Frank Patrick huddled with representatives of the National Hockey Association in the East. The conference was fruitful. The right to retain players already signed was confirmed; and the West was granted a limited power of drafting players from Eastern clubs. The most important concession was the agreement that an annual series would be held between the two leagues, with the venue alternating between East and West. So what had begun as a raiding war culminated in mutual recognition. Thereafter, from 1914 until 1926, all Stanley Cup series were contested by the champion teams of the East and West.

The first Stanley Cup series between the National Hockey Association and the Pacific Coast League was played in Toronto in March of 1914, when the local Arenas defeated Victoria Cougars in three straight games. However, just one year later, in a series played in Vancouver, the Maroons whipped Ottawa Senators in three games to become the West's first Stanley Cup holders. The total scores for the series were twenty-six goals to eight, thus proving that the Patricks had done some very good shopping in the hockey marts.

While East and West had arranged to meet in Stanley Cup contests, there still were differences to be resolved. Sometimes the causes were variations in rules, many of which were proposed by Frank Patrick.

Frank Patrick was more than just a good hockey player; he was also an innovator. He was a hockey-architect, constantly seeking new ways to make the game more attractive to fans. Some of his ideas, now accepted as routine, were very controversial at their inception. Frank is credited with introducing blue-lines on ice to indicate zones, no offside penalties in the centre zone, permitting forward passes from one area to another, and with allowing players to kick the puck without necessarily stopping play. All these and other innovations were introduced. Patrick even revised the rules in the hope of reducing whistle-blowing and encouraging continuous play.

Occasionally a new idea is instantly accepted by the hockey world, and one such change related to the time of play. Ever since shinny-on-your-own-side became hockey, the length of a game had been two thirty-minute halves. Then the National Hockey Association in 1910 thought that the stretch was too tiring, especially since substitutions were not allowed. So, with the intent of resting the players more frequently, and thus speed-

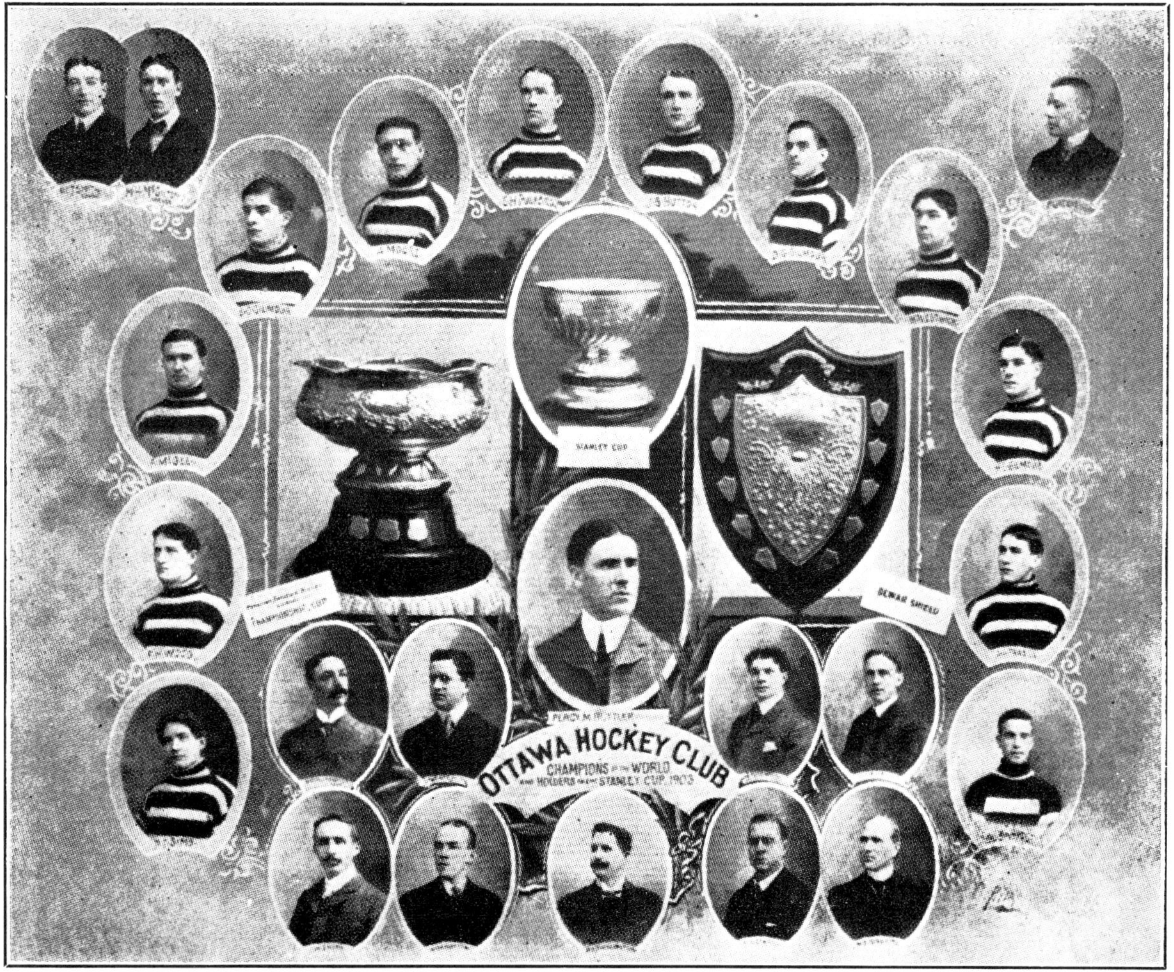

Ottawa's Famous Silver Seven Team. Stanley Cup Champions 1903-04-05.

"Cyclone" Taylor — Howie Morenz — Eddie Shore

Chuck Gardiner — Lester Patrick (in goalkeeper's equipment)

Some Were Super-Stars

ing the game, they introduced the revolutionary rule requiring three twenty-minute periods with ten minutes intermission between the periods. In so doing, they not only prolonged the playing-life of the players, but they also made it possible for the peanut and popcorn industries to increase sales.

At other times the proposals were so drastic and frequent that they were subjected to ridicule. Often they were spoofed. Once Mr. T. Emmett Quinn, president of the National Hockey Association, created consternation by proposing:

(1) To increase scoring, the puck should be painted green and reduced to half-size, thus making it more difficult for the goalkeeper to see and stop it. (2) That players should be compelled to carry rolls of bills in hip pocket, so that major fines could be paid on the spot. (3) That instead of giving a minor penalty, the referee should stop play, take the offender to the side for half-a-minute, talk to him and try to reform him.

These suggestions were duly filed.

While the Patricks were generally progressive in their ideas, they deliberated a long time before accepting the Eastern rule to reduce players from seven men to six. Pacific Coast fans were introduced to what they called "The Bob-tailed Rules" in a demonstration game between Vancouver and New Westminster. But that night a heavy fog settled over the ice, and both players and spectators were given a poor impression of the Eastern idea. Even when a Western All-Star team defeated Eastern All-Stars, in a game in which each team iced only six players, the coast folks still were not sold. They missed the backchecking of the rover and the combination play of their seven-man teams. So for many years there was usually a pre-game dispute during which the two ideas clashed. Sometimes it was resolved by playing half the game with six men to a side, and the other half with seven. Or, in a three-game series, the home club chose to play two games under its rules and the other under the visitors' rules. Eventually experience proved that six-man was faster, that the puck-carrier broke more quickly and that there was less bunching of players. So in time six-man hockey teams became nationally accepted and the factions sought other themes for their disputations.

While the rule-makers were resolving and amending the laws

and by-laws, clubs were changing in name and form, and player-raiding was still a popular pastime. But with the declaration of World War I in 1914, there were new problems. Many hockey players were early enlistments. One of these was Frank McGee, the former star centre of Ottawa's Silver Seven, who had once scored fourteen goals in a single Stanley Cup game. McGee, who was an all-time hockey great, had played part of his career with the handicap of only having one eye. Despite this disability, he enlisted at the beginning of the war and was killed at the Somme in 1916. "Scotty" Davidson, captain of the Arenas of Toronto, the 1914 Stanley Cup Champions, also went overseas with the first contingent and was an early casualty in Belgium.

The steady stream of enlistments from hockey clubs caused many changes in the personnel of professional teams. Indeed, the tide of battle and the need for overseas replacements on occasion engulfed the entire team.

At the beginning of the 1916/17 National Hockey Association season, there were enough good players in the 228th Sportsmen's Battalion to form an excellent professional team. At the time the soldiers did not know how long they would remain in Canada, but they made formal application for membership in the National Hockey Association. In a reckless moment, they posted a three thousand dollar bond to guarantee they would complete their league schedule, and with this assurance they were accepted by the N.H.A. During the first half of the season they proved they belonged, for even though they finished third, they were the highest scoring team in the league.

Early in February, the soldiers were fit and ready for the second half of the schedule. One day they had their uniforms, equipment and sticks all packed and were about to entrain for their match in Quebec. Then, without warning, their superior officers ordered a "cease-fire" on hockey nets. Instantly all further games were cancelled, and the 228th Battalion proceeded overseas to a bigger game on a larger arena, for stakes that were more important than dollars. The soldiers were, of course, disappointed at being unable to complete their schedule, but war was war. The only concession granted the players was permission to take their hockey outfits overseas, in the hope that some games might be played in London.

During the hockey season in Canada, there were some hockey episodes that brightened the dreary wartime. One of them concerned a player named "Duke" Keats who was such a good hockey star he was later honoured in the Hockey Hall of Fame. "Duke" had been a member of Toronto Blue Shirts in the 1915 season and had then enlisted with the 228th Sportsmen's Battalion. Naturally the soldiers said to the recruit: "Keats! you're our boy. We expect you to play hockey for us." The young soldier intended to play, but the Toronto club protested to the National Hockey Association that Keats, the athlete, had been signed by them, had played for them and that they were not releasing him to any club, be it military or civilian. The N.H.A. executive agreed with the Toronto club.

Keats played for Toronto while the war of words was being waged. The disagreement lasted until the final game of the first half of the season. Then military strategy intervened. On the day of the game—and not just by coincidence—Private Keats was hustled to the guard-house for confinement. Naturally he could not do much stickhandling in the hoosegow. But somehow the news of Keats' capture was promptly leaked to newspaper offices, and an indignant press howled at the gross injustice. They clamoured so furiously that it appeared civilization was on trial and that man's inhumanity to man was being unduly glorified. Rather than fight the Magna Charta, aided by the habeas corpus, the army unwillingly gave way and released Keats, just in time for him to appear on the ice and play against his own Battalion team.

While professional hockey was being played during the years of World War I, the clubs in Eastern Canada were not making money. Player raids from the Pacific coast clubs were continuing, teams had to double salaries to retain players, tempers of sponsors were becoming frayed, and threats of lawsuits and injunctions were freely bandied about. It was quite evident the National Hockey Association was sailing on rough seas and that waves of discontent were rising high. The situation was critical and could not continue. Frank Calder, the N.H.A. secretary, arranged a meeting of hockey magnates, which was held in Montreal on November 22, 1917.

The date is important in hockey history, for November 22

became the birthday of the National Hockey League. Mr. Calder, a capable Montreal newspaperman, was elected not only its secretary-treasurer but also its first president. In these capacities he invited applications for franchises, and Ottawa, Montreal Canadiens, Montreal Wanderers and Quebec were accepted, along with a team representing Toronto Arenas. However, they soon lost Quebec, because it lacked financial backing, and Montreal Wanderers were forced to withdraw when fire destroyed their Westmount Arena on January 2, 1918. So the first National Hockey League season was contested by only three clubs.

It was an interesting beginning. They divided the schedule into two halves. The first portion of the fourteen games was won by Montreal Canadiens, and the second of eight games by Toronto Arenas. Joe Malone of Canadiens made history by scoring forty-four goals in twenty-two games. In the playoffs, Toronto defeated Montreal by nine goals to seven, to become the first National Hockey League champions. Then they defended and retained the Stanley Cup by winning three of five games from Vancouver, the Pacific Coast challengers.

CHAPTER EIGHT THE AMERICAN INVASION

When the National Hockey League was born in the season of 1917/18, it was not a husky infant. Even the fans were not too healthy. These were war-time years, and in Montreal the Dominion Police were so busily engaged in rounding up military-service evaders that hockey attendance was greatly reduced. In fact, crowds were so sparse that Montreal sponsors were considering playing their Stanley Cup matches in Ottawa or Toronto. However, this was dropped when Toronto Arenas won the N.H.L. championship.

The new league had still other problems. One was that amateur games were outdrawing professional contests. Consequently salaries of professional players were not enough to warrant making hockey a full-time occupation.

Charlie Querrie, manager of Toronto Arenas in 1918, once revealed that he signed his team to contracts that totalled only $6,250 for the season. It included these amounts: Goalkeeper: Harry Holmes, $700; Defencemen: Ken Randall, $550, Harry Mummery, $600 and Harry Cameron $900; Rover: Jack Adams, $900; Centre: Corbett Denennay, $500; Left Wing: Reg Noble, $700; Right Wing: Rusty Crawford, $500. Spares: Alf Skinner and Harry Meeking, $450. Not even one of them received $1,000 for the entire season, and yet all were good enough to win not only their league but also the Stanley Cup.

Despite their ability and even the "bargain basement" salaries, the Toronto Arenas did not make money. Indeed, the following year, the cupboard was so bare that the National Hockey League itself had to pay players' salaries for the final two months to enable the club to survive the winter. At this stage, the venture had become so undesirable that Arena directors unloaded the club to five Toronto sportsmen who paid only two thousand dollars for the club name, sweaters, sticks and ice privileges. Even at this price the buyers were not boasting about the deal, for they still did not own a franchise to play in the National Hockey League.

However the other N.H.L. clubs badly wanted a team in Toronto. They sensed that someday the city, which was then an amateur stronghold, would become a profitable professional centre. In their eagerness to include Toronto, the other hockey promoters asked only five thousand dollars for a franchise. Because the Toronto sponsors had more faith in the future than they had dollars in the bank, the league arranged for them to pay the franchise money out of its profits, when and as they were earned. In response to this aid, the new Toronto owners, hoping the luck of the Irish would descend upon them, promptly changed their name from Arenas to St. Patricks. This was in the season of 1920/21, and begorra St. Pat's led the league.

The next year the Toronto club won the N.H.L. playoffs from Ottawa, defeated the challenging Vancouver club in the Stanley Cup series, paid back some of their franchise loan and upped the players' salaries. During this season, Goalkeeper "Jakie" Forbes received $1,500; Defenceman Harry Cameron, $2,200, and Forward Reg Noble, $2,000.

While these salaries were an advance, no player thought he was independently wealthy. A fine, for instance, was something to be avoided, and no one was more conscious of this than "Babe" Dye. During the 1921/22 N.H.L. playoffs, St. Patricks went to Ottawa with a one-goal lead on the round. On that mild March evening, the ice in Dey's Arena was covered with an inch of water. With such a tricky surface, Manager Querrie, in the hope of retaining that one-goal advantage, instructed his players to play a strictly defensive game. To ensure his order would be heeded, he drastically warned his team that anyone who carried the puck beyond mid-ice would be fined fifty dollars. The threat was so effective that only an over-eager "Babe" Dye, the leading goal-getter of his time, passed the point of no return. The fine was automatically imposed. When the game ended in a scoreless tie, the manager relented and forgave the sinning sniper.

During the early 1920s, the National Hockey League was growing, but there was keen competition for players. Out West there were two good professional leagues – the Pacific Coast Hockey Association, comprising Victoria, Vancouver and Seattle; and the newer Western Canadian Hockey League, including Regina, Edmonton, Calgary and Saskatoon. The demands of the two western and one eastern league invited a battle of dollars and wits in the attempt to acquire the better amateurs. Some of the so-called Simon-Pures were just as shrewd as the professional promoters. One of the most expert bargainers was Reginald "Hooley" Smith.

"Hooley" was a member of the famed Toronto Granites club which was good enough to easily win an Olympic hockey title. He was the kind of player the professionals wanted, for he was fast, colourful, had a good shot and was willing and able to take care of himself in any rough going. At the prevailing rates, he was easily worth two thousand dollars a season. But "Hooley" appraised his own value at three thousand dollars a year with a three-year contract.

Charlie Querrie knew young Smith personally and liked him so well that he determined to corral him for St. Pats. Charlie huddled with "Hooley" and cautiously offered him a contract for two thousand dollars. This, of course, was rejected. Then the wily manager slowly drew from his wallet ten hundred-dollar bills, and he spread them nicely on his desk. As "Hooley's" eyes popped at the vulgar display of wealth, Charlie leaned across the top and said, "Look at all that money, 'Hooley.' It's fresh and green. If you sign this two thousand dollar contract now, I'll give you this thousand as a bonus."

It was a terrific temptation for "Hooley." He eyed the table-cover with such intent that he almost drooled. Then he took a deep breath, faced his tormentor and said with a feigned cockiness, "Mr. Querrie, let me tell you something. I'm better than Jack Adams and Reg Noble together. You'll be farther ahead if you sell both of them and sign me at three thousand dollars a year." Now it was Querrie's turn to squirm. He rejected Hooley's proposal. But in doing so he erred, for young Smith was worth all he asked, and a couple of years later Montreal Maroons were paying him eight thousand dollars a season.

Slowly, yet relentlessly, hockey was marching on. It was growing into a sport with money-making possibilities. First it required larger and better arenas, with facilities to accommodate the many thousands who were clamouring for tickets. However, the key to most of hockey's problems was dependable ice.

The Patricks in 1911 were the first Canadians to install artificial ice in their hockey rinks on the Pacific Coast. Until then even the most important games were marred or occasionally postponed because the natural ice was unfit for play.

In one Stanley Cup series between Montreal Wanderers and a Toronto team, a newspaper correspondent reported:

Miniature ponds of water, several square yards in area, were scattered over the ice, and all the players were drenched to the skin before the game was over. Spectators who occupied places of vantage along the rails also came in for a ducking. The puck would slide to a pond, then stop dead. The onlookers were scarcely able to tell one player from another, as the latter waded-in and splashed water in clouds, in the endeavour to get possession of the puck. At half-time, tubs were carried on the ice and attempts were made to scoop some of the water into them.

Another evening, Ottawa and Victorias were playing in Montreal Arena, with five thousand spectators watching. The game was hockey, not water polo, yet:

Prior to the commencement of the match, rink attendants, armed with scoops and buckets, ladled off as much surface water as possible; but just as soon as it was removed, more appeared. As the game progressed, biggish pools near the south end increased in area; and in the second half they became lakelets.

These surfaces, while not desirable, were considered so inevitable by writers and fans that they became subjects of good-natured humour rather than contempt.

During one game in Renfrew the water was so deep that a puck really had to be fished for. Another time the puck got lost and was so completely immersed that its location was revealed only by the ripples. A writer observed: "Hall, of Shamrocks, went to drydock for repairs." He concluded his story with the report: "Thanks to the good work of the life-savers, all players were saved from drowning."

Those marine items were often lightened by the cheery sketches of sporting artists. One series depicted players in uniform swimming in the arena. Or a player with lofted stick hollering to his mates, "Wait! I have a bite." Another sketch showed two drenched players conversing and one enquiring: "Could I borrow your wringer?" It was all good clean fun, both on and off the ice. But it was not ideally suited for playing games billed for "the championship of the world."

During these years, rinks were sometimes sold out in advance sales. Until game time, there was no certainty that the match would be played. This was especially true in the month of March, when the most important games of the season were scheduled. There were times when, despite the ice-makers' best efforts, nice green grass was sprouting through holes in the surface. It was more than coincidence that the list in the Toronto newspapers of games to be played that night were usually accompanied by weather predictions.

Players, promoters and spectators endured these trials because there seemed no alternative. True, there were artificial ice rinks in the British Isles and even in the United States, but they were primarily intended for pleasure skating. However the astute Patricks, realizing that the availability of artificial ice on the warmer coast was imperative, installed the first plants in Canada in 1911 at Vancouver and Victoria. Toronto followed in 1912. But generally the East moved slowly, because the existing rinks were old and would have required costly redesigning and reconstruction. In 1921 there were still only four artificial-ice arenas in Canada. But by 1934 there were at least twenty.

Artificial ice was probably the most valuable of all scientific contributions to hockey. Prior to its introduction, rinks were cold and colourless. Windows were opened to invite arctic blasts, and spectators had to bundle up as though they had mushed to the rink on dogsled. But with the installation of artificial ice, fans could dress normally; the game was assured, regardless of spring thaws; play was speeded up; and seasons could be extended from early October until April.

The resulting longer schedules, the rising prices for tickets and the increased patronage made the profession desirable for both sponsors and players. Moreover, because artificial ice could be manufactured in any portion of the United States, American promoters became keenly interested in hockey clubs and arenas. During the early 1920s, the buying and selling of National Hockey League franchises became a popular indoor sport. It was profitable, too.

In 1920, Quebec had withdrawn from the National Hockey League, and Charlie Querrie, along with N.H.L. President Frank Calder, sold the Quebec franchise to a group of Hamilton sportsmen for seventy-five hundred dollars. "If they had only held out they could have had it for nothing," Querrie later confided. But do not feel sorry for these Hamiltonians, for five years later they resold those same rights to a New York group for seventy-five thousand dollars.

In 1924, Boston became the first American city to join the National Hockey League. That city, partly because many French Canadians were employed in the New England textile industries, had long been known as a good hockey town, and Canadian amateur teams had often visited it to play exhibition games. In addition Boston's Number One fan was Charles Adams, the owner of a successful grocery chain. It was not difficult to convince him that Boston should have its own professional hockey club.

Canadian club-owners welcomed Mr. Adams and his "cash on hand." But his team was mauled by rivals. In its first season, it won only six games in the thirty played. At times the disappointed Hub fans expressed chagrin, not by hooting and hollering, but by tossing coins on the ice. One night, a visiting Toronto St. Pats player salvaged over three dollars in small change.

Despite Boston's slow start, other cities in the United States pleaded for admission to hockey's major league. So when the 1925 season began, Pittsburgh Yellow Jackets and New York Americans were in the fold, and Chicago, Detroit and another New York faction were knocking on the door.

The outsiders were sometimes tricky when applying. For instance, "Paddy" Harmon of Chicago attended an N.H.L.

meeting in Montreal and earnestly sought a franchise. "Paddy," an old hand with money, knew the National Hockey League owners also had a liking for lucre, regardless of how filthy it might be. He was aware too that any new franchise money was divided among the clubs already in the league. So Mr. Harmon used a guile that had hitherto served him well. During the conference he carefully unloaded his satchel and casually piled a stock of fifty one-thousand-dollar bills.

"There gentlemen," said Paddy, "is my bid of fifty thousand dollars. Give me a franchise for Chicago, and all this money is yours—and now." The owners looked at each other. Instead of enjoying the prospect, they were compelled to stifle their sobs and reject the offer. Why? Well, in an earlier hour of decision, they unwisely sold the same Chicago package to a Major McLaughlin for a piffling twelve thousand dollars.

Throughout the summer of 1926, there was much feuding within and without the National Hockey League. "Tex" Rickard, a noted New York promoter, already held one franchise and was so greedy he wanted another. When Toronto's N. L. Nathanson bitterly opposed the extension, Rickard became so aroused that he threatened to invade Toronto with a competing rink and club. His bluff was quickly called. "If you do that," countered Nathanson, "I'll go down to New York and I'll erect a new Garden that will make Madison Square look cheap." And he had the wealth and influence to do it, but it was not necessary.

Then Charlie Pyle, a promoter with a yen for sponsoring sport spectaculars, offered "Tom" Duggan two hundred and fifty thousand dollars for his recently acquired New York Americans' franchise and players. Duggan, an ex-Canadian, who had bought the same privileges for only seventy-five thousand dollars rejected Pyle's pile and demanded three hundred thousand dollars.

Naturally such financial frenzy and sudden expansion aroused an urgent need for better players, and in large quantity. A rink, a franchise and a well-stocked larder of sticks and skates were not much good without bodies. Every new entry had to be manned.

At first the National Hockey League clubs approached Canada's better amateurs; but many of them were already being paid by their supposedly Simon-Pure sponsors and would not have bettered themselves financially. Fortunately for the growth of Eastern professional clubs, something important was happening out West.

In the 1925/26 season, the Western Canadian Hockey League comprised six cities—Edmonton, Saskatoon, Victoria, Portland, Calgary and Vancouver. These players were most highly skilled in their profession of potting goals. But small crowds and steep salaries made the ventures unprofitable. Additionally, many western citizens felt they would be adding to their own income as well as assisting the Canadian economy if they filled their spacious rinks with grain rather than people.

The Western demand for more storage space, together with the urge of American cities to harvest big crops of hockey players, finally resulted in the decision to disband the Western league. The rumour, as usual, preceded the definite decision. Before the grain moved in, the N.H.L. clubs, new and old, were desperately trying to make private deals for nearly all the about-to-be-harvested crop of seventy-five hockey players.

Chicago interests had contacted Portland owners and arranged to buy the entire team. Detroit magnates were dickering to take over all the Victoria Cougars players who had just won the league championship. But they hesitated when they learned they would have to pay a hundred thousand dollars for the team, fifty thousand for the ice-making plant and another fifteen thousand for Lester Patrick. Boston's Charlie Adams was even more ambitious. He offered to buy the whole league for three hundred thousand dollars. However, the other clubs soon vetoed that arrangement, for they knew that Boston would retain the brighter stars and let the rivals scramble for the lesser lights.

Some N.H.L. clubs had refrained from buying other clubs outright and had hand-picked their choices and contacted them individually. In the process, several players double-dealt. Goalkeeper George Hainsworth, for instance, had negotiated with both Montreal Canadiens and Toronto St. Patricks. Bun Cook and Bill Cook were claimed by both New York Rangers and Ottawa. Every N.H.L. club contacted Harry Oliver of Calgary.

Out of this confusion there emerged not order but even more chaos. Western clubs complained that individual players had been privately signed without the knowledge of either their club or league. Similarly, in the East, it was apparent that in the same city one group had corralled the players while another faction owned the franchise and the rink, and each group believed it held the strongest hand and refused to yield.

During the milling around, Adams of Boston produced a cancelled cheque for fifty thousand dollars to prove he had bought seven of the better Westerners. When the rivals were confronted with this evidence, they realized they had been out-foxed. They huddled, and when the conference ended, it was agreed that the National Hockey League would reimburse Mr. Adams for his outlay and that the N.H.L. would itself buy the entire Western league for two hundred and fifty-eight thousand dollars and then allocate the players to various clubs according to their needs and by the luck of the draw.

When the 1926/27 season began, there was, of course, no Western league. But there were ten teams in the National Hockey League. They were divided into two groups of five teams each. In the so-called Canadian Division, the teams were: Ottawa, Montreal Canadiens, Montreal Maroons, Toronto Maple Leafs and New York Americans. The American Division included: New York Rangers, Boston, Chicago, Pittsburgh and Detroit.

One of the by-products of the enlarging of the N.H.L. and the ending of the W.C.H.L. was that it necessitated a new type of Stanley Cup competition. Originally the Stanley Cup was a challenge trophy, and the champion clubs of most leagues could challenge the holder. The earliest Cup contests were only single games. In February of 1896, Winnipeg Victorias journeyed into a far country to play Montreal Victorias only one game (which they won two-nothing). In December of 1896, the trip was reversed, for Montreal travelled to Winnipeg and recaptured the Stanley Cup in a six-five sudden death contest.

Those twenty-eight-hundred-mile trips were tiresome and costly, just to play a solitary match that would start and finish within a couple of hours, with only a fifty-dollar trophy and a fleeting title at stake. The competing clubs realized this, and with the permission of Stanley Cup trustees, the test was lengthened to a series of two games, with total goals to decide the winner. But this arrangement also had the disadvantage that, if one team had a wide margin in the first game, then the second match failed to interest the fans. This was so apparent in 1897 that after Montreal Vics walloped challenging Ottawa Capitals by fifteen goals to two, the second game was cancelled "in the interests of hockey."

In 1900 the trustees and the interested clubs preferred to play a "best of three" series in which the team winning two games became Stanley Cup holders. This arrangement continued until March 8, 1906, and the Ottawa Silver Seven enjoyed its long run during which it turned back eight challenges. They remained undefeated until – and this might have been only coincidence—the series with Montreal Wanderers reverted to a two-game duel with total goals to decide. Under this arrangement Ottawa was dethroned by Montreal.

Through the succeeding decade, there was a frequent tinkering with rules that related to the number of games to be played in Stanley Cup competition. Sudden death, total points, best of three games were all tried. Sudden death was certainly the most decisive form, and when one club outclassed the other, it was also the least painful.

However, in 1914, when the powerful Pacific Coast champions had to cross a continent, it seemed unfair—and certainly unprofitable—to play only one game. So the competition was extended to a series of five games, which implied that the first team to win three games would have its name engraved on Lord Stanley's bowl. With the exception of two years, this three-in-five plan continued until 1927.

When the Western Canadian Hockey League disbanded in the spring of 1927, western challenges ceased, and the Stanley Cup became the sole possession of the National Hockey League. It would therefore have been sufficient to declare that the league-leading team at the end of each season would automatically become Stanley Cup holder. Not only was this too simple, it was also poor business. What happened?

Well the resulting arrangement is a little involved, but it is interesting all the same. There were then two divisions with five teams each. The second and third teams in each division played a series of two games, with total goals to decide the winner. The winner played two more games, with goals to count against the team that finished first in its division. This series resulted in a contender from both the American and the Canadian division. These two played a best-of-five series to decide who would win and hold the Stanley Cup. It seems less complicated when we recall that, in the Canadian section, Canadiens defeated Montreal and Ottawa ousted Canadiens. In the American division, Boston whipped Chicago and then New York Rangers. Finally Ottawa conquered Boston and became Stanley Cup champions.

During the decade that followed, there was a frequent shuffling of clubs and names. The Pittsburgh franchise was transferred to Philadelphia, where the Quakers lasted only one season. Ottawa was in and out and then disposed to St. Louis, where the Eagles enjoyed a very brief flight. Detroit Cougars changed their name to Falcons and later to Red Wings. Toronto St. Pats became Toronto Maple Leafs. Montreal Maroons retired. New York Americans were replaced by Brooklyn Americans, then disbanded after a year.

So, by 1942, only six teams remained: Montreal Canadiens, Toronto Maple Leafs, Boston Bruins, Chicago Black Hawks, Detroit Red Wings and New York Rangers. The same six, without additions or subtractions, comprised the National Hockey League through almost a quarter-century. Then, the winds of change aroused an expansion that doubled the number of teams. Beginning the season of 1967-68 there were new clubs in Philadelphia, Pittsburgh, St. Louis, Minneapolis-St. Paul, Los Angeles and San-Francisco-Oakland. Expansion continued in the season of 1970-71 when teams in Buffalo and Vancouver increased the membership to fourteen clubs.

CHAPTER NINE STANLEY CUP HIGH-JINKS

Hockey has always been a sport in which the unexpected is to be anticipated. Even before Lord Stanley presented his trophy, the game resulted in some unusual incidents. Often the occurrences involved a puck.

One night, probably early in the 1860's, two hockey teams were playing a game in Montreal's Victoria Skating Rink. The "puck" was a solid rubber ball of the type used in lacrosse. As it was whacked and passed, it rebounded from the ice over the low platforms at the sides, usually filled by standees, and before the hard ball was captured it smashed several windows.

All this destruction irritated the rink manager, so after three hundred and fifty dollars worth of panes were broken, his personal pains became so unbearable that he groaned: "I'll have no more of this nonsense. Give me that ball." Then he borrowed a sharp knife, cut the top and bottom sections off the ball and handed back the flat centre. "There you are," he gloated, "You can continue to play with that piece." The puck slid rather than bounced; no more windows were smashed. And thus, according to legend, the hockey puck was invented.

Another night, and still in the pre-Stanley Cup era, a hockey game was being played in the Victoria Rink, located on Huron Street in Toronto. It was a special occasion. The gallery railings were festooned with bunting, and huge Union Jacks were suspended high above the goals. In the closing minutes of the game, with the score tied, one of the attacking players lofted a high shot. The puck soared into the dimly lighted overhead area, and for a time it was out of sight. The players were confused until, moments later, the flat piece of rubber descended, bounced crazily in front of the goalkeeper and hopped between the goal posts for a score. Where had the puck gone? What had delayed its arrival? The mystery was solved when it became apparent the lofted rubber had smacked into one of the overhanging flags; it got caught in the folds of the flag and remained there until the flag uncurled and released the puck.

Pucks were frequent sources of trouble in early hockey. One night Fred Waghorne, the busiest referee of his era, was officiating at a game in a small Ontario town. At the time hockey pucks were made in two halves and cemented together. On this occasion an attacker fired a shot. While it was not as important as the one heard around the world, it did excite the immediate observers. In its flight the halves separated with one portion flying into a corner and the other sweeping right into the goal. Was it a score? The defenders said "No." The attackers yelled "Yes." The referee, with the desire to be just, yanked the rule-book out of his hip pocket and pondered. He closed the book, returned it to his pocket and declared "No Goal." His explanation was worthy of a Solomon. He reasoned: "The rules say a puck is one inch thick. The object that went into the goal was half an inch thick. Therefore, it could not have been a legal puck." The decision was protested but was upheld by hockey's law-makers. It is from such yarns that the fabric of the game is woven.

Stanley Cup series have contributed their own tales to hockey history, and while some of them have been repeated often, they do add to the folklore of a national sport. After a Stanley Cup victory in 1905, some members of the Ottawa Silver Seven were returning from a banquet in Russell House. Suddenly one of the celebrants carrying the trophy boasted he could successfully drop-kick the silverware right into the Rideau Canal. The idea was not too remote, for many of the hockey players also excelled in rugby football. So fortified by strong wine and goaded by mates, the athlete succeeded in his first attempt. The members of the gang cheerfully went to bed.

The morning after, the cup was missing. More in sorrow than in anger the players returned to the Canal, fished out the Stanley Cup and gave it to "Harry" Smith for safe-keeping in his home. The next year Montreal Wanderers won the trophy. When presentation time approached, the cup was out of sight until an

Ottawa player recalled: "Sure! I know where it is. Don't you remember the time we gave it to 'Harry' to take home? He has it all right."

Another year a Montreal Club—it might have been the Wanderers—wanted its picture taken with the Stanley Cup in the studio of photographer "Jimmy" Rice. When the scene was snapped for posterity, the team departed, leaving behind the famous cup. It remained around the studio for some months, until the photographer's mother, thinking that the bowl had neither value nor sentiment, took it from a cupboard, filled it with good, black earth. Then she planted some nice red geraniums in the earth and proudly placed it in the studio window. Later the cup was rescued by "Jimmy" and presented to its lawful defenders.

Around 1910, when Montreal Wanderers were the cup-holders, one of the players operated a bowling alley on St. Catherine Street. This time the silver bowl was not a glistening flower pot. Instead it was lodged in a showcase, heaped high with chewing gum to entice prospective buyers.

Hockey's rarest prize continued to be used and abused, to be cherished yet slighted. This was evidenced in the Big Neglect of 1924. Montreal Canadiens defeated Calgary and became cup-holders. Next night a number of players and friends gathered for a victory dinner in Canadiens' quarters in Montreal's Windsor Hotel.

After the dinner someone suggested that they drive out to Leo Dandurand's home and have a champagne party. Carefully nursing the Stanley Cup, a group piled into the Dandurand car and headed for Leo's home. While *en route,* one of the tires blew out. During the stop for repairs, the cup was removed from the car and placed on the sidewalk near the curb. Once the tire problem was solved, the passengers quickly piled into the car and continued driving to the home of their host. When the thirsty guests arrived, the champagne was ready for serving, but where was the cup? With mingled feelings of shame and concern, they realized that during the repairs, the gift of Lord Stanley had been left by the roadside. Instantly a search party was despatched, and when the rendezvous was reached after driving a mile and a half, they were overjoyed to find the gleaming trophy exactly where they had left it.

Champagne parties and the Stanley Cup have always been pleasantly associated. However, there was one occasion when the festivities were not only too costly but also held for the wrong people. Many years ago New York Rangers won the final series. Like true world champions, they planned to celebrate their victory with a champagne party, to which about thirty-five guests had been invited. However, many more than had been invited attended, for in a neighbouring reception room in the hotel a much larger dance was being held. As the evening progressed, the dancing couples strolled from their own affair into the Rangers' reservation, where they stealthily sipped the bubbling beverage from the repeatedly filled flowing bowl. It seemed as though the uninvited guests gulped more than they sampled, for the next day the New York Rangers' management was shocked into sobriety when it received a bill for thirty-seven hundred dollars.

Today the Stanley Cup is appropriately housed in Canada's Hockey Hall of Fame—when it is not required for presentation ceremonies. In earlier years, when not retained by clubs, it was often mislaid. In the absence of a regular custodian, it was occasionally left in strange hideouts. Once, after careful crating for shipment to another city, it was missing for several days. Eventually, after much searching, someone discovered it in a rarely used cubbyhole of a baggage car.

Another time the Stanley Cup was used as a psychological weapon. In 1947, Toronto Maple Leafs beat Montreal Canadiens in the sixth and decisive game for the Stanley Cup. While the fans in Maple Leaf Gardens stood and cheered, the players on both teams shook hands, then retired to their dressing-rooms. The crowd, eagerly awaiting the customary cup-presentation ceremonies, began chanting impatiently, "We want the cup! We want the cup!" But the cup was not at the Gardens. It was not even in Toronto. It was still on display in Montreal about three hundred and fifty miles away.

There was a good explanation for the absence of the trophy. Indeed, its absence had been so planned by Conn Smythe. The astute Toronto manager, following the fifth game in Montreal, reasoned in this fashion:

Leafs now lead the series by three games to two, and we need just one more victory in the game to be played in Toronto. Now if I go down to the store, where it is being displayed and take possession, the sportswriters will hear of it. There will be pictures in the papers and exaggerated stories of our confidence. Then the players would probably say to each other: "Well! the boss thinks we can't lose. He has ordered the cup back to Toronto for the presentation just after the next game. It looks as though we are sure to be champs."

Mr. Smythe also believed that removing the cup to Toronto would enable Dick Irvin, Montreal Canadiens coach, to arouse his own players. He would only need to say to them:

Smythe says the series is over and that we haven't a chance to win. He has taken the cup back to the Gardens. Let's show him up. All you have to do is win in Toronto; then you come back to Montreal for the final game. When we win that, we can have our own presentation right on Forum ice, before our own fans.

Whether or not Conn Smythe's decision to leave the Stanley Cup in Montreal was the decisive factor is debatable. At least it was a helpful influence, for Toronto Maple Leafs won at home by two to one. The trophy came along later.

A similar situation arose in the 1964 series. Detroit Red Wings had just defeated Maple Leafs in Toronto, and were about to return to Detroit for the game that might have given them the big trophy. To ensure the cup would be available if required, it was included with the equipment of the Red Wings for transportation to the Olympia. As soon as Sid Abel, Detroit coach, learned of its presence in their baggage, he ordered it removed. He instructed President Campbell to make other arrangements for its transportation. So the "spell" of the Stanley Cup still persists after seventy years. Its very presence attracts superstitions.

Stanley Cup fever has a variety of symptoms. Long ago players often scratched their signatures on the gold-lined bowl and on the silver surface. Even as recently as 1962, a Chicago fan, while a game was in progress, actually lifted the trophy from a showcase in the Stadium lobby and started walking. The pilferer almost reached the street before he was captured by a Stadium policeman.

Even when the cup itself was properly guarded, desire for its possession has evoked all sorts of emotional explosions. One year it inspired a players' strike. When the 1924/25 season ended, the Hamilton team was leading the National Hockey League, and Hamilton was given the bye into the final round. Meanwhile, Montreal Canadiens defeated Toronto St. Patricks in the semi-final series and expected to meet the Hamilton club, with the winner playing Victoria Cougars for the Stanley Cup. But this arrangement irritated the Tigers, who promptly howled.

The Hamilton players had good reason to complain. When the ten regulars signed their contracts, there was no clause relating to extra pay for playoff games. Thus, even though the players had topped the league in regular play, they were compelled to wait around at least a week, while the second and third clubs finished their semi-final round. For all the delay and for the additional playoff games, they were told there would be no extra pay.

The disgruntled players rebelled and called a meeting. They were not only skilled performers on ice but with "Shorty" Green and "Mickey" Roach they possessed excellent debating talent. The players decided, quite modestly, that their bonus for extra time should be not less than two hundred dollars a man. Then they added that their proposal was firm and that if it was not accepted they would refuse to play even if their decision resulted in individual suspensions from hockey. Green and Roach presented their arguments, and despite their colourful eloquence, the club owners and the National Hockey League governors bluntly rejected their request.

Both sides refused to yield. The League insisted that seasonal contracts included playoffs. The players denied this and stuck solidly together. Then they packed up and went home, leaving Montreal Canadiens to go west and the executives to go somewhere else. The aftermath was that all Hamilton players were duly suspended, and Victoria defeated Canadiens and won the Stanley Cup.

During the summer, the suspensions of the strikers were lifted to enable the Hamilton owners to sell the players, equipment and franchise to New York Americans for seventy-five thousand dollars. It had cost them only seventy-five hundred dollars a few years earlier. But this civil war was beneficial in that the rights of players were more clearly defined, salaries were increased, and bonuses were awarded for outstanding play.

Not many players are prepared to risk suspension for what they believe to be justice, but there have been numerous instances in Stanley Cup competition when they have delivered their own sentences. An outstanding example occurred during the 1938 series between Chicago Black Hawks and Toronto Maple Leafs. "Doc" Romnes, for instance, had previously enjoyed a reputation for clean play, and it was merited, for he had served only a single two-minute penalty. Another year he was the winner of the Lady Byng Memorial Trophy, annually awarded to the player who best combined skill and gentlemanly conduct. In the season of 1937/38, his behaviour had been a model for all other N.H.L. players. And yet, during the stress of Stanley Cup competition, without any provocation, Romnes dashed straight from a faceoff and unleashed a two-handed swipe at an opponent's head. It was so brutal that, had it struck, it would have separated the latter's chin from his shoulders. Neither before or after did "Doc" exhibit such ferocity. Indeed, the next season Romnes was traded from Chicago to Toronto and became a team-mate of "Red" Horner, whom he had so recklessly attacked.

Sometimes the emotional binge during Stanley Cup time results in tears rather than mayhem. After one Stanley Cup victory, the players on the winning team were joyously patting each other and whooping it up in mid-ice. But the goalkeeper felt differently. With the pressure of play ended, he turned his back to the jubilation, leaned on the top of the goal net and quietly shed a few tears.

Stanley Cup tension also induces an unusual reaction in the crowd. The tension is often relieved by throwing junk on the ice. More recently, arena managements discouraged the custom by threatening to eject the thrower. In some rinks they even offer to give a reward to anyone reporting an offender. The practice is both time-consuming and dangerous to the players, but in its hey-day it involved much originality. The stuff released by the tossers might have been eggs, ink, rolls of toilet paper, coins, rubber balls, playing cards, even paper clips shot from catapults.

It was an annual ritual in Detroit, during Stanley Cup games, for some undiscovered miscreant to pitch an octopus on the ice. Then, while the players and officials skated away from the many-armed mollusc, attendants gingerly shovelled the big sucker out of view. One night, in Detroit, during a Stanley Cup game between New York Rangers and Detroit Red Wings, a dark object was hurled, but when it landed it squirmed. As it wriggled some more, Marcel Pronovost, then a summer-time fishing guide, made a close appraisal and promptly identified the three-feet long thing as an eel. Even though New York's Camille Henry had been nicknamed "The Eel" because of his slippery play, he promptly denied any relationship.

Montreal fans are also famed for their good throwing arms, but their specialty is not fish but rubbers. This is not too strange, for, in March and April, worn-out rubbers are discarded anyway. Perhaps it is more convenient to dispose of them in the Forum rather than in a garbage can. But the mystery that baffles researchers and salvage crews is the fact that the number of lefts and rights rarely agrees. What happens to the lone rubber?

Most fans and participants have a personal way of revealing the Stanley Cup jitters, but there have been players who just refused to be ruffled in the midst of the storm. Alex Connell was one of them. In 1927, Ottawa Senators were an excellent team. They not only led the National Hockey League, but they also won the Stanley Cup, and Connell was their goalkeeper. In addition to being a sensational stopper, he was also a prankster and a rare mimic. During the Stanley Cup semi-final round, the Senators were playing in Montreal, and after one of the games the players had a late supper at the Windsor Grill.

That evening there was a large crowd and a splendid orchestra. Then a special treat was announced. Alex Connell, the great netminder, who was also a talented violinist, would play one of his favourite selections. The diners were astounded by the artistry of the musical athlete as he skilfully bowed the instrument then gracefully departed, with all the customary gestures of appreciation to the audience. The customers vigorously applauded. Not until long after the Connell entourage departed were they aware that the performance was faked. While Alex went through all the motions, the leading violinist of the orchestra, from behind the draperies, was actually producing the sound effects.

Often during Stanley Cup play there are flashes of banter that never reach the ears of the crowd. During a series in the early 1940s, "Nick" Metz, a quiet Toronto Maple Leaf player, who was gifted with a dry wit, had been complaining about Referee Bill Chadwick's decisions all through the game. Finally the weary official exploded. "Look! 'Nick,' I'll referee this game. Your job is to put that round black thing into the net."

Soon after Metz scored. As he skated close to Chadwick, he cracked, "You know, Bill, you're just the referee. You're not supposed to coach us players."

"Turk" Broda was one of the most colourful players to ever perform in the National Hockey League. Without even trying he was always headline material. Much of his esteem was attributed to a coolness under fire.

During a game in a Stanley Cup series between Toronto Maple Leafs and Detroit Red Wings, "Turk" earned a shutout. At the conclusion, Toronto fans were excitedly shouting, and the players were moving toward their goalkeeper to give him the traditional whacks and thumps. But instead of awaiting the mauling and greeting, "Turk" dashed from his net and was eagerly salvaging from the ice a few cigars that a well-wisher had tossed in his direction. When the players finally reached Mr. Broda, he was not in any mood to blushingly exclaim, "Aw! Shucks, fellows. I wasn't really that good." Instead, while thousands cheered and mates exulted, "Turk" was verbally denouncing one of his defencemen who had accidentally skated over and crushed one of the gift stogies.

Stanley Cup time is much more than a series of games that decides the hockey championship of the world. It is also a period when spectators and participants, aroused by alternate jolts of victory and defeat, are shocked into behaviour quite foreign to their normal way of living. Symptoms of Stanley Cup fever are many. The contagious disease has struck when a usually silent fan turns into a roaring lion breathing defiance to everyone within sound of his voice. It has struck when a swashbuckling player reverts to docility with fear of making a mistake that will lose his team the game. There is no known cure!

CHAPTER TEN SERIES TO REMEMBER

The story of the Stanley Cup is not restricted to the activities of colourful individuals. It teems with the stories of great clubs which have matched their skills in series that are long remembered.

One notable struggle occurred more than sixty years ago. Even as early as the turn of the century, there was intense hockey rivalry between the best of the east and the west. It actually began early in 1896, when Winnipeg Victorias challenged cup-holding Victorias of Montreal and defeated them in a sudden-death game by a score of two to nothing. The result was a shocker for the east, for few observers believed the western players had acquired the skill to match the maturity of those in Montreal, Ottawa or Quebec. However, the Winnipeg triumph was short-lived, for in December of 1896 the Montreal Vics went West and regained the Stanley Cup in a cliff-hanging six to five game. These stirring contests continued, for the West persistently challenged. In 1900, Montreal Shamrocks were the Stanley Cup holders, and Winnipeg Victorias hoped the change in defenders might also improve their fortune.

The Western club left Winnipeg with a send-off fit for a king, and their trip to Montreal was telegraphed from station to station. Along the way enthusiasm heightened by the mile, until it was reported that every city within a day's travel of Montreal would have some representative or other at the series. In the early pre-game fanfare, an ardent Montreal writer predicted that: "Captain Trihey and his Shamrock lieutenants never faced a foe that will be more worthy of their steel and hickory than the one which is now speeding eastward with big physiques and stout hearts." The lofty forecast proved very true.

Remember the year was 1900. Queen Victoria was still on the throne. Hockey enthusiasm was so rampant that eight thousand spectators watched Winnipeg Victorias win by four to three. The second game was viewed by a capacity crowd with many hundreds milling around and unable to get through the doors of the arena. The game, too, was as good as the first, but this time Shamrocks won by three to two.

The third and final match was played on the day that Kimberley was relieved in the Boer War. Again the crowd filled every nook and cranny. Prior to the start, the atmosphere grew so foggy that the referee borrowed a megaphone and requested that the spectators, for the good of both the players and themselves, discontinue smoking.

The game was later described as the fastest and finest ever played. With only a minute of play remaining, the series was even and the score was tied. Then Shamrock's Captain Trihey, who was both a hockey star and an eminent lawyer, fired the shot that was heard across Canada—especially in Manitoba's capital.

However, in typical western fashion, Winnipeg Victorias did not retire to hockey's wailing wall and mourn their loss. Instead they strengthened their team, and just one year later, in January of 1901, they again steamed East, determined to upset the Shamrocks.

This time checking was closer and hitting was harder, even though a referee and two umpires were on duty. An observer reported:

> Winnipeg's Bain made a run all alone. Wall of Shamrocks made some extraordinary lifts. Then both of them got into a mix-up and were sent to the fence. The game was rough. Sticks on both sides were cut to razor-like effectiveness and, in the slashing, ankles were temporarily rendered useless. Players on both teams tried to see how near to the fence a man might be shouldered without being charged with manslaughter.

In such rugged fashion Winnipeg won by four to three.

The second game was just as bitterly contested. Penalties were many, and some players resorted to guile. At one time, after a strenuous sortie, Wall of Shamrocks lay on the ice. But he received little sympathy from the referee, who presumed he was using the sit-down strike to gather a second-wind. Time proved the official was right, for when Wall got up, he played sensationally. When the game ended, Winnipeg was ahead by two to one, and the Stanley Cup again found a Western home. The two teams had been so evenly matched that, after three games in 1900 and two in 1901, the total scores in goals was only sixteen to fifteen. In none of the five matches was the winning margin more than a single goal. Both clubs also prospered financially, and Winnipeg's share of the 1901 series was fifty-six hundred dollars.

In 1905 there was a Stanley Cup series which was not esteemed for close competition or great play—yet it was one of the most memorable in sports annals. It all began in late 1904, in the land of the midnight sun. In distant Dawson City, there were many adventurous young men who had left their Eastern homes to moil for Yukon gold. In the East they had played hockey, and some had been very good. In the far North, where ice was everywhere, they donned skates, whacked pucks and enjoyed dreaming they were Canada's best. True, it was mainly a vision, but there was enough fact in it to induce Colonel Boyle, a wealthy prospector, to finance an almost incredible journey. The players must have included some superb pleaders in lost causes, for they not only obtained Boyle-backing but they also convinced the Stanley Cup trustees they knew how to bang a puck into a net. The Ottawa club did not rate the Yukoners very highly. But how could the Silver Seven say they were the world's best when they had not even played a champion team from the land where "ice was born"?

With their hopes as high as the temperature was low, the challengers left Dawson on December 19, 1904. The team included: goalkeeper — Forrest, Three Rivers; point — Johnston, Ottawa; cover point—Dr. McLennan, Cornwall; rover—Fairbairn, Portage La Prairie; centre—Smith, West Selkirk; right wing—Watt, Aylmer, Quebec; left wing — Kennedy, West Selkirk; spares—Martin, Ottawa, and Hannay, Brandon.

The party, during their four-thousand-mile trek, used every kind of available transportation. They began with some members walking and others riding bicycles. After a few miles, the wheels broke down and everyone "footed" it to Whitehorse. Each day they covered from thirty-three to forty-six miles. Each night they slept in a Northwest Mounted Police post. After nine tiring days they reached Whitehorse. A storm on the White Pass delayed them two days. When they reached Skagway by railroad, they were informed that the steamer which had waited twenty-four hours for their arrival had been forced to leave just two hours earlier. They were compelled to stay around for three days awaiting the next boat to Seattle. Then they entrained for Vancouver, and from there to Ottawa.

Their hockey baggage was light. They carried only boots and skates. In Ottawa they purchased the rest of their equipment and their uniforms, which appropriately were coloured with touches of gold on black and white. The Dawson team was small and light, averaging only 150 pounds each, and the team's assets were mainly desire and skating ability. They were also encouraged by the promise that, should they return with the Stanley Cup, the folks back home would reward them with one thousand dollars.

The series began in controversy, for the leg-weary travellers who arrived in Ottawa a day prior to the scheduled opening requested a week's delay. They certainly needed time to meditate and practice—and perhaps pray. But Ottawa had league obligations, and other challengers were waiting for their opportunity to test the Silver Seven. So on January 13, 1905, the first game began with His Excellency the Governor General dropping the ceremonial puck. For twenty minutes the challengers gave their all, but they gradually softened under pressure. The final score was Ottawa nine—Dawson City two.

It was generally believed that the team from afar would do better in the second game. But during the three-day lapse, one of the visitors down-graded the great Frank McGee, who scored only once in the first game. He was entitled, of course, to belittle the Ottawa centre, but the criticism boomeranged. In the second match, McGee made hockey history when he scored fourteen goals, with eight goals in succession. Ottawa thus overhwhelmed Dawson City by twenty-three to two. The team that travelled the farthest was beaten the most. The Stanley Cup trustees should have spared them such humiliation.

A vastly different series was played in 1909, and it was three years in the making. In 1906, Montreal Wanderers ended the reign of the Ottawa Silver Seven, one of hockey's greatest teams. Since then, both clubs made so many personnel changes that only two of the fourteen players who participated in the last 1906 game were still with their former teams in 1909. So the revival of competition was between clubs rather than individuals—but the desire for revenge was still acute.

Enthusiasm for the big game, with the Stanley Cup at stake, did not need much fanning. Even though prices of tickets were sharply increased, there was a complete sell-out of reserved seats. Some speculators placed advertisements in the papers and made profits of three hundred per cent.

On the night of the match, hundreds stood in line for hours prior to game-time, awaiting the opportunity to stampede through the rush-entrance and search for standing-room. Some of the more daring crawled out along the beams extending above the throng and perched there from the opening whistle to the final blast.

The game itself matched the enthusiasm. Checking was hard, heavy and constant. The play bristled with sensational rushes by such stars as Taylor, Ross, Lake, Smaill and Kerr. Both defences adopted the new aggressive style of attack, even to shooting on goal.

There was a considerable delay before starting. Judge of Play "Joe" Power tossed a coin, which Wanderers called correctly, and they were given the choice of the goal they would defend. Then while the crowd impatiently yelled "Play Ball!" Referee Russell Bowie hunted for two capable goal-umpires. He actually had to leave the ice and climb up into the stands to coax two men to fill the posts. At 9:13, the game began.

The ice was "as smooth as polished marble," and from the drop of the puck, the play swept from end to end. Ottawa scored first at 4:50. Bruce Stuart, Ottawa Captain and rover, added another goal just forty seconds later. At one time Ottawa had three players serving penalties, yet at half-time the score was three-all.

In the second half, a player temporarily retired to get a new shoe lace, while another went off to replace a broken skate. Some players were injured, and others were winded, but play continued with Ottawa as the aggressor. When Wanderers had two men "on the fence," Kerr scored to give Ottawa a four-three lead. Still pressing, they added additional goals and thus gained revenge for the defeat they had suffered three years earlier.

The spectacle following the victory is best described by an eye-witness. It indicates the extent of Stanley Cup fever more than a half-century ago.

With the ringing of the gong, spectators leaped to the ice. The old Ottawa cheer which had urged the wearers of the red, white and black to victory, on scores of occasions, again rang out with increasing volume. It was the happy shout of a delighted crowd, expressing its happiness after three long years of waiting. As the Ottawa players started to leave for the dressing-room, they were surrounded. Bruce Stuart, nursing an injured knee, pleaded with his admirers to be more careful. Lake, whose face and mouth were badly cut and swollen, together with Walsh and Gilmour, were carried into the dressing-room. Taylor, who had played with a foot bound in batting and lint, snugly encased in a special boot, protected on the inside by a broad welt of hard leather, was seized and raised shoulder high. While he was being lofted, rooters robbed him of his stick and gloves and retained them as souvenirs. Inside and outside the arena, far into the night and morning, the rejoicing continued.

In 1919 there was a Stanley Cup series that was not only hard-fought but it was never even completed. That year Montreal Canadiens won the National Hockey League title, and Stanley Cup trustees ordered them to play in Seattle against Metropolitans, the Pacific Coast champions. It seemed a long journey, and the Black Flu was ravaging the continent, but Canadiens were prepared to defend the cup against all challengers. During their trip to the West, they played exhibition games, which enabled them to practise skating and gather a few shekels. At Brandon, they permitted "Joe" Hall to visit his home for a few days, but when he rejoined the team at Seattle, he became ill and was hospitalized. Shortly "Bill" Couture and "Jack" McDonald, who had roomed with Hall, were also feeling unwell.

The series began with Seattle, under Western rules, winning the first game. The second, under Eastern rules, was won by

Canadiens, with Lalonde scoring all four Montreal goals. Seattle captured the third match, and the fourth was a scoreless tie, even after twenty minutes overtime.

Prior to the fifth game, more Canadiens were suffering from influenza. "Jack" McDonald had gone to the movies that afternoon, and during the show everything suddenly went black. When he came out, he told manager Kennedy how he felt. That night, even though dressed to play, he just sat and watched. However, when the game went into overtime, and some of his mates were tired and ill, McDonald felt he should make some contribution to his team. So he jumped in at centre and carried the puck into Seattle's end of the rink. He faked a pass to Lalonde and another to Odie Cleghorn, and when the Seattle goalkeeper came out to intercept him, he eluded the thrust and scored in the empty net.

This goal won the game and tied the series. The tie was never broken. On the day of the intended final match, five members of Canadiens and their manager were not only sick but seriously ill with temperatures running as high as 105 degrees. McDonald and Hall were the most dangerously affected, and "Joe" Hall subsequently died. In the Stanley Cup records, the reference reads:

1918/19—No decision. Series halted by Spanish influenza epidemic, illness of several players and death of "Joe" Hall of Canadiens from flu. Five games had been played when series was halted, each team having won two and tied one.

Under these circumstances, Seattle might logically have been awarded the Stanley Cup, for they were fit and ready to play the sixth game. But Frank Patrick, President of Pacific Coast Hockey League Association, sportingly declined to make any claim. The teams agreed to equally share the proceeds of all games, and the series ended without a decision.

In 1933, there was another Stanley Cup game which, while it eventually did conclude, had many characteristics of a continuing serial. It all began in Maple Leaf Gardens at 8:30 P.M. on April 3, 1933. Toronto Maple Leafs and Boston Bruins were deadlocked in a Stanley Cup semi-final game, and a decision had to be reached that very night to enable the winner to play New

York Rangers in Madison Square Garden on the following evening.

Through the regular sixty minutes, play was so even that only a disallowed goal eluded either goalkeeper. After three periods it was a scoreless draw. Following the usual rest, the teams returned to the ice, and the spectators remained to observe the anticipated quick thrust that would end the series for either Bruins or Leafs. That moment of decision was not forthcoming through twenty, forty, sixty, eighty and even one hundred minutes of overtime play. Once "King" Clancy scored, but Referee Cleghorn disallowed the goal on an offside call.

The game began at 8:30 the previous evening, and even at 1:45 the following morning both teams were still struggling to get just one goal. At that moment the spectators were reading morning newspapers; players were falling frequently and rising slowly. Proposals were offered that the referee toss a coin to decide the winner; also that both teams remove their goalkeeper, and the one that scored first would advance to the Stanley Cup final round. President Frank Calder rejected all suggestions and ordered the game to be won and lost on the ice, in accordance with National Hockey League rules.

Four minutes later, Boston's "Eddie" Shore passed the puck toward "Joe" Lamb; but Toronto's "Andy" Blair, weak in the knees but alert in mind, anticipated the play, poked out a long stick, intercepted the puck and whipped it across to "Ken" Doraty, the smallest of all players in the National Hockey League. Doraty, in full flight, swooped in on goal, fired, and the puck bulged the net just inside the far goal-post. The red light flashed. The referee blew his final blast. Doraty dashed to retrieve the puck. The players left the ice, and the crowd flowed out into the early morning. Two hours later the Leafs were on their way to New York to begin the final Stanley Cup round.

But not even this prolonged Toronto-Boston game holds the Stanley Cup endurance record. Three years later, on March 24, 1936, an even longer match was played between Montreal Maroons and Detroit Red Wings. It was a close, hard-checking game for the full regulation time. But when the three twenty-minute periods ended, the result was a scoreless tie. The teams continued through the fourth period without any decision. The

New York Americans—"Red" Dutton (later N.H.L. President) at right.

Manager Conn Smythe discusses strategy with "King" Clancy, "Red" Horner, "Flash" Hollett and George Hainsworth.

Stanley Cup action during 1941 Boston-Toronto series

Art Ross and Lester Patrick attend Hockey Hall of Fame opening.

Montreal Canadiens' famous Punch line, "Rocket" Richard-Elmer Lach-"Toe" Blake.

"Hap" Day—coach of five Stanley Cup champions.

"Gordie" Howe, Detroit Red Wings' Super-Star with Toronto' Johnny Bower defending.

fifth, the sixth and the seventh were also scoreless. Toward the end of the eighth period, after almost 160 minutes of play, a Detroit goal seemed certain. "Marty" Barry, a smart Red Wing centre, made a perfect pass to left-winger Herb Lewis. Lewis cut in sharply and fired a shot that had Lorne Chabot beaten all the way. But the puck struck on the inside of the post and rebounded to Maroons' "Hooley" Smith. "Hooley" scooted for the Detroit net, slipped the rubber to Northcott; "Baldy" shot, and Normie Smith, in Red Wings goal, had to jump fast to get a pad on Northcott's drive. Then Detroit's Doug Young snatched the puck, dashed down the right boards and almost scored when he caromed a shot off Lionel Conacher's skate. The puck rolled toward Chabot. Young dove for it, but before he could get his stick in place, Chabot slid out and smothered the puck. It was a very close call as the eighth period ended.

After the ten-minute intermission, the ninth session began. At four minutes and forty-six seconds, history was made—for at this moment the previous all-time distance-record was broken. Less than two minutes later, Detroit's Normie Smith repulsed a savage four-man Maroon attack. "Hec" Kilrae snared the rebound and skated away fast with rookie "Mud" Bruneteau. Bruneteau, who had scored only two goals in the entire season, flashed behind the Montreal defence. Blond Kilrae flipped the puck to him. The youngster, in full flight, dodged around Chabot, as the goalkeeper slid out, then calmly poked the puck in the open net.

A combined groan and sigh escaped from ninety-five hundred fans who had remained at the Forum nearly six hours. They watched a match in which Normie Smith, Red Wings' goalkeeper, in his first playoff game, stopped ninety shots without a miss. They also had the satisfaction of sitting-out the most enduring of all hockey matches. The record still stands.

In other cup series miracles had "come to pass." In 1938, Alfie Moore, an unwanted goalkeeper, was conscripted by Chicago Black Hawks to replace an injured netminder. He played so sensationally that the Hawks management repented, paid him well and presented him with an inscribed gold watch, as a recognition of his skill and daring.

In 1942, Toronto Maple Leafs lost the first three games of

their Stanley Cup final round to Detroit Red Wings. They were playing the fourth and presumably last match in Detroit, and they were trailing in the third period. At that moment they were less than twenty minutes from defeat and almost two hundred minutes from victory. Yet against such terrific odds, they rallied to win four games in a row and recapture the cup.

There was another great series between Montreal Canadiens and Toronto Maple Leafs in 1951. It was such a bitter battle that the first four games continued into overtime before a winner emerged, and so did the fifth. In the latter match, with only a minute remaining, Leafs tied the score; during the overtime, Toronto's "Bashing Bill" Barilko whirled his two-hundred-pound frame through the air to pick-up "Howie" Meeker's pass. As Barilko landed, he whipped a hard rising shot into the upper reaches of the Montreal net; and, with four victories in five overtime games, Toronto Maple Leafs, for the first time in ten years, won the Stanley Cup. Unfortunately a few months later Barilko lost his life while returning on a plane from a fishing holiday.

All through the 1950s, Montreal Canadiens were riding so high that they competed in ten consecutive Stanley Cup finals and won five in a row. In every series they toppled records as though they were pins on a bowling alley. In one continuous stretch they were unbeaten through eleven games. In one match they scored three goals in fifty-six seconds, and "Rocket" Richard was finally making hockey history in every game he played.

The drama of the Stanley Cup did not end with the dethroning of Montreal Canadiens in 1961. They were succeeded for three years by Toronto Maple Leafs who also contributed a few thrills. In the final game of the 1963/64 series, the Toronto club played without the services of injured left-winger McKenney—while defenceman "Bobby" Baun, defenceman Carl Brewer, centre "Red" Kelly and right-winger George Armstrong were bandaged, strapped and inoculated with pain-killers. Yet the wounded and the healthy played such an inspired game that they shut-out their younger, speedier rivals and earned a third successive Stanley Cup title for the Maple Leafs.

There are no limitations—in either time or plot—to the thrills and spills of Stanley Cup competition.

CHAPTER ELEVEN INDIVIDUAL HISTRIONICS

The excitement of Stanley Cup competition does strange things to individual players. Some go tense, nervous and irritable and play poorly, while others are spurred by the challenge and rise to the importance of the occasion.

"Eddie" Gerard, an Ottawa defenceman of the 1920's, was one of the fortunates who enjoyed crucial games. Indeed, his willingness to play anywhere at anytime inspired the following story. In 1922, Vancouver Millionaires, western champions, were playing a Stanley Cup series in Toronto against St. Patricks, the N.H.L. winners. Vancouver won the first and third games, and in the latter game St. Pats were crippled by the loss of two injured defencemen who would be out for the remainder of the contests. It thus appeared reasonably certain that Vancouver would handily win the oncoming fourth game and take the cup back to the coast.

There was a possibility that the Toronto team might not be able to assemble a team. Rather than default, "Charlie" Querrie, St. Pat's manager, approached Lester Patrick, the Vancouver manager, and sought permission to borrow "Eddie" Gerard, whose Ottawa club had finished its season. Lester was aware that "Eddie" was a good defenceman, and his first inclination was to bluntly refuse. But Querrie argued that even with "Eddie" on their team they still did not expect to win and just wanted to give the fans a good show. On that presumption, Lester, who was acting for his brother Frank, eventually weakened and consented to the use of Gerard as a replacement for the injured players.

In the fourth game, the one that St. Pats were supposedly playing just for fun, "Eddie" was sensationally outstanding, and the Toronto club won by six to nothing. In the fifth and decisive game, the Ottawa import was again a star, both defensively and on attack. Certainly Gerard had come to play and not merely fill a gap. Thus through kindness, Vancouver lost the Stanley Cup.

In the dressing-room after the final game, Querrie congratulated "Eddie" on his fine play and inquired what price he placed on his services. "You don't owe me a cent, Charlie. I had a lot of fun," the player replied. He really meant what he said and refused the five hundred dollars he might have received for his excellent performance. Querrie was equally insistent Gerard should be rewarded, so St. Pats later presented a valuable diamond pin to the star who was willing to play "just for fun."

Next year Gerard had the personal satisfaction of playing in Vancouver, for his own Ottawa Senators who won the Stanley Cup in a series with Edmonton. Fortunately "Eddie" was spared the distress visited upon Cyril Denneny, one of his team mates. It all happened on the long trip home after the victory. At the time prohibition was abroad in the land, but someone generously gave coach "Pete" Green a bottle of liquor for celebration. Not deeming it wise to immediately participate, Green carefully hid the bottle in a little leather duffle bag and locked it in his berth. During the trip the coach nursed his secret until the night before the arrival in Ottawa. He then decided the time was appropriate for a get-together, brought out the bottle and offered Cyril Denneny the first swig. The player drank a mouthful, then hastily dashed for the washroom, holding his throat and stomach. Earlier some other players had discovered the coach's hiding place and drank the contents, then refilled the bottle with soap and water.

"Eddie" Gerard, who really enjoyed Stanley Cup pranks and contests, had an opportunity in 1928 of repaying Lester Patrick for the favour "The Silver Fox" had extended him back in 1922. In the spring of 1928, New York Rangers and Montreal Maroons were playing the second game in the final Stanley Cup series at

Montreal Forum. Maroons won the first game, and early in the second period of a scoreless second game "Nels" Stewart, a hard shooter, drove the puck toward Rangers' goal. The puck smacked the New York goalkeeper close to his left eye. A scramble ensued, Chabot dropped to the ice and the referee quickly stopped play. The netminder, unconscious and bleeding profusely, was rushed to Royal Victoria Hospital. It was apparent Chabot was through for the series.

At the time, several goalkeepers who had played for other teams were watching the game from Forum seats; and New York's manager, Lester Patrick, sought permission to use one of them as a replacement. Maroons' manager refused his consent, and the two teams temporarily returned to their dressing-rooms while Rangers considered their problem.

The New York Club was without a substitute, and some of the players facetiously suggested that the manager might himself don the pads. But Lester was forty-four years old; he had played goal only once in an important game, and that had been a generation earlier. However, after some deep thinking, the manager astounded his players by declaring, "All right. I'll do it."

Probably the strongest influence prompting the veteran to reach the decision was that he recalled giving his consent for "Eddie" Gerard to be used as a Toronto replacement six years earlier. And Gerard, now the Maroon manager, had refused to return the courtesy. This really irritated the New York manager. When the players realized Patrick's intention, they protested vigorously and pleaded with him to get someone—anyone else. All the while the determined manager donned the equipment discarded by Chabot and, followed by his players, skated slowly to the goal. A few practice shots were fired in his direction, and play resumed.

The Rangers were aroused to protect not only their goal but also its guardian. All through the remainder of the period, even though the Maroons "volleyed and thundered," there was no score by either team. After the intermission, with increasing confidence that their veteran manager would do a good job, they attacked more vigorously, and "Bill" Cook fired the first goal of the game, to give New York a one to nothing lead. This score gave the team quite a lift, for they were aware that the "boss" was risking limb and maybe life in their common cause. However, the one-goal margin did not stand-up, and with only six minutes remaining, "Nels" Stewart, whose earlier shot had flattened Chabot, fooled Patrick and the score was tied.

That goal was discouraging, for the veteran was tiring from exertion and the weight of equipment. As well, the need to continue into overtime added to the concern. For seven minutes the Rangers became a defensive powerhouse; then Frank Boucher threaded through Maroons defence, drew out their goalkeeper and whipped the winning goal into the unguarded net. As the game ended, the jubilant Rangers hoisted Lester Patrick on their shoulders and carried him into the dressing-room.

This modern version of "Horatius at the Gate" is a good example of Stanley Cup histrionics. To complete the story, Rangers were allowed a replacement for the remaining games, and New York won its first Stanley Cup title.

For some reason, it has often been goalkeepers who have "passed the miracles" in big Stanley Cup games. Perhaps this is so because the netminder is the key to success, like the baseball pitcher or the football quarterback. Certainly, cup history is saturated with outstanding displays of "Gardiens-de-buts," much in the fashion of Frank McCool.

In the autumn of 1944, "Turk" Broda was in the army, and Toronto Maple Leafs desperately needed a goalkeeper. They endeavoured to buy or trade but could make no deals. In their distress, Lorne Carr, Leafs' good right-winger from Calgary, informed the management that Frank McCool, an Albertan goalkeeper, had been discharged from the Armed Forces because of stomach ulcers. Even though goalkeepers and ulcers were a hazardous combination, Leafs invited the twenty-six-year-old McCool to their training-camp. Partly because of the player's natural ability, but also because of the immediate need, Frank was signed to a Toronto contract. He played well through the season and was voted winner of the Calder Trophy as the best rookie of the year.

Despite this honour, McCool's performances had been spotty. When the Stanley Cup final series between Detroit Red Wings and Maple Leafs began, there were many observers who thought goalkeeping was Toronto's weak spot. However, like many other forecasters, both before and since, the prophets were proven false.

In the first three games, for a total of 180 minutes, not a single red light flashed above the Toronto goal. Detroit won the next two matches, and also the sixth, even though McCool was unbeaten through sixty minutes of regulation time and fourteen minutes more of overtime. The series was then tied at three victories each. The seventh and decisive game was played in Detroit, and despite his unexcelled record of four shutouts in six regulation games, McCool was really on the spot. Red Wings, after losing the first three, turned back the onslaught and won the next three.

The situation would have given concern to even the most complacent netminder, and McCool was never a "cool, calm and collected" type. In that game to end all games, Frank allowed only one goal in the first fifty minutes, but his ulcers were screaming for help. Halfway through the final period, McCool was so uncomfortable he sought relief, left the ice and retired for ten minutes. He returned to struggle against the foes within and without. When "Babe" Pratt scored to give Leafs a one-goal margin, even McCool's ulcers cheered. Toronto won that game and the Stanley Cup. The series' hero was Frank McCool who allowed only nine goals in seven games—quite a contrast to his seasonal average of more than three goals per game.

At other times, the big man in a short series is the forward who, during regular play, is a mill-run type. "Sudden Death" Hill belonged in this group. When "Mel" Hill was a youngster, he attended a New York Rangers' training camp. The management believed he had talent but considered him too frail to withstand the rigours of a full season and still have enough stamina to endure the Stanley Cup playdowns. So Hill was sent home. This decision was not only wrong in fact, but it later boomeranged to defeat Rangers in Stanley Cup competition.

After the New York rejection, "Mel" endeavoured to sell his services to other N.H.L. clubs, and Boston Bruins agreed to give him a contract. He had not been considered a scoring threat, and it was intended he would do the back-checking for line-mates "Bill" Cowley, who was a masterful playmaker, and Roy Conacher, an excellent goalgetter. In this lesser but essential role,

"Mel" did a good job. But his propensity for scoring important goals did not bloom until the Stanley Cup playoffs in 1938/39, when Bruins faced Rangers, who had earlier turned thumbs down on him. Hill's performances during this series were fantastic.

In the first game, at the end of regulation time, the score was tied. Overtime continued, and almost sixty minutes later, Cowley passed to Hill, and the latter swooped in on Rangers' goal and fired the winning shot for Bruins. The second game resembled the first. It too was tied at full-time and continued into sudden-death overtime. After more than eight minutes had elapsed, Cowley again flipped the disc to the flying Hill. The player, who was considered too frail for long combat, whipped the rubber into the New York net for another Bruin victory.

These feats were not bad for a reject. If revenge was Hill's driving motive, he had already earned his reward. But there was still another victory to be earned. The series had been extended to seven games, and the physical strength of the participants was waning. This was the time to test whether anyone was fragile. Hill was not only on trial physically, but Rangers, recognizing his talent for scoring important goals, placed a double-check on him. Once more, the two teams were so evenly matched that they were deadlocked one to one at the end of sixty minutes. After the usual intermission, the almost exhausted players resumed their weary struggle. They continued through another forty-eight minutes (108 in all), when none other than Saskatoon-born Melvin Hill—for the third time in one series and each time in overtime—ended the game and the round with a well-executed goal. Not by chance did this amazing sharp-shooter earn the apt nickname of "Sudden Death" Hill.

There are many other instances in Stanley Cup play in which the hero was earlier "unhonoured and unsung." It was smallish "Ken" Doraty, who had scored only five goals all season, who ended the night-long Toronto-Boston overtime game. It was rookie "Mud" Bruneteau, who had scored but twice all year, who fired the only goal in the longest hockey match ever played. In the 1951 Stanley Cup series, it was Bill Barilko, a stout defenceman, who banged the goal that won the cup for Toronto Maple Leafs over Montreal Canadiens. Marcel Bonin, while playing in twenty-five Stanley Cup games for both Detroit and Montreal, never scored a goal. Then in the 1958/59 series, again with Canadiens, he suddenly caught fire and blazed ten goals to easily lead all scorers.

During the 1963/64 regular season, Toronto's "Bobby" Baun was a solid defenceman with a reputation for being one of hockey's hardest hitters. In the terms of the Royal Canadian Mounted Police, he was famed for always "getting his man." But scoring was something else, for Baun's annual total averaged about four goals. In the forty-seven Stanley Cup games he had participated in during earlier years, he scored only once. Yet he was destined to become a scoring hero.

It happened this way. Toronto Maple Leafs and Detroit Red Wings were playing the sixth game in the final round in Detroit Olympia. After thirteen minutes in the third period, the score was tied. Red Wings were flying, and Maple Leafs appeared to be fading. A Detroit victory would ensure them possession of the Stanley Cup. Earlier Baun had been cracked in the ankle, and after a few minutes, while facing-off with Howe, he heard a crack. His right leg collapsed, and he had to be removed from the ice on a stretcher. It seemed inevitable that the "Boomer" was through—not only for that game but also for the seventh, should that match be necessary. It was a tough break for both the player and the club.

However, the Leafs continued to hold Detroit in check until regulation time expired, and the match continued into overtime. In the intermission, Baun received a local anaesthetic to kill the pain. Without knowing the extent of the injury, he determined to play. When the game resumed, Olympia fans, television viewers and especially Detroit players were startled to see a revived Baun skate to his defensive position. But their surprise grew into amazement when after one minute and forty-three seconds overtime, the crippled Leaf—playing on borrowed time, with a record of only a lone goal in forty-seven playoff games—fired a hard shot in the direction of the Detroit goal. While winging on its way, it ticked the stick of "Bill" Gadsby. Then it glanced into an unguarded portion of the Detroit net as though steered by radar. Only when the Stanley Cup series ended in a Toronto victory did Baun consent to an x-ray. Then his injury was confirmed to be a hairline fracture of the ankle.

Still is would be wrong to presume that all Stanley Cup heroes are those usually found in supporting roles. Just as often the leading players during the regular season have proven beyond all doubt that they too excel in the short cup series. "Rocket" Richard, for instance, was always a sensational player.

Here is one of the "Rocket's" many exploits. It is the second period of the seventh and last game of the 1952 semi-final round between Montreal Canadiens and Boston Bruins. Richard was checked heavily. He fell head-first on the ice and sprawled unconscious, with blood trickling from a cut in the forehead that later required six stitches. In Richard's description: "I never knew what happened. Suddenly everything went black. I didn't recall anything else until I woke up in the medical room." Despite such a crash, even though wobbly in his legs and foggy in his mind, the "Rocket" resumed playing in the third period. Then with four minutes remaining and the score tied—with the Forum crowd cheering his every move—Richard made a most sensational play.

In mid-ice, Bouchard laid a flat pass right on the stick of the flying "Rocket." In full flight, with body crouched and skates flashing, Richard swooped across the centre line, bobbled the puck for an instant, picked it up again and swerved to the right as he crossed Detroit's blue-line. It appeared for a moment as though he would end in the corner. But he cut sharply toward the Detroit goal, deked a defender out of his boots, curved to the centre and fired a bullet-like puck that the goalkeeper never saw until he turned around and fished it out of the net.

The play was so awesome that in a combination of exhaustion and excitement Elmer Lach, Canadiens' centre player, staggered to the boards, draped his arms over the railing and collapsed. After the game, Lynn Patrick, who was observing, commented: "I never saw a better goal. When Richard saw his chance and cut for the net, he looked like only one thing, a rocket. That's how he got his name, and it fits."

Great players not only sparkle in Stanley Cup play, but they also don't scare easily. This freedom from fear was portrayed in a game played at Maple Leaf Gardens between Detroit Red

Wings and Toronto Maple Leafs. In an earlier game played in Detroit, "Gordie" Howe collided with "Tod" Sloan, and the latter suffered a broken shoulder and was definitely out of action for that season. Many Toronto fans criticized Howe for the incident, and one of them became so incensed that he telephoned two Toronto papers and threatened them "Don't worry about Howe and Lindsay tonight. I'm going to shoot them."

Lindsay and Howe were warned about the crackpot, and while Gordie was not personally disturbed, he was concerned that his ailing mother might be upset, so he phoned to Saskatoon and assured her there was nothing to worry about. Lindsay, in turn, became fighting mad and scoffed at the whole affair, calling the threat the stupidest thing he had ever heard. Then to prove that they were not the least bit scared, Lindsay and Howe gave such outstanding performances that Detroit overcame a two-goal deficit and earned a five-four victory. Lindsay scored both the tying and the winning overtime scores. And when the last shot was fired, "Ted" turned his stick up, cocked it like a rifle and began sniping in pantomime at the crowd.

In the drama of the Stanley Cup, the winners of hockey's Oscars for best individual performances are not restricted by age, height, weight, position or previous experience.

CHAPTER TWELVE SOME WERE SUPER-STARS

While the Stanley Cup is long in years, its true worth is not in beauty or age but as a symbol of the achievements of great players who fought so hard to have their names engraved on its elongated silver base. Without the efforts of an army of talented athletes, intent on defending or challenging for the famous bowl, it might have remained the meaningless example of the silversmith's art.

Within the covers of a score of books, it would be impossible to sketch the career of all those whose contributions have been noteworthy. The players selected for this chapter might well be matched by others. But these six are representative of three hockey eras and were greatly esteemed by their contemporaries.

"Cyclone" Taylor and Lester Patrick were leading players during the first twenty years of this century. "Eddie" Shore and "Howie" Morenz were worthies in 1920-1940 decades. "Rocket" Richard and "Gordie" Howe have been leaders in more recent years.

FRED "CYCLONE" TAYLOR

Fred "Cyclone" Taylor was born in Tara, Ontario, in 1885. He grew up on ponds and band-box rinks in the Listowel area. Because surfaces were small and players many, he was forced to stickhandle his way through a maze of young legs, if he hoped to get a shot on the rocks that served for goals. Because his early hockey was played outdoors, he had to first clear snow from the ice and then skate against heavy winds. In the process, through sheer necessity, young Fred learned to skate fast, to control a puck and to endure from sunrise to sunset.

Taylor's fame as a junior attracted the early attention of the professional Houghton Hockey Club, then playing in the International Hockey League. Still a teenager, he accepted the offer, despite the fact he had to leave home and compete against older players. At times the veterans were rather harsh in their sponsoring of the lad.

One night two players undertook to guide the rookie on a tour of Houghton's free-lunch counters. During the expedition they took him to a lavish cafe, and everyone enjoyed the grand meal. On departing, the guides walked ahead, leaving Taylor at the rear. As he was about to leave the manager stopped the lad and abruptly asked, "Who's going to foot this bill?"

"What bill?" Taylor inquired. "Isn't this a free lunch depot?"

"Free nothing," the owner retorted. "There's just $7.25 coming from you. You're sure a green one. You must be from Canada."

"You're dead right I am," the lad agreed, as he emptied his pockets. "And the more I see of this place, the happier I'll be to get back there."

Happy or unhappy, Taylor became the all-star rover on what they chose to call the All-American Hockey Team which was composed entirely of Canadians. The Houghton paper then wrote of the teenager. "He is the sensation of the year and the fastest skater in the game. He stars at either rover or defence, is fast and aggressive, and there is scarcely a man in the league that he cannot elude."

In 1907, players returning from teams in United States began praising the young "Cyclone," and Canadian clubs started coaxing him for his signature on a contract. Ottawa, which had earlier lost the Stanley Cup, were rebuilding, and Taylor looked to be the keystone in the "comeback arch." But there were two Taylors playing in the International League, and the other Taylor had unfortunately earned a police record. He was the one who erroneously discouraged the Ottawa management, but soon the real Mr. Taylor stood up to be recognized.

At the time "Cyclone" was also a skilled piano-tuner. When Ottawa offered one thousand dollars for his services, he was prepared to work it out either on ice or on a key-board, but it had to total one thousand. Ottawa agreed, but before Taylor played a game for them, the Renfrew club offered him a bigger bag, with a lot more "sugar" in it. The player was dickering, when an Ottawa representative barged right into the conference room and warned Taylor he had better stop talking right away. He did, for the lawyer had "Cyclone's" signed contract right in his pocket, and the lawyer was prepared to show it to a judge.

Taylor was a member of the Ottawa club in 1909 when they regained the Stanley Cup from Montreal Wanderers. He was so proud of the victory that he asked the club for permission to borrow the cup so he could take it back to Listowel, his home town, and show it to the folks. Permission was given, and on the day of the Listowel reception, "Cyclone" received a telegram from his team-mate Fred Lake. It read: "Tell the folks all about the cup, but don't forget to remind them I won it for you."

The next year, Renfrew Millionaires again communicated with Taylor in the dollar-sign language. "Cyclone" understood this kind of talk, and through many weeks the newspaper headlines of Ottawa and Renfrew blared: "He Will;" "He Won't." "He Is;" "He Isn't." It was an exciting game while it lasted. Finally money spoke louder than words, and Renfrew signed the erstwhile Listowel flash for a reported twelve hundred dollar salary, plus a permanent position to be worth another twelve hundred.

Taylor had played well for Renfrew. After one game it was reported: "Fred Taylor gave one of his most acrobatic performances and provided endless amusement to the gallery. Time and again, he doubled back on his tracks and left the opponent who was alongside to check him, standing still."

However the Renfrew club and the other teams in their association soon learned they were "paying too much for their hockey whistle," so they disbanded and a new league was formed. In the break up and revival, the new clubs drew lots for the Renfrew players, and Wanderers assumed Taylor's contract. The switching did not please "Cyclone." He became so annoyed he stayed out of all hockey for a year. However, in 1912, he heard the call of the West and journeyed to the Pacific coast, where he played brilliantly with Vancouver Millionaires until his retirement in 1921 at the age of thirty-six. Since then Fred "Cyclone" Taylor had been close to the hockey scene. He was chosen to turn the first sod in the ceremonies in 1960 leading to the erection of the Hockey Hall of Fame.

LESTER PATRICK

Lester Patrick, the Silver Fox, was a contemporary of "Cyclone" Taylor, sometimes with him but more often against him. Like Taylor, Lester was an early hockey itinerant who wore the uniforms of many clubs—but always with distinction. He was born in 1883, in Drummondville, Quebec, and happened to be in Brandon, Manitoba, in the winter of 1903/4, in good time to play for the Brandon club in the Stanley Cup series against the Ottawa Silver Seven. Even at this early age he was recognized as the "thinking man's player." Certainly he was credited with many ideas that gave hockey a new look.

Lester had originally been a rover and, as the name implied, he roved all over the ice. But one day a defenceman became ill, and young Patrick took his place. This was one occasion when hockey history was made, for Lester, instead of stopping attacks and giving the puck to a forward, or lifting the puck up into the dim lights, resolved to do some rushing on his own. The old hands were shocked by the unusual performance, but their amazement turned to praise when the roving defender scored a goal. As the news of the venture spread, the horizons of defencemen were greatly extended. The sceptical rivals soon adopted the new style of rushing and shooting.

The Edison of hockey had another idea. Until his day, hockey players were positioned in lacrosse fashion with goal, point and cover-point lined up vertically. That did not seem right to Lester, so he experimented with the idea that point and cover-point should be placed opposite one another, with each defenceman being primarily responsible for defending his own side of the ice. Experience proved this theory was sound, and eventually point and cover-point became left defence and right defence.

All the while Lester was doing much more than upsetting

tradition, for he was also playing superb hockey. In the 1906 series, when Montreal Wanderers ended the long reign of the Ottawa Silver Seven, it was young Patrick who, in the decisive game, scored the three goals earned by his team which enabled Wanderers to win their first Stanley Cup. Under Lester as captain, they repeated their victory in 1907 and 1908. Later, with younger brother Frank, he signed with Renfrew Millionaires at the fabulous salary for those times of three thousand dollars each for a schedule of only twelve games.

The sinecure, of course, was too good to last. When the Renfrew bubble burst, the two Patricks went West. Instead of thumbing through scrap books and polishing their trophies, the brothers planned a new league on the Pacific coast. But to make the dream come true, they first had to arrange financing, build arenas, obtain players and whip up fan enthusiasm.

At the time Lester and Frank were still in their twenties. With parental backing and personal energy, they organized the Pacific Coast Hockey League, built Canada's first artificial-ice arenas and persuaded a flock of good eastern players to sign contracts with teams in Victoria, Vancouver and New Westminster. Frank, who was an equally famous player and theorist, managed Vancouver Millionaires while Lester directed Victoria Cougars. Despite keen competition between East and West for players, the Vancouver team, in 1915, was good enough to win the Stanley Cup and to be billed as the "world's best." Lester's record was even more remarkable, for he played on or managed teams in fifteen Stanley Cup series, and in seven of them his club was victorious.

The contributions of Lester and Frank Patrick both to Stanley Cup history and hockey in general gave new life to the game while it was idling at the crossroads. Between the two of them, in addition to improvements already mentioned, the Patricks were credited with the idea of scoring assists along with goals; with the substitution of an entire forward line instead of individual changes; with the removal of offsides in centre ice; with the right to kick the puck without penalty; and with the use of left-hand shots on right wing and right-handers on left. During the past thirty years, Murray ("Muzz") and Lynn, sons of Lester, have been playing, coaching or managing National

Hockey League clubs. The Patricks have indeed been Hockey's Royal Family.

HOWARTH MORENZ

About the time Lester Patrick and Fred Taylor were beginning their professional careers, there was born in the Ontario town of Mitchell a boy whose name was registered as Howarth Morenz. Howarth's unusual name was later to cause some excitement in the sports world, for a government clerk presumed his name to be a girl's and thus wrote "female" in the records.

The young lad grew up close to the scenes of "Cyclone" Taylor's boyhood. He enjoyed a similar environment of ponds and rivers, and later moved with his parents to Stratford. In this noted hockey centre, young Morenz became a sensational junior. Indeed, he was so outstanding that opponents declared no one so good could be so young. So they protested Howie's age and in their investigation they discovered that Howarth was registered as a girl.

"There you are," they gloated, "he sure is over age. If he wasn't they wouldn't be playing him under his sister's birth certificate." Shortly the Ontario Hockey Association was considering the protest. But they quickly rejected it when they learned a clerical error had been made at the time of recording the birth. So Howarth, while smart for his years, was still a junior.

When "Howie" became twenty-one, hockey sponsors everywhere knew that he was much beyond the ordinary and that he had all the attributes to make him another "Cyclone" Taylor, whom he resembled in so many ways. Naturally the Stratford club wished to retain Morenz for their own senior team, but already professional clubs were spreading their nets.

One of the most persistent bidders for "Howie" was Leo Dandurand, manager of Montreal Canadiens. It had been rumored that Leo had offered Morenz $850 in cash and a season's contract for twenty-five hundred dollars. When the Stratford club became aware of this, they pressured the player and persuaded him to revoke any agreement and remain in

Stratford. However Dandurand confirmed he had already paid the money, that he had a signed contract and that he would take the case into the law courts if there was any interference. Unwillingly Morenz consented to turn professional, and it was probably a wise decision. He was much too good for local opposition, and he needed keener competition worthy of his talent.

It did not take "Howie" long to convince the professionals that he belonged. "Joe" Malone, an all-star in his own right, was one of the first to recognize the fact, and as he later recalled to a sportswriter:

In the season of 1923/24, I took a look at a new kid in Canadiens' training camp at Grimsby, Ontario, and I knew right then I was ready for an easy chair. His name was "Howie" Morenz. In practice, he moved past me so fast that I thought I was standing still. I then knew it was time for me to quit.

Morenz was not big statistically, for his height was five feet nine inches and his weight 165 pounds. But these figures are deceiving. He was solidly constructed, never spared himself and had enough power to sweep aside all who dared obstruct him.

Morenz began his professional career with Canadiens and continued with them through eleven seasons. At the end of his first year, Ottawa Senators and the Montreal club met in a two-out-of-three series to decide which team would advance into Stanley Cup rounds against western Canadian champions.

This was a time of trial for the rookie, but when the series ended, friend and foe had to admit "Howie" was not a kid to be ignored but rather a professional to be respected. In his first playoff game, he swooped in and picked up a rebound. With two Ottawa defencemen draped around him, he flipped the puck into Senators' goal for the only score of the game.

In his second playoff match, playing on Ottawa ice before a hostile crowd, the twenty-one-year-old scored twice, and each in a different way. For the first, he stole the puck off an Ottawa player's stick in mid-ice, then split the defence and fired a rising shot that the goalkeeper never saw. For his second goal, he stickhandled from end to end without an opponent touching the puck, then calmly tipped the disc into the net. During his first playoff series, Montreal Canadiens scored five goals. Morenz scored three of them and assisted on the fourth. The Flying Frenchmen then defeated Vancouver Maroons, and continued to whip Calgary in the final round. In this game Morenz scored three more goals. In his first professional year, he earned the right to have his name engraved on the Stanley Cup.

All through his playing years he was a streak on skates and a player who never spared himself. Some of the tales of his prowess possess a Paul Bunyan tinge. The story is told that during a Stanley Cup game in Montreal Forum two opposing defencemen decided they would have no more Morenz nonsense, so they planned on his next rush to use him as the filling in their sandwich.

They did not have to wait long. Seconds later Morenz broke alone and came dashing toward the burly defenders.

"This is it", shouted one.

"O.K." echoed the other.

"Howie" looked up, sensed trouble and pretended he was going to break them apart. Then, at the last moment, he poked the puck between them, swerved sharply to the right, circled them, snared the loose puck and blasted a winning shot. As he went around the net and looked back, he could see the two huskies still sprawled on the ice, recovering from their collision.

Morenz was such a fierce competitor he never became reconciled to defeat. Elmer Ferguson, a Montreal sports editor who knew him well, wrote of him:

One night in a playoff game in Boston, Canadiens lost in overtime when little "Cooney" Weiland, playing centre against Morenz, banged in a long drive. At six o'clock the next morning, there came a knock on my door. I opened the portal and there stood Morenz, dressed in his street clothes. It was still dark and a surprised host said a bit testily, "What's the idea? Where are you going so early?

"To bed," said Morenz wearily. "I've been walking the streets all night, trying to forget that goal. We lost and it was my fault." And the kid was sobbing.

"Howie's" career had an abrupt and unfortunate end. In 1934, he contemplated retiring but was traded to Chicago Black Hawks and was never happy in that environment. The following season, still fretting, he was transferred to New York Rangers. But, before the 1936/37 season began, Morenz was reunited with his beloved Montreal Canadiens. They were his team, and he knew it. He was happy to again wear the uniform of the club that meant so much to him, but this was soon to be the avenue to his death.

On January 28, 1937, while playing against Chicago Black Hawks in Montreal Forum, he fractured a leg and was, of course, hospitalized. He never left the hospital, for he suffered a heart attack and died on March 8, at the comparatively young age of thirty-four. The funeral service, attended by seventeen thousand sorrowing fans, was conducted in Montreal Forum. Many more thousands mourned along the route of the cortège as it wound slowly up the slopes of Mount Royal. With his passing, Montreal Canadiens retired forever Number 7, the uniform that Howie Morenz had worn with such distinction.

EDWARD SHORE

In the same year that Howarth Morenz was born in Ontario, a prairie child was born in Saskatchewan. There was a similarity in their upbringing, for both boys were raised in centres where population was small and outdoor ice abundant.

"Eddie" Shore developed surely but slowly. It was not until he was twenty-two-years-old that he became a professional with Regina Caps in the Western Canada League. The next season he played with Edmonton, and he looked so good that when the W.C.L. disbanded, Shore was considered so desirable that many National Hockey League clubs tried to buy him early rather than take a chance on drawing his name from a hat. In claiming his services, Boston became lucky. The pride of the prairie was signed for "Charley" Adams' Bruins. Through fourteen seasons, Shore was such an outstanding defenceman that he was elected to the All-Star first team seven times. He was also a four-time winner of the Hart Trophy, annually awarded to the player in the National Hockey League considered the most valuable to his club.

While the records reveal Shore's greatness, his true worth never depended on totals, for he had individual assets that figures could never indicate. He was a fierce competitor. He was also a hard-hitting defender who hurled his 190 pounds into an oncoming attacker then, without delaying to pick up the pieces, gathered the puck on the end of his stick and started a foray of his own.

Elmer Ferguson, a shrewd hockey observer once wrote of Shore:

> He gave no quarter and he asked none. One night in 1929, Montreal Maroons deliberately set upon him. A long-reaching jab with a stick-blade tore open his cheek. Another sliced his chin. He was hammered, pounded, cut; and just at the end, a Maroon player cut across Shore and deliberately gave him a sickening smash in the mouth, which knocked out several teeth and felled the Bruin in his tracks. He was carried off, and five minutes later, his wounds temporarily doctored, he was standing silently beneath the showers. Expecting an outburst, I said, "Rough going, Eddie." Through bloody, swollen lips he answered laconically, "It's all in the game. I'll pay off."

Shore was a man with a flaming temper who impulsively perpetrated hockey-crimes that he afterwards sincerely regretted. He spent much of his ice-time "getting even" and was high in the ranks of penalty-servers. He was a great guy to have on your side but a foe to be both feared and respected. And yet Eddie had a softer side that was best known only to intimates.

A sports writer once recalled that his most poignant recollection of Shore was not the sight of his histrionic flare on the ice but rather the fact the burly Bruin played a saxophone. The recorder was once rooming next door to Eddie, in Ottawa's Château Laurier, during a Stanley Cup series. He remembered that the hockeyist-turned-musician always played "Roses that Bloom in Picardy" on the saxophone, and that he always got stuck on a certain note in the third cadence. The repetitious error so impressed the sports writer that for many years thereafter he could never sing that popular song without repeating Eddie's error.

When Shore's playing years ended, he did not turn his questionable musical talent into a career. Instead he invested all his hard-earned savings into the purchase of hockey clubs and developing them into profitable enterprises. In this undertaking, he played on, coached and managed his own teams and has given employment to scores of players.

In his official capacity, the "boss" has been alternately harsh and soft with his staff. Some critics, perhaps facetiously, contend that taskmaster Shore collected enough fines from his hirelings to pay his own salary. Others recall many instances when he generously and quietly aided those in need. But scores of players, who have been coached by Shore, pay tribute to his knowledge and patience.

MAURICE "ROCKET" RICHARD

The Stanley Cup bears the names of most of hockey's greats, and many of them have been blessed (or cursed) with colourful nicknames. The list includes: Cyclone, The Silver Fox, The Big Train, Sudden Death, Bad Joe, Dynamite Twins, Moose, Babe, King, Bucko, Turk, Butch, the Big M and Bingo. While each is linked with some characteristic of its owner, no nickname is more apt than that of "Rocket" when it is linked with Maurice Richard.

In the season the career of "Howie" Morenz ended, a young French Canadian, who had been born in Montreal, was attracting the attention of hockey's talent scouts. Maurice Richard started playing shinny on river ice as soon as he could stand on his skates. It appears most great athletes have the unusual flare to do instinctively what others must laboriously learn through coaching and practice. Young Richard was one of those with the magic gift. When he joined his first team, he already had that special touch.

In the year that Morenz died, the lad who was eventually to replace him in the esteem of Montreal fans joined the Poquette Juveniles. Each year, always a star, he climbed into a higher category. At eighteen he was a member of Verdun juniors, and a year later, still an amateur, he played with Canadian Seniors.

Unfortunately young Maurice was plagued with injuries, sometimes quite early in the season. One year, in his first game, he was heavily bodied and suffered a broken ankle. The next winter he fell heavily and broke his left wrist. Observers agreed he was a prospect with ability and promise, but the rumour persisted that he was too brittle for National Hockey League competition. Even so, Montreal Canadiens invited him to their training-camp.

At that time the twenty-one-year-old rookie was not only a shy youth but he also spoke little English, and this added to his aloofness. However, the fact he could shoot a puck from either right or left seemed more important than the ability to speak two languages. Certainly his prowess could score more goals, and in 1942 he was the only prospect signed by the big club. Right from the season's opening he played well, and he was hailed as the likely winner of the Calder Trophy, annually awarded to the year's best rookie. But that dream ended abruptly in late December, when Maurice was checked heavily, spun around and crashed into the boards. The spot was very near the one where "Howie" Morenz was injured a few years earlier. For the second time in two years, young Richard suffered a broken ankle.

This was no way for a newcomer to reach stardom. Assuredly on the basis of this, few persons would have predicted that this accident-prone youth was destined to become the holder of almost every scoring record in hockey history. But time works wonders, and during the discouraging years, Richard had two strong influences working for him. One force was that he never lost confidence in himself. The other was that Montreal Canadiens' management recognized his potential worth and were willing to patiently await its maturing.

At last Richard received a break he really enjoyed, and it came unexpectedly. One day Coach "Dick" Irvin decided to experiment with a new line. The line comprised: centre Elmer Lach, who spoke only English; right wing Maurice Richard who specialized in French; and left wing "Toe" Blake who was fluently bilingual. Right then, one of hockey's most notable forward lines was born, and Richard's promise became a reality. In this particular season, in one Stanley Cup playoff game against Toronto Maple Leafs, Canadiens won by five to one and Richard scored all five goals. At the end of the game, with the three stars to be named, the selector created a stir when he announced: "Richard, Richard and Richard."

In the years that followed, the "Rocket" once scored fifty goals in a fifty-game schedule. He was also elected to either first or second N.H.L. All-Star teams fourteen consecutive times. When he retired he held or shared the record for most goals in a season, most points in a game, most goals in a lifetime, the longest consecutive scoring streak and most "hat-tricks" in regular games. In Stanley Cup playoffs—he participated in fifteen—his impressive record included most goals, most winning goals, most assists, most total scoring points and the greatest number of playoff games.

Insofar as hockey is concerned he was, until his playing years ended, the "mostest and the greatest." For eighteen years he thrilled fans in all National Hockey League cities. He could arouse hatreds, incite demonstrations and bring down both the wrath and the cheers of spectators. Yet he persisted until the only records left to break were his own. Still it is one of sports' little ironies that records are made only to be broken.

GORDON HOWE

After Montreal Canadiens' Number 9 was permanently retired, another Number 9 on the Detroit Red Wings began an ascent to even greater heights. There were contrasts in the careers of both contenders for hockey's top marks. Richard was an Easterner, born in Montreal, the largest Canadian metropolis; Howe was a Westerner, born in the little town of Floral, Saskatchewan. Richard was a compact 5′10″, weighing around 170 pounds; Howe, at maturity, measured 6′1″ and weighed about 200 pounds. The "Rocket," as his nickname implied, was an explosive player, who seemed to come from nowhere, to suddenly release a blazing scoring power; in contrast, "Gordie" appeared more relaxed in his play, for he combined his strength with considerable finesse.

Howe is a good example of the way Western Canadian youngsters grew up a generation ago. The hockey training may not have been as polished as the synthetic approach of training in comfortable ice-arenas with professional coaching, but in its cruder way it produced solid players who were eager to play and needed the money.

When Gordie's family moved from their Floral home to Saskatoon, the lad learned to skate on any available slough that was big enough to permit a few kids to play shinny. His first pair of skates were hand-me-downs from an older brother, and only a generous supply of woollen socks saved him from taking a walk right inside the roomy boots. Sticks were not easily obtained but, in the manner of kids everywhere, he used plenty of care and tape to always have one available.

When young Gordon, then tall and loose-limbed, was attending Saskatoon's King George School, the principal doubled as hockey coach. At first the lad was a goalkeeper, but he soon changed to defence and then to forward. In the winter when the fifteen-year-old Howe captained the team, they won all eleven games and outscored opponents by 106 goals to six. During his schoolboy years, Gordie never missed an early morning practice on the school's outdoor rink, regardless of the weather. At the same period, he was also playing with non-school peewee, bantam, midget or juvenile teams.

While still a student, he attracted attention from the older sportsmen, who knew what a real hockey player looked like. One of them gave Gordie a puck, a stick and shin-pads. Even when the season ended, the boy did not completely desert hockey, for his parents later recalled that during the summer months he was so intently practising shooting that "he loosened most of the boards on one side of the house."

His determination to succeed, together with his natural ability, began to pay off when he starred for the young Bruins team, sponsored by the Lions Club, and won the Saskatchewan championship. Through his developing years, the youngster was never pampered by club or coach. The only possible exception to this is trivial when compared with the courtesies now extended to junior players. It seems that one night, when Gordie was carrying skates and equipment from his home to the rink in an old battered and gaping suitcase, he lost one of his skates. It had to be traced and retrieved before he could play. After the mishap, a benevolent coach treated him to a new duffle bag.

When only fifteen, young Howe had been skating, stick-handling and scoring for nine or ten years, and there were many indications that a great player was in the making. At that age, "Al" Ritchie, one of Canada's shrewdest observers of sports talent, was so impressed that he arranged for Gordie to attend

New York Rangers' fall training-camp in Winnipeg. Then, just to prove how wrong even the most astute appraisers can be, Lester Patrick, in a decision he must have regretted for the rest of his years, took a couple of looks at the gangling kid and advised him he was too young and should return home for further growth and development.

This rejection could have discouraged the ambition of the boy, but the flame of desire was burning so fiercely that one disappointment could not quench it. Neither did it disturb the scouts of other professional teams. Indeed Fred Pinkney, who was then prospecting for Detroit Red Wings, snatched the opportunity to get Gordie's approval and his parent's signature on a Detroit contract. Promptly he was assigned to Guelph (Ontario) juniors, but a regional dispute arose and he was forced to remain out of competition for a year. But even in practice he proved much too good for junior hockey. The following winter, still only seventeen, young Howe became a member of Omaha Knights, a Detroit farm club in the United States Hockey League. He did not stay down on the farm very long, for the next season at the age of eighteen, he became the youngest-ever rookie in the National Hockey League. He is now in his twentieth year with the same club.

There are N.H.L. players who were just beginning to crawl when Howe began his Detroit career. During the years, he was beset with nearly every kind of injury to which a professional hockey player is subjected, including a skull fracture that might have ended his hockey when only twenty-one years old. Yet despite his disabilities and the constant fresh waves of challengers, he is still tops in his profession.

At the moment Gordie Howe has played more N.H.L. games, scored more goals and earned more assists and total points in league play than any other player in hockey history. In addition, in Stanley Cup competition, he has played in more series, made more assists and accumulated a higher total of points than all other contenders.

He has other accomplishments too. Six times he won the Art Ross Trophy, annually awarded to the N.H.L. scoring leader. Four times he was voted the most valuable player in the entire league to his team. Twenty-one times he was elected to either first or second All-Star teams. It is no longer news when Gordie Howe wins a hockey honour. The news comes when he misses recognition.

And still Howe goes on. Every time he assists, scores or even appears on the ice, he makes it harder for challengers on-the-up to equal his marks. He still takes his regular playing turn, kills penalties and is the key attacker on Detroit's power-play. He skates easily, paces himself nicely, shoots from either hand and has a mind to match his powerful frame. Like Ole Man River, Gordie Howe, at the age of forty-three, just keeps rolling along.

There is no measuring rod for comparing hockey greatness. Players in the old days were as brilliant as are those in the 1960s. Each in his own time did things that enabled him to surpass his contemporaries. And so it will continue, as the stars of today become the celebrities of the morrow.

CHAPTER THIRTEEN

TORONTO MAPLE LEAFS

On the evening of November 12, 1931, the largest crowd until then to ever attend an indoor event of any kind in the city of Toronto streamed through the turnstiles of the brand-new Maple Leaf Gardens, Toronto's new palace of sport.

It was an important event, for it pushed professional hockey into a prestige-status so that the game could now be enjoyed in surroundings usually reserved for opera and theatre. In the pre-game ceremonies, the bands of the 48th Highlanders and the Royal Grenadiers played "Happy Days Are Here Again." The Toronto Maple Leafs were presented with huge floral horseshoes. The players on the Chicago Black Hawks and the home team lined up along their blue-lines. The civic leaders orated. The fact the Leafs were beaten did not add to the joyousness of the occasion, but even this was forgotten in the boost to the morale of the sportsmen of Toronto.

The opening was not something casual. It was prompted by an incident that occurred five years earlier. During the winter of 1926/27, every American city that boasted a rink, a hockey puck and a couple of goal-nets was clamouring for admission into the National Hockey League. Five clubs in the United States were already in the fold, and many others were trying to lift the latch. It was a time when every Canadian professional club could have been sold at prices yielding handsome profits.

In that year, St. Patrick's club, which operated the Toronto franchise, was not doing well at the gate or on the ice. The owners were not only disappointed, but they were also aware that it was a good time to sell. One of the interests then pleading for franchise and players was based in Philadelphia. Being close to the U.S. mint, the interests offered St. Pat's owners a healthy two hundred thousand dollars for assets and rights that had earlier been bought for seven thousand dollars. The offer was tempting and was ready for signing.

Then up rose doughty Conn Smythe. Conn was a unique combination of warrior, engineer and sportsman. In his student years he captained the University of Toronto juniors when they won the Ontario championship, and he then went overseas with the entire team to do battle in World War I. He earned a commission with the 40th Battery and was fighting with them when he won the Military Cross. He later transferred to the Royal Air Force and was mentioned in despatches. Later he was shot down and captured. He escaped, then retraced his way to assist a comrade and was recaptured. There was no doubt about his willingness to fight, and neither was there any uncertainty about his keen interest in all sports, especially hockey. Indeed it is a combination of these two characteristics that led to the building of Maple Leaf Gardens.

When Conn returned from the First World War, he continued coaching and managing good hockey teams. Some won national titles and another became Olympic champions. Because of those successes he was invited by Colonel John S. Hammond to gather and coach New York Rangers on their entry in the National Hockey League. He assembled an outstanding team, but before they played a game, Conn was replaced by Lester Patrick, who was considered a better showman. The dismissal stung the proud Smythe, and he vowed he would build a team of his own that would be better than the one he had lost.

To Smythe a vow has always been much more than a faint-hearted wish. It is a firm pledge that rages until it is properly resolved. So when he learned St. Pat's owners wanted to sell, he was immediately concerned. He did not want the franchise to leave Toronto or Canada. He did not want to lose the opportunity to build a hockey empire that would appease his wrath.

Promptly Smythe gathered a few friends, and they contacted

St. Pat's owners, who were four well-known Toronto businessmen—J. P. Bickell, N. L. Nathanson, Paul Ciceri and "Charlie" Querrie. They were willing to listen, but they were also insistent that the Toronto offer had to match the two hundred thousand dollar bid from Philadelphia. They compromised to the extent of offering a temporary option of thirty days on payment of ten thousand dollars. While the option was in effect, Smythe and associates tapped all accessible financial sources but could raise only one hundred and sixty thousand dollars. With hat in hand and tongue in cheek, they again called on St. Pat's owners.

"We can't get more than one hundred and sixty thousand dollars," Smythe began.

"We still want two hundred thousand dollars," the owners' spokesman replied.

Then Conn gave them forty thousand dollars worth of professional advice, "You fellows are good Canadians and you already have a terrific profit. Besides, you all live in Toronto and you have many friends. Surely you don't want to walk down the street in your hometown and have the neighbours snub you because you sold out to foreigners. Haven't you any civic pride?"

Well this was different. Indeed the four owners were very fine citizens, and they eventually said farewell to the forty thousand dollars they might have received. So for one hundred and sixty thousand dollars (seventy-five thousand dollars cash and eighty-five thousand dollars to be paid in ninety days), Conn Smythe and his buddies owned St. Pat's name, players and franchise. If the new owners had been primarily interested in a quick profit, they could easily have made forty thousand dollars for themselves, for the same Philadelphians, whose earlier proposal had been rejected, again made the same offer to Conn Smythe. But, apart from the ethics involved, Conn remembered he was still pledged to build a team to defeat New York Rangers.

That promise was still far from fulfilment. To create a new public image, the name St. Patricks was changed to Maple Leafs, an emblem always esteemed by Mr. Smythe. The design on the new jerseys was to be a green maple leaf bearing the name Toronto in small white letters.

These changes, however, were not nearly as important as the personnel of the team. Conn soon found that some of the players were "over the hill." Others were young and willing but simply did not have enough ability. Three years later only two of the originals "Hap" Day and "Ace" Bailey remained.

Meanwhile Smythe was busily scouting, trading and scheming to exchange rowboats for battleships. He was selling players he did not want and used the dollars to buy others he preferred. He began developing his own material, and he produced such great prospects as Conacher, Jackson and Horner. Sometimes he was fooled by rival "gypsies," but in various ways he was constantly coming closer to the kind of team he wanted. Even so, he still had one great need, for he lacked a dynamic player, someone with experience to steady the youngsters, to give them inspiration in the dressing-room and leadership on the ice.

At the time the Ottawa club had some good players, but the crowds were not large, and the management needed money. All N.H.L. clubs had designs on "King" Clancy, but the clubs resisted the seemingly high price placed on the dashing defenceman. While others were bargaining, Smythe agreed the price was fair; but first he had to sell the proposition to his own directors. So he secured a five-day option, went to work on his associates, then startled the hockey world by purchasing Clancy's services (with the player's approval) for thirty-five thousand dollars cash, plus two average players valued at fifteen thousand dollars. In 1930 the fifty-thousand dollar expenditure seemed a gamble, but it has been paying dividends for most of thirty-four years, for Clancy is still a loyal and capable Toronto Maple Leafs executive.

At the start of the 1930/31 season, Leafs were improving and they appeared to be the team most likely to succeed. But manager Smythe still had problems. "We aren't doing right by these players," he confessed to his directors. "We have the makings of a good team, but we aren't paying them enough. If they belonged to American clubs, their salaries would be much higher."

"What's the answer?" one of them asked.

Conn explained, "This Mutual Street Arena seats only eight thousand people. If we want to get more money for the players, improved accommodation for the fans and increased profits for ourselves, we have to get a rink that can seat twelve thousand at least". While this idea was being considered, he added, "And what's more, even if I have to put up my own building, I'm going to get it in time for next season".

He was reminded that the club contract with Mutual Arena did not expire for another year, and they were obligated to forfeit one thousand dollars for every unplayed home game during that period. He did not need to be told that the country was in the depth of an economic depression, that unemployment was prevalent and that banks were trying to take money in rather than pay it out. But Conn shrewdly rebuked the doubters by stressing that men needed jobs, building costs were low and the jittery economy was pleading for a shot in the arm.

Conn, as usual, got his own way. With the help of his directors, he was able to obtain a suitable, central site. By a judicious mingling of coaxing, coercion and logic they raised one and a half million dollars at a time when capital was being hoarded. Later, when he learned that costs were exceeding estimates and that another two hundred thousand dollars was needed, he received aid from workers, who agreed to take a fifth of their wages in Gardens stock, and from suppliers, who accepted shares for a portion of their bills.

If Smythe had been the kind of person who heeded discouraging words, he would have dropped the whole project. Frequently he was told: "You'll never raise the money." "You'll never have it built in time." "You'll never fill it when you do build it." However, the chance-taker confounded them all, for he found the dollars, the Gardens doors opened exactly on schedule and the building was crowded to capacity. Were the manager and promoter content at last? Not quite, he still had to produce a team to humble New York Rangers.

The first season in the Gardens started badly. Leafs not only lost the opener to Chicago Black Hawks, but they continued to slump so severely that by the end of November they were last in the eight-club league. Conn tried to make suitable trades, but rivals avoided him because their earlier swaps had boomeranged. When exchanges were impossible, Smythe tried to buy and offered seventy-five thousand dollars for "Howie" Morenz; and was refused. Finally, when new players were unavailable, he decided on another coach and replaced "Art" Duncan with "Dick" Irvin.

Honoured Members, Hockey Hall of Fame. Opening Day—September 5th, 1959.

1. Red Dutton; 2 Lloyd Turner; 3. Frank Goheen; 4. Ching Johnson; 5. Aurel Joliat; 6. Frank Boucher; 7. Al Pickard; 8. Bill Cook; 9. George Hay; 10. Duke Keats; 11. Dit Clapper; 12. Eddie Shore; 13. Conn Smythe; 14. King Clancy; 15. Wm. Northey; 16. Frank Foyston; 17. George Dudley; 18. Frank Fredrickson; 19. Lester Patrick; 20. Newsy Lalonde; 21. Frank Nighbor; 22. Joe Malcne; 23. Herb Gardiner; 24. W. A. Hewitt; 25. Hugh Lehman; 26. Art Ross; 27. Cyclone Taylor; 28. Dickie Boon; 29. Claude Robinson; 30. Moose Johnson; 31. Paddy Moran.

Jean Beliveau, Captain Montreal Canadiens, displays the Stanley Cup.

Irvin was a great hockey player, but his talent for developing young players was still to be proven. But "Dick" was a dedicated teacher who knew the fundamentals of hockey and took his job seriously.

One afternoon when in New York, Irvin invited "Andy" Blair to go to a show with him. Later another player enquired: "How did you like the show, 'Andy'?" Blair was compelled to answer: "I didn't hear or see much of it. But I sure learned how to check 'Normie' Himes."

Under Irvin's guidance, the whole team perked, and within a month they had climbed from last place to first. They continued to play well all that season. Then they defeated Chicago Black Hawks in the Stanley Cup semi-final round and, in spring 1932, were destined to meet New York Rangers in the final series.

This was the meeting that Smythe had anticipated for five years. It was peculiar in that the first three games were to be played in different cities, and the series was to end when one club won three games. The first match was played in New York and Leafs won by six-four; the second was played in neutral Boston and Leafs were victors by six-two; the third and decisive game was played in the new Maple Leaf Gardens, before a crowd of fifteen thousand, and Leafs triumphed by six-four.

That final victory was doubly welcomed because Toronto Maple Leafs won their first Stanley Cup honours and because Conn Smythe had avenged his dismissal by Rangers. The fans were so pleased that they milled in and around the Gardens for more than an hour, cheering the players and congratulating the manager. Thus 1931/32 was a complete year for the Toronto club. The fans enjoyed the improved accommodation, the players received higher salaries, and the shareholders, despite having to pay twenty-two thousand dollars for unused arena rental, still earned an increased dividend.

All through the 1930s, the Leafs' roster was constantly changing. Veterans were retiring; youngsters were breaking in; the Jackson-Primeau-Conacher line was thrilling the crowds all around the league. Every season produced one of those scenes to be recalled for generations to come. It could have been the night Boston Bruins and Toronto Maple Leafs endured through 164 minutes until a goal was scored. Then there was the "Ace"

Bailey Night, when every club in the N.H.L. sent its best players to play a benefit game for the "Ace". Prior to the face-off, manager Smythe publicly addressed the injured player and said: "Allow me to present this sweater which you have worn so nobly and long for the Maple Leafs. No other player on our clubs will ever use this number." And Toronto's Number 6 was retired forever.

Then there was the rollicking "King" Clancy Night, when all the leprechauns paid a St. Patrick's tribute to the popular player. Later there was the "Alfie" Moore occasion, when officers of Chicago Black Hawks and Toronto Maple Leafs gave each other cuffs on the ears.

It was in the same decade that Conn Smythe was at his battling best. In his book *Hockey Night in Canada,* Foster Hewitt recalled:

> Smythe in the 1930s was a dynamic leader. Around the circuit he was defending his players verbally and physically. Using logic when possible and fists when necessary, tossing pucks on the ice to attract the referee, waving arms, hurling his hat, dashing across the ice, racing around the rink, stomping through corridors, the Leafian boss was a powerful, roaring force, in an era when his contemporaries were also at their shouting best.

Another "Do You Remember" night occurred in Boston. Smythe resented the dull, listless defensive game the Bruins played in Toronto. So the next time Leafs visited Boston, the Toronto manager spent sixty-three dollars and placed this advertisement in a Boston paper:

> ATTENTION HOCKEY FANS!
>
> If you're tired of seeing the kind of hockey the Boston Bruins are playing, come to the Garden tonight and see a real hockey club, the Toronto Maple Leafs.

"Art" Ross was naturally displeased with the display, and he appealed to the league to fine Smythe a thousand dollars. Actually the Boston manager should have been grateful, for the game attracted the largest crowd of the season.

While Conn was having fun and the Toronto team was playing well, they were unable to win the Stanley Cup through the entire ten years following the Ranger Revenge, but the "touch" returned in April 1942. Toronto Maple Leafs traditionally did things the hard way. For some hidden reason, success has rarely come easily. Usually the team does better when the wind is a gale and the waves are rolling hard and high than when fanned by gentle zephyrs and a calm sea. This was especially so in the 1942 Stanley Cup series.

This was a wartime year, but hockey carried on with Federal approval and the wishes of overseas troops. The two finalists were Detroit Red Wings and Toronto Maple Leafs. The first two games were played on Toronto ice, but the Wings won both of them and returned to play the next two matches in their own Olympia.

In the third game Detroit showed even greater superiority, for they walloped Leafs by five-two. "Eddie" Bush, one of their defencemen, scored one goal and had four assists to establish a playoff record for defencemen. At this point Leafs lost three straight games and, with the fourth to be played in Detroit, they looked to be ready for the final thrust. Never before in all Stanley Cup history had a team lost the first three games and recovered to win the historic bowl.

Naturally, Toronto coach "Hap" Day was disappointed with the performance of his club. But by this time he had discovered the cause. In 1942 there was still no centre line in mid-ice. The Detroit coach had shrewdly planned for his players to advance to their own blue line and fire the puck ahead into the Toronto defensive zone. He then used younger, faster skaters to swoop down the ice, harass the Toronto defence into making bad passes and pick up loose pucks. It was not pretty hockey, but it was effective. To counteract it, Day decided to drop two of his older and slower regulars, and replace them with "Don" Metz and "Ernie" Dickens, a couple of speedier youngsters.

Day did something else. All coaches know that a psychological angle can often induce miracles, and the inspiration can come from the most unexpected of sources. It can emanate from an opponent's sarcastic deprecation, a rebuke from a sportswriter, the gift of four-leaf clovers, a horseshoe or perhaps a lucky penny. "Hap" Day wondered where he could find such an uplift. Then just before the fourth game, he received a letter from a fourteen-year-old-girl. In the letter the young girl expressed her complete confidence that Leafs would eventually win. She added that she was praying for their success. The letter was so simple and sincere that, in the dressing-room, prior to the game, coach Day read it to the team. When he finished, "Sweeney" Schriner, one of the older players, arose and said with some feeling, "Don't worry about this one, coach. We'll win it for that little girl."

They did! In that fourth game, Red Wings were leading by two-nothing early in the second period; then Davidson and Carr tied it for Toronto. In the third period, Liscombe of Detroit scored what seemed to be the game- and series-winning goal. At that moment Leafs were three games down and trailing in the fourth with only ten minutes remaining. It seemed only a miracle could keep them alive. With the flame of victory barely smouldering, Apps tied the score three-three. Then a newcomer, "Don" Metz, never considered a prolific scorer, fired the clincher, and Leafs were still in the series.

The surprise ending caused Detroit fans and players to go berserk. Grosso and Wares were fined for berating the referee. Manager "Jack" Adams punched the official and was suspended by President Frank Calder who had personally to receive police protection. These wild outbursts did not help the morale of Detroit players, and neither did the loss of their coach, who had to be replaced by a less-experienced leader. So for a variety of reasons the rout of the Toronto club was delayed.

Leafs won the fifth game by nine-three, and the newly formed line of "Don" Metz, "Syl" Apps and "Nick" Metz scored six times. Their victory was not a fluke, for when the Toronto team returned to Detroit, with excellent goalkeeping by "Turk" Broda, they shut out Detroit by three-nothing. Both clubs came back to Maple Leaf Gardens for the seventh and decisive game. In the presence of more than sixteen thousand spectators, Toronto Maple Leafs earned the privilege of having the players' names engraved on the big bowl. It was a comeback unmatched in Stanley Cup history.

This achievement sparked the Toronto club, and all through the 1940s, Leaf teams were powerful. They won the Stanley Cup again in 1944/45 and, after a one-year lapse, they won the trophy in three successive years—in two of them by four straight victories.

Those successes did not just happen, for they involved a constant appraisal of playing material. It was always one of Conn Smythe's axioms—and he had many shrewd ones—that "you can't win this year on what you did last year." So even in 1947, when Leafs were enjoying the fame resulting from two consecutive Stanley Cup triumphs, Smythe did not stand pat.

At the time "Max" Bentley was not only the N.H.L. scoring champion, he was also an excellent playmaker. He was credited with having "a shot so accurate it could thread a needle." But "Max" belonged to Chicago Black Hawks and, with his brother Doug, was a crowd-pleaser in all arenas. Moreover, Chicago was drawing well at home and was not crying for dollars. But Chicago did have one real need, and this was more bodies. Their farm system was not producing, and replacements were needed for several positions.

Toronto needed Bentley, and Chicago needed quantity. Smythe knew he had to give to get. So he said to "Bill" Tobin, "I know you don't want to break up the Bentley combination, but, for 'Max' alone, I'll give you five players and each is high-class N.H.L. calibre. I'll let you have three forwards—Stewart, Poile and Bodnar—and two defencemen—Goldham and Dickens. What's more, if you ever want to return Goldham, I'll give you twenty-five thousand dollars for him."

The five for one offer was a deal in which each club would get what it wanted. After a little hemming and a lot of hawing, it was completed. Who won? Well, Chicago Black Hawks were greatly strengthened; but Toronto Maple Leafs, with Max Bentley firing important goals, won the Stanley Cup three times in the next four years.

However, teams can fall apart faster than they can be built up, just as wreckers can destroy in days a building that once required months to erect. Similarly, through the 1950s, while Montreal Canadiens, Detroit Red Wings and Chicago Black Hawks were winning the honours and hosting the champagne parties, Toronto Maple Leafs were slowly rebuilding for another drive to the top.

In 1957/58, the Leafs finished last in the league for the only time in their long history. Then, as they had done a quarter century earlier, they changed coaches and brought in George "Punch" Imlach. Unlike most other N.H.L. coaches, "Punch" had never played other than junior hockey. But in minor leagues he was a successful executive and was credited with the development of the skilled Jean Beliveau.

The selection of Imlach was surprising, for his excellence had not been shouted from the roof-tops. Yet it proved to be one of the smartest decisions ever made by Leafs management. This assertion needs no embellishment or qualification, for the facts tell their own story. In 1958, Leafs were last. In 1959, under the new coach, they advanced to fourth, and reached the Stanley Cup final round. In 1960 they climbed to second but were again beaten by Montreal Canadiens in the Stanley Cup final. In 1961 they were second once more in the League race, they lost to Detroit Red Wings in the playoffs. There was a change in Toronto management that year. Conn Smythe retired, and his son Stafford took over the presidency and, along with associates Harold Ballard and John Bassett, became responsible for the operation of all Maple Leaf Gardens enterprises.

Then, with "Punch" Imlach coaching and managing, and "King" Clancy assisting, Toronto Maple Leafs won the Stanley Cup in three successive years. But even during their success the club had fallen into the dangerous and traditional custom of winning the hard way. The 1963/64 Stanley Cup series typified this habit of "coming from behind."

In 1964, Leafs finished third when the season ended, so they began the first cup round against Montreal Canadiens who were leading the league. After five matches, Canadiens were leading by three games to two and needed only one more to win the round; but Leafs won the sixth game to tie the series. The seventh and all-important match was played in Montreal, and Leafs eked a slight lead, then grimly held on to snatch the victory and advance into the Stanley Cup final round against Detroit Red Wings which had beaten Chicago Black Hawks.

All through the 1964 Toronto-Detroit series, there was a constant, relentless ebbing and flowing of fortune. At times, one team would seem assured of success. But before they drank the wine of victory, the cup would be snatched from their lips. Never were the clubs separated by more than a single game, and many of the contests were in doubt until the last minute of play. It required a stout heart to even watch the thrillers, let alone participate in them.

With Red Wings leading by three games to two, and the sixth game being played in Detroit, Leafs were forced to win or immediately begin their long summer vacation. Their position was similar in the previous Montreal series. Once more they contrived to win, and they proceeded to the seventh game.

Throughout the 1964 series there was a controversy over the coaching theories of Detroit's Sid Abel and Toronto's "Punch" Imlach. Abel was a relaxer. He reasoned that the Wings, having completed a long seventy-game schedule and having just ended a tough seven-game series with Chicago Black Hawks, deserved good rests between playoff games. So in the belief that relaxation was the best remedy, he arranged for the players to take it easy, to go sight-seeing and even to visit race-tracks and generally rid their minds of hockey.

Imlach held to the opposite theory. Even though many of his key players were veterans and were beginning to reveal the ravages of time, "Punch" insisted on a strenuous daily practice, whether or not they won the previous night, no matter how rugged the game had been. Sometimes they went directly from their plane or train to Gardens' ice. Imlach had many critics who believed that the coach would pay the penalty of defeat for overworking his players. But as well as being a very determined manager, he was a successful one, and it is risky to fault a champion.

However on the day of the seventh game, it seemed "Punch" had gone once too often to the Fountain of Youth. An hour before game time, Kelly was limping badly from a strained ligament in his left knee. On the way to the Gardens he announced he would not be in the game. George Armstrong was nursing a painful shoulder injury. Carl Brewer had missed a couple of games in the series and was playing with a distressing rib separation. "Bobby" Baun was impaired by a leg injury which x-rays later revealed to be a hair-line fracture of the fibula. "Don" McKenney was out for the series with a torn knee ligament.

In the midst of all these disabilities, as the criticism of Imlach mounted, the stock answer of the coach was, "There is no substitute for hard work. We're up for this game and we're in shape to win it." Time proved him right, although the team doctors deserved assists. Crippled Kelly, Baun, Brewer and Armstrong, with pre-game injections of pain-killers, plus booster shots during intermissions, not only played well but they performed so brilliantly that Leafs shut out Red Wings by four-nothing and won the Stanley Cup for the third straight year.

In April 1965, Toronto's three-time Stanley Cup streak ended, and the two-year reign of Montreal Canadiens began. Then, in 1966/67, a surprising Maple Leaf team recaptured the historic trophy for the fourth time in six seasons. But the downfall was as sudden as the elevation for, in 1967/68, the Toronto club, the Cinderellas of the previous year, didn't even get into the playoffs. That humiliation had not been experienced in a decade and it hurt. Prior to the end of the season, Leafs management began planning, trading and buying, in preparation for another climb up the hockey ladder.

Progress was slow. In 1968/69, Leafs finished fourth in their division and were eliminated in the first Stanley Cup round. In 1969/70, still experimenting, under the direction of General Manager Jim Gregory and coach John McLellan, they finished a lowly last in their eastern group. However, in 1970/71, with the addition of Plante, Parent and Baun, the whole team improved. Leafs climbed from seventh to fourth place, qualified for the Stanley Cup playdowns and showed signs of again becoming a powerful club.

CHAPTER FOURTEEN MONTREAL CANADIENS

The head of the professional hockey family, the grandfather of all National Hockey League clubs, has to be Montreal Canadiens. Its origin dates back to 1909, in the days when "Jack" Johnson was the world's heavyweight boxing champion and "Christy" Mathewson was baseball's hero. The same year there was a feud between two professional hockey leagues in Eastern Canada. One group, the National Hockey Association, comprised Montreal Wanderers, Renfrew, Cobalt, Haileybury and Montreal Canadiens. Some of the clubs were wealthy, for they were sponsored by Noah Timmins and "Amby" O'Brien.

The rival forces in the Canadian Hockey Association did not have as much gold or silver. But the teams from Ottawa and Quebec, together with Montreal Shamrocks, Montreal Nationals and All-Montreal, did have some twenty-four-carat players.

As soon as schedules were announced, the contending clubs began raiding each other's rosters. "Cyclone" Taylor, one of hockey's immortals, was lured to Renfrew from Ottawa. The Renfrew Millionaires signed Lester Patrick and brother Frank Patrick for three thousand dollars each for a season of eight games. In an emergency, they offered Hay Millar of Edmonton one thousand dollars for a single game. In the turmoil, Montreal Nationals sued Montreal Canadiens for alienation of Didier Pitre's services.

The opening of both groups was delayed until New Year's Day for the formation of ice. It did not require more than two weeks operations to convince most clubs that continuing the war would financially ruin many of the teams. Sensibly the two groups agreed to unite and form the National Hockey Association. Montreal Wanderers, Renfrew, Cobalt and Haileybury became charter members; then Ottawa and Montreal Shamrocks were accepted. Finally there was an appeal from a number of French-Canadian sportsmen who wanted to enter a team composed entirely of French-speaking players. It was apparent such a club would have a loyal following and the club was awarded the seventh franchise. The Montreal Canadiens, wearing their red, white and black uniforms, played their first N.H.A. game early in January of 1910.

When Les Canadiens, now in their sixty-second season, began their professional life, hockey was a seven-man game, with point, cover-point and rover included in the line-ups. Time of play was divided into two thirty-minute halves, and no substitutes were allowed. There were no blue lines, red lines or circles marked on the ice. And even if there had been, the colours would have melted with the first thaw. Actually lines were not needed, for forward passing of the puck was illegal. Neither were there farm teams and organized scouting. After the mining moguls retired, professional salaries rarely exceeded one thousand dollars for the season.

The Montreal Canadiens are not only the oldest club but they are also the founding fathers of other clubs. One of their early missionary tours involved spreading the gospel of professional hockey in Toronto. Toronto had always been a good city for baseball, lacrosse and amateur hockey, but before World War I the burghers had never given healthy support to professional hockey. This neglect worried the sponsors of National Hockey Association clubs who knew there were riches ready for tapping. So the Easterners proposed an invasion of Toronto's territory. Montreal Canadiens, along with Montreal Wanderers, volunteered to lead the attack. Just prior to Christmas of 1912, the two clubs arranged for a game to be played in the new artificially iced Arena Gardens Rink.

The announced intention was to play a nice game, introduce Toronto to the new six-man hockey and create such a favourable response that Toronto fans would demand representation in the

National Hockey Association. It was a seemingly worthy gesture, and it was anticipated that, in the spirit of the season, Peace on Ice would prevail. However, goodwill did not ensue, for the contending missionaries, instead of making converts, almost killed each other.

It was the roughest, toughest game ever played in Toronto. The *pièce de résistance* of the grand exhibition was staged when Canadiens' "Newsy" Lalonde collided with Wanderers' "Odie" Cleghorn. Both were driving full speed ahead. When they crashed, both "Newsy" and "Odie" were knocked to the ice and temporarily dazed. While the first antagonists were sprawled over the ice, Sprague Cleghorn skated over to them and, without further cause, deliberately swung his stick at Lalonde, giving him a gaping head-wound which began gushing blood. Promptly the referee fined the Wanderer twenty-five dollars but made no attempt to eject him from the game. The horrified Toronto crowd wildly demonstrated until the offender was removed from the ice. Within an hour the National Hockey Association officers, who had been informed of the bad propaganda, slapped another fifty dollar fine on Cleghorn, together with four weeks' suspension without pay—a total loss of $675. There was even more punishment, for a Toronto detective obtained a warrant for Sprague Cleghorn's arrest. He was summoned to court and fined some more. All because brotherly love is so deep.

A rather amusing sidelight to the incident has a little moral in it. It reveals the indifference of hockey players at that time. After the game, "Charlie" Querrie, manager of the arena, hurried to Agnes Street Police Station to provide bail for both Cleghorn and Lalonde, who had been compelled to go along with the officer. He was amazed to find both lodged in one cell and shooting crap. They even coaxed the bondsman into the game. He yielded and lost.

Despite—or perhaps because of such violence—the game impressed Toronto fans. Within a year there was not one but two Toronto teams in the National Hockey Association, along with Quebec, Ottawa and two Montreal teams. It might reasonably be claimed that Montreal Canadiens were godfathers to professional hockey in Toronto, even though they almost strangled the child at birth.

Montreal Canadiens won their first Stanley Cup title before the National Hockey League came into existence. In the season of 1915/16, their coach and manager was George Kendall, who was better known as Kennedy. He was an erstwhile wrestler who loved hockey and was a shrewd promoter. In his operations he frequently clashed with Sam Lichtenhein who owned the rival Montreal Wanderers. One year the pair debated the respective drawing powers of Canadiens and Wanderers and eventually talked themselves into a five thousand dollar wager. When the season was about to end, the comparative attendance figures were very close. Indeed they were so near that Kennedy bought one thousand dollars worth of tickets with his own money, then gave them away so he might win the much larger stake.

Under Kennedy's guidance, the Canadiens of 1915/16 were a strong, colourful team. "Jack" Laviolette was really a Flying Frenchman, for he skated so fast that his toque frequently flew off as he dashed down the ice.

"Newsy" Lalonde was another member of that early Montreal Canadiens' team, and apart from his scrappy habits, he was highly esteemed for his hockey ability. He later earned the distinction of being voted Canada's best lacrosse player during the first half-century. Lalonde featured in nearly every game he played. But no manager could succeed with a whole team of "Newsys," for the manager would likely find too many players in the penalty box!

Much of Montreal Canadiens' first Stanley Cup victory could be attributed to goalkeeper George Vezina. Half a century ago a netminder had to remain upright, and was penalized if he sprawled on the ice, so the job was more than ordinarily hazardous. Vezina, whose manner was so cool that he earned the nickname "Chicoutimi Cucumber," almost died in action. Still playing for Canadiens, in a game against Pittsburgh in November of 1925, he became ill after the first period and died four months afterwards from tuberculosis. Later, in his memory, the owners of Montreal Canadiens presented the Vezina Trophy as an annual award to the goalkeeper on the N.H.L. team with the fewest goals scored against it.

During the eight years' lapse following Canadiens' first Stanley Cup victory, there were many changes in the team personnel, for only one of the original champions remained. Rules, too, were revised, for kicking the puck was allowed; ice-surfaces were divided into three zones; assists were recorded in scoring statistics; goalkeepers were permitted to pass the puck ahead to players in their own defence zone.

The league, too, changed, for the National Hockey Association became the National Hockey League, and out West there were two major leagues. So in 1924, Canadiens had to defeat successively Ottawa, Vancouver and finally Calgary to become Stanley Cup holders. The fact that they won each series in two straight games and had only six goals scored against them indicates they were one of hockey's great teams.

It was during the Calgary matches that one of the Western players received a sharp rebuke from Referee "Art" Ross. Probably irritated by the fact that his team was taking a trimming, the player shouted at the official, "The Stanley Cup will never go West as long as you're refereeing." Ross moved a little closer to his accuser and replied, "I don't know when the Stanley Cup might go West. But I'm sure of one thing, it will never go to Calgary so long as you're in the nets."

Some idea of the length of Canadiens' long lifeline can be gleaned from the knowledge that, even after the Flying Frenchmen twice won the Stanley Cup, not one of the other clubs now comprising the N.H.L. even held a league franchise.

In the year Canadiens won their second title, a group of Montreal sportsmen financed and erected a new arena. The number included Hon. Donat Raymond, Sir Edward Beatty, Kenneth Dawes, Herbert Molson, Major McDougall and William Northey. At a time when insurance companies refused to back what they considered speculative enterprise, Mr. L. H. Timmins personally assumed all the mortgages and assured the erection.

The site of the new Forum was almost historic ground. In earlier years, when it was an empty lot, there was a depression in its centre, and as snow melted and froze, a fair ice-surface remained. It was on this pond that such celebrities as "Art" Ross, Frank and Lester Patrick and Russell Bowie learned to play hockey.

The Montreal Forum, when it opened, pioneered in indoor sports stadiums, where hockey was the principal revenue-producer. It was erected seven years prior to Maple Leaf Gardens and antedates all other N.H.L. arenas.

Thus 1924 was a big year in the life of Montreal Canadiens. They repeated their Stanley Cup victories in 1930 and again in 1931. Then, through more than a decade, they suffered in both prestige and dollars. In 1935, the outlook was so dreary that consideration was given to removing the team and franchise to Cleveland.

At the time, as tenants of the Forum, the club was obliged to pay a rental of forty per cent of gross receipts to the Canadian Arena Company. One year, after winning the Stanley Cup, they had a surplus of thirty-five thousand dollars, but they lost all this and five hundred more in the celebration festivities. The transfer of the club to Cleveland was much more than talk. But before it became a reality, the Canadian Arena Company agreed to pay Leo Dandurand and "Joe" Cattarinich, Montreal Canadiens' owners, one hundred and sixty-five thousand dollars for the club franchise, players, name and equipment. It was not a high offer, but Leo and "Joe" had racing interests elsewhere, and they had paid only eleven thousand dollars for the same assets in 1921. So it was not a bad deal. Even more important, the Montreal Canadiens did not have to migrate to United States.

Following the 1935 sale, the Habitants had one good season, when they led the league. Then they slumped so badly that in four successive years they never finished higher than sixth. In one year they earned only ten victories in forty-eight games. That was no position for the proud club that had included in earlier years many of hockey's most illustrious French-Canadian names: Vezina, Le Seuer, Laviolette, Pitre, Lalonde, Joliat, Gagnon, the Lepines, the Bruneteaus, the Manthas and many other notables. Their brilliance, speed and stickhandling, even in defeat, had thrilled the throngs. They deserved, in the late 1930s and early 1940s, a return to their good old days.

It sometimes happens that the best tonic for a hockey team is a change in coaches. That was true in 1930, when Toronto Maple Leafs replaced "Art" Duncan with "Dick" Irvin. It was to be tested again in 1940, when the same Irvin was invited to coach Montreal Canadiens, and he talked it over with Conn

Smythe. Even though Smythe was always a devoted team-man, he was also interested in maintaining a solid league. At times he traded or sold players he admired. But he knew that when he strengthened a lesser club, competition would improve, crowds would increase and his Toronto Maple Leafs would share the prosperity.

When the opportunity came, Smythe was aware Montreal Canadiens needed a lift, and he consented to Irvin becoming their coach. "Dick" was a man with many interests and skills. In his youth he had been a good Winnipeg amateur hockey player. One night, in an Allan Cup final series, he scored all nine goals earned by his team. During World War I he served as a despatch rider. When he returned to Canada, he became a professional hockey player with Regina Capitals.

When Irvin's playing career ended, he had a brief coaching term with Chicago Black Hawks, but any such association around 1930 was dangerous. One morning, after a game in which the Hawks were beaten, "Dick" visited the sumptuous office of owner Major McLaughlin. The coach lamented, "For the life of me, Major, I don't know what's wrong with this team." "I'll tell you what's wrong with it," snapped the Chicago boss. "All you have to do is to look in that big mirror." Irvin reflected, and he soon joined the Hawks' legion of lost coaches. Then he quickly moved to Toronto, where he helped Leafs win the Stanley Cup in his first year.

"Dick" was witty and wise and became an excellent after-dinner speaker. Sometimes he spoofed the talents of a coach. "Coaches are often praised for incidents in which they had no part," he admitted. "One night, Canadiens were tied with Boston Bruins in a close game. 'Toe' Blake wasn't doing too well. I decided to take him off. But before I could get a replacement on the ice, he scored the winning goal. That was master-minding for you."

Another time, at a dinner, he was asked, "What is meant by sudden-death overtime?" Dick thought for a moment, then explained, "It's like this. When your team gets the first goal, it's sudden; but when your opponents get it, it's death."

"Dick," in addition to his hockey knowledge, was also a breeder of birds, many of which won international honours. He often remarked that hockey's birds and the feathered variety had much in common, and many coaching ideas were applicable to both. However, "Dick" Irvin did not win hockey fame because of bird-breeding or off-ice quotes. During fifteen seasons with Montreal Canadiens, his teams won the Prince of Wales Trophy for league leadership four times in a row. Only once in fifteen years did Montreal Canadiens fail to make the Stanley Cup playoffs.

All through Irvin's tenure, he was aided by at least two great influences. One of his blessings was the presence of the Richard-Lach-Blake line, a threesome which he invented to pack power and scoring success right from its inception. Another helpful association, even though it will never be mentioned in a statistical column, was the advice and co-operation of manager Frank Selke.

Selke, in his younger years, was associated with junior hockey. Through his success with teenagers, he became an ally of Conn Smythe. When Maple Leaf Gardens opened, he accepted an executive position and remained in various capacities, through fifteen seasons. During these years he was a colleague of "Dick" Irvin, and the two had much in common, even to the interest in breeding birds. About five years after Irvin became Canadiens' coach, Selke also moved to Montreal to become manager and later managing director.

Selke earned his honours, for he was a sound organizer, an excellent judge of young material, and he had the faculty of working well with others. He was an unusual hockey executive in that he rarely blasted rivals or engaged in bitter controversy—he preferred to take a good look at a problem before making a decision. He was a wise counsellor to Irvin, who at times became moody and often attributed success or failure to "the unseen hand of destiny."

When at the age of sixty-four, much in the fashion of New York Yankees' "Casey" Stengel, Irvin accepted the challenge of returning to a coaching job with Chicago Black Hawks, he was replaced by "Toe" Blake. Blake had played brilliantly with Montreal Canadiens for thirteen seasons, during which he was a member of "The Punch Line." He won the Lady Byng and Dr. Hart trophies and was elected to many All-Star N.H.L. teams as first or alternate left-wing. He was thus familiar with Canadiens' style and learned much from "Dick" Irvin.

Blake's coaching record was remarkable. Under his direction, Canadiens won the Stanley Cup five successive times, an unmatched accomplishment. In regular league play, regardless of frequent changes in personnel, Montreal led the N.H.L. eight times in ten years.

"Toe" Blake was more volatile than most coaches and he had the advantage of being fluent in both French and English. However, he preferred to pay fines in English currency for he was assessed $2,000 for one fracas, and the penalty was paid in dollars rather than napoleons or francs.

In May of 1964, there was a more or less peaceful revolution in the upper echelons of the Montreal Canadiens. The reins of office were handed to younger executives, with Frank Selke still available for counselling and "Toe" Blake continuing as coach.

Despite the changes in management, Montreal Canadiens continued to roll. Under the guidance of President J. David Molson, General Manager Sam Pollock and Coach Toe Blake, the club won the Stanley Cup in 1964/65. In 1965/66, after heading the league during the regular season, they whipped Toronto Maple Leafs in the semi-final Stanley Cup round in four straight games. In the final series with Detroit Red Wings, they began by losing the first two games played on their home ice. However, while most observers were predicting a continuing collapse, Canadiens came roaring back to win four straight games.

This penchant for roaring back has long been a trait of the "Habs". Midway through the 1967/68 season Canadiens were last in their N.H.L. group. Then, in the midst of the gloom, big Jean Beliveau became "hot" and carried the whole team with him. In an amazing about-turn, the club climbed steadily to the top and won the Prince of Wales Trophy. They then swept through three Stanley Cup series, defeating Boston, Chicago and St. Louis, while losing only one game in thirteen.

In 1968/69 season, after Blake's replacement with coach Claude Ruel, Montreal's supremacy continued. They finished first in their division, then defeated New York Rangers and Boston Bruins to capture their fourth cup in five years. At that time, they seemed destined to prolong their supremacy through many more seasons. Yet, surprisingly, in 1969/70 for the first time in twenty years, they slumped so badly that they didn't even qualify for the playdowns.

However, in 1970/71, with Al MacNeil coaching, there came a resurgence of power. With a combination of mature players and a flock of youngsters, Canadiens swept into third place in the eastern division. Then, in one of hockey's greatest upsets, they first overcame the supposedly unbeatable Boston Bruins and in the semi-final round, they eliminated Minnesota North Stars. Finally, in a seven-game series against the Chicago Black Hawks, the amazing Canadiens repeatedly came from behind, eventually to win the Stanley Cup for the fifteenth time. Their rise had been as sensational as their earlier decline.

CHAPTER FIFTEEN EARLY AMERICAN CLUBS

BOSTON BRUINS

In 1924, Boston Bruins became the first American-owned club to play in the National Hockey League. This occasion was not, of course, the beginning of hockey in the United States, for even as early as 1896, there was a four-team amateur league operating in New York City. More than sixty years ago, Canadian players were emigrating from Montreal, Ottawa, Quebec and Toronto to play for American teams comprising the world's first undisguised professional hockey league. Even then the better Canadian-manned teams, some of them Stanley Cup holders, barnstormed south of the border, wherever a hockey stick was recognized as something more than a shillelagh.

These early American professional leagues did not last long, partly because the players were Canadians, and there was more money to be made on Canadian rinks. Also the Stanley Cup was building a tradition, and it was desirable to have one's name engraved on the silver bowl. When the American leagues folded, it was customary for such teams as Ottawa, Montreal Wanderers, Quebec Bulldogs and Montreal Shamrocks to play exhibition games in New York and Boston. Usually they played a two-game series, with total goals to decide. The players not only saw the sights of the big cities, but they also shared in the stakes offered by promoters which on occasion were as high as twenty-five hundred dollars.

In the era of early-American hockey, Boston was always prominent. One reason for Boston's interest was that many French Canadians drifted down to New England's textile mills, and they were anxious to watch their familiar game. In 1910, Ottawa, the Stanley Cup holders, played a series with Montreal Wanderers in the new Boston Arena. In 1916, Boston Athletic Association team won the American Amateur Hockey League. Incidentally, this was the club that "Babe" Ruth, baseball's immortal slugger, wanted to join. Indeed, he was so interested that he reported for a trial, but after a good belt on the shins, he decided that "the diamond was a man's best friend."

When World War I ended, amateur hockey returned to Boston in an arena rebuilt following a fire in 1918. Much credit for the revival in the early years can be given to Conn Smythe who annually took University of Toronto teams to the Hub to play matches against Harvard and Boston University. These weekend contests were so popular that crowds lining up for tickets extended for blocks. The games also encouraged Mr. Charles Adams, a keen and wealthy hockey fan, to buy a National Hockey League franchise in 1924.

This initial venture was much more than a financial gamble for Mr. Adams. Upon its success or failure depended the future of professional hockey in United States. Boston was to be a laboratory, and if the experiment failed, then other cities would grow wary. When Mr. Adams began his project, he did not have a single player and he did not have a coach. The only thing that seemed assured was that the colours of the team's uniforms would include brown and gold, because these were the hues that decorated the fronts of the chain of grocery stores owned by Adams. However he soon contacted "Art" Ross, a man who knew how hockey should be played and where good players could be found.

A contemporary of the Patricks and "Cyclone" Taylor, Ross was born in the Montreal suburb of Westmount. He was prominent in baseball, football, lacrosse and even motorcycle racing before he concentrated solely on hockey. In his playing days, he was a member of three Stanley Cup winning teams. His services were keenly sought, even though he was a shrewd bargainer. When he retired from hockey after seventeen professional years, he refereed many games including a Stanley Cup series. When

Mr. Adams was crying for help, "Art" Ross was operating his own sporting-goods store in Montreal.

Ross accepted the Boston challenge, but soon realized that the Bruins were a team without a body, so he was forced to become a triple executive—scout, coach and manager. This was a chore for even the knowledgeable Ross. It was said later that in his first season he had three teams: one that was on the ice; one that was fired and on its way home; and one that was on its way to replace the departed. This was not much of an exaggeration, for Ross took a look at more than twenty prospects.

This was discouraging to the only American club in the National Hockey League. None of the five Canadian teams showed sympathy. When the season ended, Bruins won only six games in a schedule of thirty and were a distant last. This was a bad way of building local support, and it would not impress other American cities that there was gold in hockey pucks. Fortunately the fans proved loyal and hopeful, Ross was willing and optimistic, and Mr. Adams had no desire to scuttle the ship. In 1925/26 they were all partially rewarded, for the team won more games than it lost and finished higher than New York Rangers, Toronto St. Pats and Montreal Canadiens.

It was during this season that Ross and his old friend "Charlie" Querrie, then managing St. Pats, were publicly feuding yet privately respecting one another. Boston fans were not only stridently vocal but also slightly violent. One night, in Boston, Querrie was sitting with St. Pats players, when some rebel hurled a monkey wrench in his direction. The fan's aim would never have earned him a place among the top ten scorers. The unharmed Querrie picked up the wrench and took it home. Later he went to the trouble and expense of having the discarded tool silver-plated and a small watch inserted in the handle. With some blarney about being kind to those who hate you, he presented the souvenir to Ross. It was typical of this period in sports that, while grudges were frequent, few were so deep that time could not cure them.

The Bruin boss appreciated Querrie's gift, but soon he would receive a boon that would mean much more to himself and his club. When the Western Canada Hockey League showed signs of disbanding, Mr. Adams, on the advice of his man Arthur, paid fifty thousand dollars for the services of seven players—Shore, Frederickson, Keats, Briden, Halderson, Oliver and Frank Boucher. This arrangement was the buy of the year. Indeed, it was so good that other N.H.L. clubs objected to the purchase and insisted on reimbursing the quick-acting Mr. Adams with the sum he paid, then placing the names of the players in a league pool. Even then Bruins remained lucky, for they drew Shore, Frederickson and Oliver, who were such good players that Boston began climbing to the top. Four years after the Adams-Ross duo introduced Boston to professional hockey, the Bruins were Stanley Cup champions. Their success encouraged other American clubs. In 1927/28, instead of four Canadian teams, there was a ten-team league, with two divisions of five each, named Canadian and American.

All through the 1930s, Boston had great teams—Thompson or Brimsek in goal; Shore and Siebert and associates on defence. They had such famed lines as "The Dynamites"—Gainor, Weiland and Clapper – and the Kraut line – Bauer, Schmidt and Dumart. From 1928 to 1941, they led the league ten times. They were easy to look at but awfully hard to beat. During the thirty-years' tenure of Art Ross, the Boston club competed in eight Stanley Cup final series. When the veteran retired in 1954, at the age of sixty-eight, he was succeeded by the forty-two-year-old Lynn Patrick, son of the illustrious Lester, who enjoyed a half-century of combat and debate with Arthur Howey Ross.

Lynn Patrick was reared in a hockey environment, yet his favourite early sports were basketball, football, baseball, rugby and bicycle-racing. His first objective was not to fill a goal-mouth with pucks but rather a human mouth with teeth, for he contemplated a career in dentistry. Eventually he determined to give hockey a try. At twenty-one, rather late for a beginner, he moved from Victoria to Montreal, where he practised eight hours a day until he finally found a place with the Montreal Royals.

Lynn was a natural athlete with a powerful physique. He was aware he could not match the artistry of his father, but he continued to develop until he was given the opportunity to play professionally with New York Rangers. He quickly proved he not only inherited talent from his father, but he also earned the right to compete on his own merits. Before he retired to serve in

World War II, he was elected left-wing on the National Hockey League All-Star team. When war ended, Lynn coached New York Rangers and afterwards became coach and eventually general manager of Boston Bruins.

The 1940/41 season was a memorable one for Boston. That year they topped the league in regular play and continued to defeat Toronto and Detroit to become Stanley Cup champions. Then, through 29 cold winters, Bruins discouraged a generation of fans by never recapturing either the league title or the big bowl.

However, in 1969/70, the drought ended. With a combination of shrewd trades, new coaching and the arrival of super-star Bobby Orr, Boston again won the Stanley Cup. In 1970/71, Bruins dominated the regular season, established 37 new league records and seemed destined to be hailed as one of hockey's all-time great teams. Prior to the opening of the Cup matches they were widely believed to be certain winners; yet, surprisingly, Boston was eliminated by Montreal Canadiens in a first-round, seven-game series that thrilled millions of listeners and viewers. Despite their unexpected downfall, Boston Bruins will continue to command the respect and maybe the envy of all other National Hockey League clubs.

NEW YORK RANGERS

In 1925, New York Americans had bought Hamilton's N.H.L. franchise for seventy-five thousand dollars and were playing their home games in Madison Square Garden. This nettled Colonel John S. Hammond, who preferred to have a team owned by the Garden using its facilities, so he arranged to buy the second New York franchise.

Although the new group had a franchise and a place to play, it had neither players nor a name. At first, they considered calling the team Tex's Rangers, in recognition of "Tex" Rickard, a Texan and a noted promoter, whose enterprise led to the building of the Garden. Wisely, however, with a gesture to the well-known Texas Rangers, the club adopted the name of New York Rangers.

But a name cannot score a goal. It was soon apparent that gathering a team would be much more difficult. When Colonel

Hammond discussed this problem with his Boston friend, "Charlie" Adams, the latter suggested that the likeliest person in the world to gather and coach the New York team would be Conn Smythe of Toronto. In Mr. Adams' opinion, the amateur clubs that Conn had annually taken to Boston were the equal of any professional team. Colonel Hammond accepted the advice of his friend, and a willing Smythe was soon scouting Canadian ponds and rinks in a search for high-class players.

Conn certainly knew what a hockey player looked like. By various means, he magically produced a team that was great before it was even iced. Five of the starting line-up were: Chabot, goal; Abel and Johnson, defence; "Bill" Cook and "Bun" Cook, the nucleus of a forward line. They were easily worth three hundred thousand dollars, yet the astute Smythe signed them for a tenth of that sum. They proved to be so good that, with a few additions, they won the Stanley Cup in their second year.

Before they played their first game, however, someone not too well informed convinced Colonel Hammond that, while the team was all right, Madison Square Garden needed a showman to sell it to the public. So the Garden vice-president dismissed Smythe and hired Lester Patrick to coach, manage and promote New York Rangers. At the time the firing and hiring seemed unfair and unwise. But eventually, for both Conn and Lester, as well as hockey in general, the action proved beneficial.

New York Rangers played their opening game at Madison Square Garden on November 16, 1926. The result was a one-nothing victory over Montreal Maroons, who were then Stanley Cup champions. Rangers were not a team that had to grow; they were mature right from inception.

Like most great hockey teams, the New York club was blessed with an outstanding line whose success inspired the whole club. For almost a decade, Rangers were the beneficiaries of the famed Cook-Boucher-Cook trio. Certainly in this case too many Cooks did not spoil the hockey dish.

"Bill" Cook was born in Brantford, and his brother "Bun," (who would scarcely be recognized by his actual names of Frederic Joseph) was born in Kingston. The Cooks earned their early reputation in the "limestone city," but later they went West to play with Saskatoon Shieks. When the Western Canada League was about to fold, Conn Smythe signed the brothers to a Rangers' contract, while Ottawa-born Frank Boucher was purchased by Boston. When it became apparent the Cooks needed a competent centre to complete their line, the brothers recommended Boucher, an ex-mountie who played on the coast with Vancouver, and Rangers willingly paid fifteen thousand dollars to the Bruins.

Many of hockey's outstanding lines are designated by such appropriate names as: The Dynamite Line, The Kid Line, The Kraut Line, The Big S Line. But the New Yorkers' line was never tagged. They played together for ten years, during which they scored 522 goals in regular play and another forty-two in Stanley Cup competition. Frank Boucher, in his career, won the Lady Byng Trophy annually awarded to the N.H.L. player who best combines skill and sportsmanship so often that the governors finally gave him the cup "for keeps" and replaced it with another. When the trio disbanded—Bill Cook was then forty years old—all the players became successful coaches or managers on other professional clubs.

Through nearly thirty years, Lester Patrick continued to coach, manage and ultimately become a Madison Square Garden vice-president. During those years, his teams broke several records, but one gave him much personal satisfaction and will probably never be broken. It relates to the fact that his two sons, Lynn and Murray, both played on New York Rangers teams, and that each made the grade on his own records and not because the head-man was his father. The Patricks were a closely knit family, in which the sons respectfully, yet familiarly, addressed their esteemed father as Lester.

New York Rangers reached an early peak in 1940, when their team was unbeaten, either at home or away, through twenty successive games. It was not attributable to luck, for the team earned the phenomenal goals-against record of only 1.6 per game. That same year they defeated both Boston Bruins and Toronto Maple Leafs to win the Stanley Cup.

However, in the more than thirty intervening years, Rangers have never recaptured the Stanley Cup. They have been well-coached and managed and, despite shortcomings, have been enthusiastically supported by New York fans. In 1970/71, Rangers won more games and scored more goals than in any previous season; yet they finished second in their group and were eliminated by Chicago in the semi-final Cup series. It now appears that long-deferred hope is about to become a reality.

CHICAGO BLACK HAWKS

During the fifties and sixties, while Bruins and Rangers were deep in hockey's valley, Black Hawks were enjoying the view from the hilltops. Indeed, the latter club has been so consistent that only once since 1961 has it missed the Stanley Cup playoffs. This was not always true. In 1926, Major Frederick McLaughlin obtained a National Hockey League franchise at the bargain price of twelve thousand dollars. The club was named Black Hawks because the Major, during World War I, was a member of a famed unit of the U.S. 33rd Division, which bore that honoured name. The soldier liked the title and the associations it recalled. Black Hawk had another distinction, for the name was that of a celebrated Indian Chief, famed for being the greatest orator of his race. There have been many winter nights during the past almost forty years when it seemed that the talent of the Chief descended upon those hockey braves who bore his name and crest.

In the founding years the Hawks suffered from a handicap. While Major McLaughlin was prominent in society and finance, he was not conversant with the hurly-burly of hockey. Because of his unfamiliarity with the game, he listened to strange voices and hired and fired ten coaches within six years. Many of these were good hockey men who knew their profession. Given time they might have been successful, but some of the others were real characters.

In 1932, one of the major's choices was Godfrey Matheson. There were conflicting stories relating to the signing of coach Matheson. One source said the Major had met him on a train, was impressed with his personality and hired him as coach without knowing much about his hockey knowledge. Len Bramson, an observant sports-writer, once described the new Chicago coach:

He was a studious, almost ascetic-looking man. He herded the Hawks to Pittsburgh for training, and on the first day he turned-up with shin-pads over his trousers, elbow pads around his knees, a tassel-cap on his head and two buckets of pucks. The first practice was unique. Matheson kept flipping pucks on the ice, and the players skated by and shot them at the net. But he wouldn't let "Charlie" Gardiner go in goal for fear he would get hurt by one of the flying pucks.

After a few hours, Matheson picked a team of six players and while the others sat on the bench he told them, "Now this will be my first team. I want you to watch them, paying particular regard to each individual, so that you can adapt yourself to his style. Then, if you have to go into the game, you'll be able to fit in."

For the next few days, the first team skated up and down and tauntingly yelled, "Don't you guys wish you could make the first team?" All the while the reserves sat along the boards, loafing, smoking and doing nothing to keep in shape.

Things did not improve. Around the third day, Matheson began working on new plays and one of them was a shocker. The biggest Black Hawk was 230-pound "Taffy" Abel, who was a defensive gladiator but never a goal-getter. The smallest player was "Mush" March, a very fast skater, who could also stickhandle and shoot. It was Matheson's idea that March would skate helter-skelter into opposing defences and split them apart, while the ambling Abel would trail the brave little block-buster, pick up the loose puck, fire his deadly shot and, or course, score a goal. Well it did not work out that way. Soon so many unfavourable reports drifted back to Chicago that the coach was fired even before the season began.

Matheson's successor also had some peculiarities, for Emil Iverson was a physical educationalist at Wisconsin University. He knew little about hockey for his specialty was muscles. Unfortunately the exercises he advocated were not suitable for athletes playing hockey. So Mr. Iverson soon followed Mr. Matheson down the long trail leading to oblivion.

The third coach of the year was jovial, capable "Tommy" Gorman. No one doubted the Irish Canadian's ability to get the most out of hockey players, for during his coaching and managing years he eventually led four teams to Stanley Cup triumphs:

Ottawa Senators, Chicago Black Hawks, Montreal Maroons and Montreal Canadiens. "Tommy" was not only shrewd and capable, but he also had a characteristic that some call determination and others stubbornness. Because of his refusal to yield, he once made hockey history.

In March of 1933, Chicago Black Hawks were playing in Boston and Referee "Bill" Stewart made a decision which Gorman did not like. As the debate continued, the participants became increasingly adamant. Gorman pulled his Hawks off the ice and sent them to the dressing-room. Stewart looked at his watch and gave "Tommy" one minute to get them back into the game. At the end of sixty seconds, the Boston team lined up and Stewart dropped the puck at mid-ice. Boston's "Cooney" Weiland skated down the ice and scored in the empty Hawks' net to break the two-two tie. This was possibly the only time a National Hockey League game was forfeited, and it went into the records as a one-nothing Boston victory.

In Black Hawks' early years, something newsworthy was always happening. There was the time when Major McLaughlin conceived the idea that he could and would produce a team composed entirely of American-born players. It did not take too long to convince the visionary that, if he fired all his Canadians and signed only Americans of proven professional ability, he would probably have to play all his games with about three players—a goalkeeper, a defenceman and a forward. He was spared that necessity just in time to avoid a catastrophe.

Another season Black Hawks were responsible for production of the hockey drama entitled "The Goalkeeper Nobody Wanted." The theme involved Alfie Moore, a netminder who was scorned yet became a hockey hero. The occurrence began when "Mike" Karakas, Chicago's regular goalkeeper, suffered a broken toe in the previous game. Hawks arrived in Toronto without a netminder available for the first game in the 1938 Stanley Cup final.

Chicago asked Leafs for permission to use New York Rangers' "Dave" Kerr. The home club promptly refused, for Kerr was the Vezina Cup winner and probably hockey's best goalkeeper. With that refusal, the Chicago management went searching for another replacement, and the only one available seemed to be "Alfie"

Moore. Moore had considerable minor league experience, but had never risen to N.H.L. eminence. However, as insurance, a scout asked Moore to appear at the Gardens in the event he was required.

Moore eventually appeared, but so did Kerr, and a bitter dialogue ensued between the rival managers. Indeed, it was so acrid that when words ended fists flew in the "Battle of the Corridor."

At that moment, Hawks had not the least desire to use Moore. The players, knowing "Alfie" was a Toronto resident and suspecting he did not have the ability to do the job, openly expressed their mistrust. When Moore let it be known that he too did not care whether or not he played, and was only in the room because he had been invited, the Chicago attitude softened. After all, it had to be Moore or an empty net.

However the fears of the Hawks were heightened when, after two minutes play, Moore was beaten and Toronto led by one-nothing. Chicago appeared headed for an artistic licking. But this never happened, for Moore played sensationally and repulsed all attacks for the remaining fifty-eight minutes. When the final whistle blew, Hawks were winners by a three-one score, and the unwanted goalkeeper became a Chicago hero. When manager "Bill" Tobin asked "Alfie" what he thought his services were worth, the player bravely asked one hundred and fifty dollars. "That's not enough," said Tobin, as he peeled three hundred dollars from his roll and thrust the bills into the hands of the grinning Moore. The next night the regular custodian, Karakas, was fit to return to the net. But "Alfie" was not forgotten. When the series ended and Chicago Black Hawks celebrated a Stanley Cup victory, Moore was invited to attend the party, where he was presented with a valuable gold watch, suitably engraved.

Not all Chicago's early problems related to goalkeepers. Sometimes their main concern was lack of public support. Originally the Major tried to sell hockey to "the carriage trade," and the Women's Junior League sold many thousands of tickets for the opening game. But high society did not support repeat performances. In the season of 1927/28, the average attendance was under five thousand. To improve the humble figure, "Joe" Farrell, "Bill" Tobin and "Dick" Irvin visited stores, restaurants, taverns, barber shops and gave free tickets for the privilege of placing signs in windows. It was truly a pioneer promotion. Ultimately it paid off so handsomely that, in 1946, with an average attendance of 17,600, the Hawks broke all N.H.L. attendance records. About this time tickets were so valuable that a cemetery caretaker offered "Joe" Farrell a free burial plot if he could arrange for him to buy two season tickets.

Much of Chicago's upsurge was initially due to Manager "Bill" Tobin who, through the lean years and the fat ones, tripled as coach, business manager and general manager. More recently, Stadium crowds have reached the capacity allowed by Chicago civic authorities. The teams have matched the fan enthusiasm, for in 1961/62 they won the Stanley Cup and in 1966/67 they finally captured the Prince of Wales Trophy, a distinction that had eluded them through forty years. More recently, under the direction of manager "Tommy" Ivan and coach "Billy" Reay, Hawks have always been crowd-pleasers. The heroic efforts of many individual stars, including "Tony" Esposito, "Stan" Mikita, and "Bobby" Hull, have encouraged Chicago fans to pack the Stadium in record-breaking numbers.

In 1970/71 season, it appeared the Hawks, after winning the western division, might recapture the Stanley Cup. In the playdowns they whipped both Philadelphia Flyers and New York Rangers. In the final series they were never behind in the round; but eventually lost to Montreal Canadiens by a single goal in the seventh decisive contest, played in hot-house temperature on May 18, 1971. It was an historic date.

DETROIT RED WINGS

In 1926, a group of Detroit businessmen, including such well-known names as Ford, Kresge, Scripps and Fisher, were awarded a National Hockey League franchise. After paying about one hundred thousand dollars for the rights, they were still without a name, a place to play and a team.

Hockey, of course, was not exactly new in Detroit. In 1910, Detroit teams played matches in the arena; and some of the contests must have been far removed from the days of chivalry. After a game between Detroit and Duluth teams, a sportswriter reported:

Hockey isn't for nice boys, even though it is perhaps the most scientific of outdoor sports. Body-checking is one of its worst evils. A player going at full speed meets another; and if the attacker doesn't use extreme caution, he will probably be carried away on a stretcher. Tripping is not allowed, but it is impossible for a referee to detect all such fouls. A clever tripper can upset opposing players and runs only a remote chance of being caught. A favourite trick of Canadian players is to skate behind or past an opponent, and while so doing barely touch the heel of the other. It looks accidental but, in many cases, the man who goes down stays there until assisted from the ice. When players are disposed to be ugly, there are many tricks to be used.

This was the practice in 1910. In 1926, the Detroit syndicate was not seeking new ways to upset people. Instead they were more concerned about the availability of players who could stand up. Fortunately, because of the collapse of the Western Canada League, Detroit sponsors were able to purchase the Victoria club, and as the latter was called Cougars, it seemed appropriate to use the nickname, especially as it was free.

The problem of where to play was a little more difficult. At the time the Olympia, a new sports palace, was being constructed. But construction was not completed in time for Detroit's first home game on November 18, 1926. So the Cougars played their home games all that season in Windsor, Ontario.

The new project was born in adversity. The Cougars, during the first year, not only finished last among the ten teams but also suffered an eighty-four thousand dollar loss. Distress signals were soon flying, and one who observed them was a thirty-one-year-old hockey player named "Jack" Adams. In later years, Adams was familiarly referred to as "Genial Jawn." But in his playing heyday, he was better recognized as a hard-hitting, rabble-rouser. He was a powerful ally but a tough foe. When he chopped down your stick, it stayed down. One of his more memorable fistic duels occurred when he fought Sprague Cleghorn in the presence of the Duke of Devonshire, then Canada's Governor General. Adams always thought His Grace was rooting for him.

However, it was not because of pugnacity that the applicant won the position of Detroit manager. Instead he impressed N.H.L. President Frank Calder with his hockey knowledge, his desire to win and the gift of inspiring others. All those factors encouraged Mr. Calder to quickly say, "Jack! I think you're just the man for the Detroit job." And he was—for thirty-five years. During all that time the names Adams and Detroit were so linked that they became interchangeable.

Adams did not waste much time in looking around his new office. Instantly he started trading and buying. In his first day he made two deals and announced he would also coach the club. The Cougars did not exactly leap from the barrier, and even changing the name to Falcons did not score more goals. But crowds improved, the Falcons started to flap their wings and soon they were leading their American division of the N.H.L.

In 1933, Mr. James Norris, Sr., a millionaire shipowner and grain-broker, purchased the Detroit club. In his youth in Montreal, he was a good hockey player. When he moved to Chicago, he was still such a hockey enthusiast that he became owner of the Chicago Shamrocks then playing in the American Hockey Association. When Mr. Norris resided in Montreal, he was a member of the Montreal Amateur Athletic Association and always admired its purposes and its symbol. So one of his first decisions after buying Detroit Falcons was to change the name to Detroit Red Wings and to adopt as the crest the Winged Wheel so long associated with the M.A.A.A.

Mr. Norris also made another early decision. He warned coach Adams: "You will be on probation for a year." Whether the threat scared or inspired "Genial Jawn" was never revealed, but certainly something startling happened for, in both 1935/36 and 1936/37, Detroit Red Wings not only topped the N.H.L. but continued to win the Stanley Cup: Mr. Norris must have been satisfied with his coach and manager, for even though Jack Adams never had a contract, he stayed on and on and on until his retirement in 1962.

In sports, permanent success is impossible. A club at the bottom improves slowly, and gradually climbs until it reaches the top. Then it has no place else to go. There are no more worlds to conquer, and it slowly declines to the bottom of the ladder. Few clubs are spared this up-and-down pattern. Yet Detroit Red Wings broke the tradition when, from 1948/49 until 1955/56, they won the National Hockey League championship and the

"Cyclone" Taylor and Foster Hewitt
at Hockey Hall of Fame Sod-turning Ceremony.
N.H.L. President Clarence S. Campbell presents Hall of Fame Plaque to veteran player and executive "Jack" Adams

"King" Clancy and Private "Smoky" Smith, V.C., with centres "Billy" Taylor and "Milt" Schmidt; opening night—Maple Leaf Gardens—1945.

Montreal Canadiens, Stanley Cup champions 1970/71

resultant Prince of Wales Trophy through seven consecutive years.

Much of Detroit's lifetime success can be attributed to their good fortune in acquiring and developing powerful lines. In the 1930s, they were blessed with the threesome of "Larry" Aurie, "Marty" Barry and Herb Lewis. They were succeeded by the unusually named "Liniment Line," composed of Abel, Grosso and Wares. The origin of "Liniment" might be associated with their ability to "rub it in" to opponents. Much more likely it was related to the frequent injuries of its members. "Count" Grosso, for instance, was very accident-prone. One season he suffered a bone-separation in his left wrist. He wore a cast, secretly hidden beneath his glove, lest his opponents become aware and "work" on its weakness. Another year, during a Stanley Cup series, Grosso played with a wrist broken in not one but two places. Yet, in a single game, despite the disability, he scored three Detroit goals.

A few years after Abel, Grosso and Wares disbanded, Detroit was blessed with one of hockey's all-time great lines. It was appropriately named the "Production Line," and its membership was composed of three players, each with a distinctive personality. "Ted" Lindsay was a hard-checking, firebrand type who could both provoke and attack. "Sid" Abel was a brilliant and experienced play-maker. "Gordie" Howe was strong physically, an excellent puck-carrier and a high scorer. In the 1949/50 season, the trio finished one-two-three in the N.H.L. individual scoring race, and as a line they garnered a phenomenal 215 points. Howe, who began his professional career in 1945, is still hockey's most versatile player. "Ted" Lindsay, who had earlier retired, made a strong comeback with Detroit Red Wings, during the 1964/65 season, when 40 years old.

"Sid" Abel, the centre of the famed Production Line, continued playing until the end of the 1952 season when he coached Chicago Black Hawks for two years. He later returned to his beloved Red Wings and became coach and general manager.

During Abel's eleven-year tenure as Detroit coach, Red Wings qualified seven times for Stanley Cup playoffs and, in four of them, reached the final round. However, in recent years the club has suffered through injuries, retirement of veterans and slow progress by rookies. Even more disabling, there have been several trades that misfired, plus constant feuding amongst players, coaches and management. In the 1970/71 season, this battling so reduced team morale that a once mighty club, which had in earlier years led the National Hockey League in seven successive seasons, finished a lowly seventh in the Eastern Division. Yet, despite the sorry showing, Detroit fans remained so hopeful and loyal that the total attendance figures were the second-highest in all Detroit history. Such confidence deserves an early reward.

CHAPTER SIXTEEN THE EXPANSION YEARS

Through many years, the governors of the six original National Hockey League teams had considered expanding the group. It wasn't a decision to be hastily reached, for many problems were involved. Primarily, the N.H.L. was a cozy association of men who had prospered financially and enjoyed their sports contacts; moreover, attendances were near capacity and a continuing prosperity seemed assured. Even so, there was a growing demand for other large cities to be included in hockey's major league. There was also the threat of a rival setup competing for the same player personnel. Eventually the six original members agreed to expansion; but first there were many vexing problems to be resolved.

It was desirable to start with a reasonable balance so that new clubs would not be overwhelmed by those long established. But — were there ample reserves to man six new teams with about 125 acceptable players? Would the recruits come from junior clubs, minor league teams or from a surplus on existing N.H.L. teams?

There were other problems, and scheduling for over 450 games was one of them. Instead of being a compact group located between Chicago and New York, two of the newcomers would be situated on the Pacific Coast, thus necessitating long flights and sudden weather changes. Moreover, some clubs preferred Saturday night games while others were sold on Sunday fixtures. Additionally, schedules had to avoid dates customarily allotted to ice shows, circuses, rodeos, wrestling matches, basketball games and sundry sporting or cultural affairs requiring use of the same arenas.

Some cities were already prepared for the coming of major hockey but others, such as Los Angeles and Oakland, had yet to be sold on hockey, its rules and its heroes.

There were also varying methods of financing the new clubs. Some were takeovers by established clubs, with ample funds and a knowledge of what was to be expected; others were sponsored by groups who, while inexperienced in hockey, were presumably able to finance a team through founding years. However, not all predictions proved reliable, for a couple of the new clubs were ultimately in need of dollars.

Some of the expansionists had money but required experienced hockey men who enjoyed desirable contacts and who were capable of appraising playing material. Fortunately, many such managers and coaches were available, but there were wide differences in their ideas of the kind of team they wanted.

In the original drafting it was soon apparent that most managers were seeking sound goalkeepers. Some clubs favoured mature players in the hope they would "get the jump" on rivals who would have to experiment with untried material. Still others, contemplating the future rather than the present, preferred players in the early twenties, presuming they would develop through the years and become stronger while veteran-manned teams would skid. Again, some managers sought strong defences with the objective of holding the original six clubs to low scores; but just as many voted for players who were offensively-minded, who could skate fast, shoot hard and provide fan excitement.

Despite the disparity of motives, some clubs suffered while others prospered. Even though management had, in 1967, used its best judgment, it is noteworthy that four years later only 24 of the 120 draft choices were still playing for their original clubs. The rise or fall of the expansion teams is interesting history.

ST. LOUIS BLUES

In 1967, when the N.H.L. exploded from six clubs to twelve, St. Louis Blues were early in line, waiting for the doors to open. St. Louis was a lively sporting city, with a surprisingly long interest in hockey. As long ago as 1934 it even had a slight contact with the National Hockey League, for it took over an Ottawa franchise; but the Eagles lasted for only a season. Still, the desire for major league hockey had never really died, and when expansion was first mooted the Missourians quickly produced not only dollars but the noisiest and most loyal fans in the country.

The St. Louis club, well-organized and soundly financed, was initially astute in obtaining Lynn Patrick and "Scotty" Bowman to manage and coach. Bowman, who was replaced by Sid Abel at the end of the 1971 season, began with a team that finished third in the Western division in its first year; then he shrewdly acquired such veterans as Glen Hall, Jacques Plante, Doug Harvey, Dickie Moore and Camille Henry. While some rivals believed "Scotty" was recruiting for an Old Folks Home, the old-timers were manfully stemming the tide and winning games. Through contacts made when he earlier coached Montreal Canadien junior clubs, Bowman was also privileged to make so many good deals that, at one time, he had nine former Canadiens on his roster.

When the veterans eventually "ran out of steam," St. Louis management didn't hesitate to develop and swap. Sometimes their deals seemed rather reckless, especially when they traded Plante to Toronto and Berenson and Ecclestone to Detroit; but despite the many exchanges the club finished second to Chicago in 1971. The faithful fans are still awaiting the opportunity to view the names of their heroes on the collars of Lord Stanley's Cup. Meanwhile, the Blues' supporters are streaming through the turnstiles; the organist is grandly bellowing the inspiring "When the Saints Come Marching In" and some year there will be complete rejoicing in St. Louis.

PHILADELPHIA FLYERS

Like the St. Louis club, Philadelphia had an earlier membership in the National Hockey League, for, in 1930, they took over the Pittsburgh franchise but retained it for only one year. However, that bitter experience had long been forgotten in 1967 when Philadelphia sponsors assembled ample financing and capable officers and became one of the so-called expansion clubs. They already had an arena, and Bud Poile and Keith Allan began scouting for material. One of their early results was to purchase Quebec Aces, a solid team which had just won the American Hockey League title.

With such a firm foundation the Flyers were already assured of a respectable team and, unlike some rivals, were not completely dependent upon the N.H.L. draft. Even so, they chose wisely and came out of the draw with some excellent prospects, including Doug Favell and Bernie Parent, two of the most promising young goalkeepers in all hockey.

In their first season Flyers led the Western division, but their success was not maintained. In 1968/69 they ended third; in 1969/70 they retreated to fifth. However, in 1970/71 under coach Vic Stasiuk they regained some lost prestige, finished third, but were beaten by Chicago Black Hawks in the first round of the Stanley Cup playoffs.

Through the years, the Philadelphia club has been defensively strong but rather weak on attack. They also had such a leaning toward tie games that, one season, a third of their matches ended in draws. Despite those shortcomings the Flyers are attracting capacity crowds and the sponsorship is eminently profitable to its owners.

PITTSBURGH PENGUINS

Professional hockey had an earlier arrival in Pittsburgh than in any other expansionist city, for nearly seventy years ago many Canadian stars drifted down to that city in search of hockey fame and fortune. Later, in 1925, Pittsburgh had a team in the National Hockey League and the tenure lasted four years, when the franchise was transferred to Philadelphia. Then, after nearly forty years in minor professional hockey, fans and sponsors were keen to join the N.H.L. in the 1967 expansion.

In the beginning, Penguin's management preferred to draft for instant experience rather than hoped-for promise. They promptly picked up such mature players as Bathgate, Boivin, Angotti, Dea, Schinkel, Fontaine, Ingarfield and Binkley—all in their thirties. They had anticipated that those veterans would give them a sudden thrust; but the strategy failed.

In their first two N.H.L. seasons, Pittsburgh finished fifth in the Western division. In 1969/70 management believed that a change of coaches would result in improvement, so they replaced "Red" Sullivan with "Red" Kelly. The latter stressed hard checking and sound positional hockey, two characteristics for which he had been noted in his own playing years. Some of that coaching "rubbed-off" and Penguins soared to second place and qualified for Stanley Cup playoffs. However, the success didn't continue for, in the 1970/71 season, the club was plagued by injuries and again slumped to a sixth-place finish.

Despite the retreat, attendances improved but still were well below the numbers required to break-even financially. For some months the N.H.L. kept the club afloat until, at the end of the 1970/71 season, new owners bought the franchise and players. "Red" Kelly is both capable and popular and, with success in drafts and more healthy bodies, prosperity could quickly return to Pittsburgh Penguins.

MINNESOTA NORTH STARS

Minnesota has long been an area in which youths have enjoyed skating and crowds have enthused over hockey. Consequently, when the opportunity to join the N.H.L. became available, ample financing was assured and the 15,000-capacity Metropolitan Sports Centre in Bloomington was ready for use. Moreover, North Stars had obtained the services of "Wren" Blair, who was initially prepared to serve as both general manager and coach.

Blair, an experienced hockey leader, drafted skilfully, made many shrewd swaps and, even more important, had acquired the professional rights to many members of Canada's Olympic hockey team. He also enjoyed friendly contacts with Montreal Canadiens, who always seemed to control a surplus of high-grade material. Through the years, North Stars obtained such famed Montrealers as Worsley, Harris, Larose, Grant, Rousseau and Drouin – almost an entire starting team. Naturally, through this wheeling and dealing, there has been such a shuffling of bodies that only two members of Blair's original squad remained on the team in April 1971.

Despite the "coming and going," the North Stars have missed the Stanley Cup series only once in four years; and, in 1970/71, their second round playoff games with Montreal Canadiens thrilled millions of hockey lovers. In return for their fine hockey, Minnesota fans have supported the club so staunchly that average attendances have exceeded 14,500 and many games have been sellouts. Equally impressive is the promise that Minnesota may soon be harvesting its home-grown hockey crop, for more than 45,000 players are now registered in the state.

BAY AREA (OAKLAND) SEALS

No expansion club has experienced a rougher introduction into the National Hockey League than that suffered by the Oakland club. Initially there were many problems to be resolved, for hockey was a new game in the Bay Area. Moreover, the owners had little hockey knowledge; management had planned a defensive team, and fans had to be sold on the sport.

Before the 1967/68 season was far advanced, all those factors became serious difficulties. The game didn't catch on, and attendances were scanty; financiers became discouraged and sought new sponsors. Additionally, Bert Olmstead, a no-nonsense type of coach who demanded the utmost from his players, finally gave up. It was no surprise that in the first year the Seals scored fewer goals than any of the twelve clubs and finished a lowly last.

Such a situation could not long endure and, through intervening seasons, the club name was changed and the Van Gerbig interests sold out to colourful, enterprising Charles Finley, a gentleman with a penchant for introducing new ideas.

What happened to the team? The hard-driving Olmstead was replaced by Fred Glover who had spent many years as player-coach of the Cleveland Barons. Management then went into a trading spree in the hope of ensuring more fire-power; and it was rewarded. In their second season, Seals were so improved that they won fourteen more games, scored sixty-six more goals, finished second in their division and qualified for Stanley Cup playoffs.

When that second season ended, Oakland's future seemed

very bright; however, the record was not maintained. In 1969/70 Seals slipped to a fourth place finish and in 1970/71 ended seventh in the Western division with the fewest points in all fourteen National Hockey League clubs. Still, the Oakland area is good sports territory, and once the team gets lucky in drafts and trades the crowds will increase, and owner Finley will add to his already substantial resources.

LOS ANGELES KINGS

Prior to 1967, one of the early applicants for an N.H.L. franchise was Jack Kent Cooke. Cooke, a native Torontonian, once had youthful ambitions to become a professional hockey player but those yearnings were later rejected for a career in promoting sport. After sponsoring baseball and football teams in Canada, Cooke moved to Los Angeles, where he soon became involved in baseball, basketball and football and needed only hockey to round out his sports empire.

At first, N.H.L. governors felt that problems relating to transportation and scheduling were insoluble; but impresario Cooke, with a combination of personal charm and ample cash, impressed the tough Eastern owners. To strengthen his proposal he promised that, if accepted into the N.H.L. family, he would build the finest arena in the league. It is now history that Los Angeles was approved and that "Cookie" kept the faith by expending sixteen million dollars to erect a gorgeous Forum, with capacity to seat comfortably 16,000 spectators.

A place to play was one objective and so was the necessity for gathering a respectable team. In typical aggressive fashion, Cooke purchased the entire Springfield Indians hockey club and used its roster to found his Kings; then he drafted to obtain more bodies. For the purposes of managing and coaching he obtained the services of two experienced hockey men — Larry Regan and Red Kelly.

Originally, it was presumed that the club would prosper because so many expatriated Canadians who resided in Los Angeles would flock to the Forum to enjoy their native game. However, the forecast was too optimistic for the attendance during the entire first season was only 360,000. Even so, the team was comparatively good, for Kings finished second in the Western division, just one point behind the leading St. Louis Blues.

However, that was the high spot, for never since has the Los Angeles club matched that success. In an attempt to stem the tide of defeat, there were several coaching changes, for "Red" Kelly was replaced by "Hal" Laycoe, who was himself superseded by Regan. There was also considerable player-trading and, in the process, Kings lost such very colourful personalities as Shack, Duff, Wall, Campbell, Irvine and White. So drastic were the changes that, in a four-year span, only four of the original team remained. In the 1970/71 season the club scored more goals than in any previous season, but their weak defensive power prevented them finishing higher than fifth in their section.

Cooke's charges have the arena, the management and the dollars; but they still lack the talent to ensure success on the ice.

VANCOUVER CANUCKS

When the National Hockey League, in 1967, expanded from six to twelve clubs, one of the most disappointed applicants was the Vancouver hockey club. Amongst the many causes for their chagrin was the fact that its supporters had known professional hockey through at least half a century. Indeed, back in the winter of 1914/15, Vancouver Millionaires, playing in their own artificial ice arena, won the Stanley Cup and were hailed as world champions. During the following decade many Vancouver teams participated in Cup playdowns against Eastern Canadian winners.

More recently Vancouver was represented in the Western Hockey League. Thus, pride suffered when their application was rejected in the 1967 expansion. However, disappointment changed to pleasure when, in 1970, along with Buffalo, the Vancouver club became a member of the National Hockey League.

Unlike some other newcomers, Canucks entered with a capable, already-made team. In 1969/70 Vancouver had won the Western Hockey League by a wide margin and had continued to capture the Lester Patrick Cup in the playoffs. So, before Canucks played a single N.H.L. game the roster included eleven players from that 1969 championship team.

Moreover, they drafted wisely; they were fortunate in obtaining the services of General Manager "Bud" Poile and Coach "Hal" Laycock; and they had sound financial backing. With all those early advantages, Canucks began the 1970/71 season with the promise of being the team most likely to succeed. Through some weeks they maintained a good standing; but injuries to key players, including Captain Kurtenback, together with the stress of long journeys, lessened their power. Only in the doubtful category of earning the most penalty minutes did they top the league.

Despite their sixth-place finish, loyal Vancouver fans gave such enthusiastic support that the average attendance not only exceeded 15,000 but was also augmented by off-rink private television showings. Major league hockey in the British Columbia city has already proven to be both exciting and profitable.

BUFFALO SABRES

Buffalo sponsors, like those in Vancouver, after experiencing many years in minor professional hockey, were keen to advance into the National Hockey League in 1967; but others were preferred. Later, when the owners of Oakland Seals became financially discouraged, the wealthy and public-spirited Knox brothers offered monetary aid with the hope they could eventually transfer the Oakland franchise to Buffalo. That intent didn't become a reality and Buffalo had to await the 1970 expansion when, along with Vancouver, they became members of the fourteen-team N.H.L.

The Sabres were blessed with ample funds, a hockey-oriented following and "Punch" Imlach, an astute leader who became both general manager and coach. Buffalo was also fortunate in winning the toss to select the first draft choice and their prize was "Gil" Perreault. Unlike many other starry juniors, this youth was chosen to play in the All-Star game and also broke the all-time record for most goals ever scored by a first-year player.

While Imlach started with a promising team, he soon noted where improvements could be made; so, through trades and purchases, he added more experienced players. As the season advanced, Sabres became a team which, on some nights, could match the best in the league. On one such occasion, in Boston, they scored seven goals and broke the Bruins 27-home-game winning streak. When the schedule ended, Sabres were fifth in their division and had the appearance of a team which Imlach had predicted could eventually become the first expansion team to win the Stanley Cup.

When the Knox-owned Buffalo club was granted its 1970 franchise, the only available arena accommodated fewer than 11,000, which was much too small for N.H.L. standards. However, assurance was given that the existing facilities would be increased to 15,000 for the second season. That promise was fulfilled, and it seems apparent that Buffalo area fans will flock to the enlarged Auditorium.

In review, the N.H.L. expansions of 1967 and 1971 have generally proven so satisfactory that league governors have expressed interest in adding another two teams and thus ensuring a better-rounded sixteen-team association.

CHAPTER SEVENTEEN

IN THE DAYS OF THE "KING"

Probably no sportsman has enjoyed more intimate Stanley Cup associations than Francis Michael ("King") Clancy. "King" has been an N.H.L. player, referee, coach or assistant manager through more than forty years and is recognized as hockey's most-quotable executive and *raconteur*.

"King" was born in Ottawa in the year that the famed Silver Seven was beginning its long run of Stanley Cup victories. The lad was destined for athletic fame from early childhood, for his father was one of Ottawa's football greats in the era when teams had fifteen players and the three-man scrum heeled out the ball. So esteemed was Clancy, the Elder, that junior was proud to inherit his dad's nickname—"King."

Another factor forcing the younger Clancy into sport was that Ottawa was the then national centre of sport. In "King's" short-pants years, the lad who did not play hockey, football or lacrosse was often very lonesome.

Even though Ottawa youngsters lived in an environment in which goals and touchdowns were the standards by which they were rated, success still had to be earned. In winters, the embryo Stanley Cuppers sometimes played their games on canals and rivers, where wind-blown ice was keen and the goals might be miles apart. It was an achievement for the young ankle-benders to even skate the distance between the markers without worrying about offsides or bodily contacts.

Later, when the city of Ottawa erected hockey boards (often

erroneously referred to as cushions), it was necessary for the players to do their own ice-cleaning. Before play could begin, each team removed the snow from its own half of the rink. Even during half-time intermissions, instead of relaxing, the lads again shovelled the surface so that play could continue. While the effort tended to turn enjoyment into a form of hard labour, it strengthened legs and arms and improved lung-power. In the process, Ottawa was able to boast that in a single decade no fewer than twenty-two professional players graduated from its Do-It-Yourself hockey school.

Clancy himself matured so quickly that when only fifteen years old, and still an office boy for the *Ottawa Free Press,* he was playing both left-wing and defence in the Ottawa Senior League. He played so sensationally that when the youthful "King" reached the ripe old age of seventeen, weighing a soaking-wet total of 131 pounds, he became a professional. Normally such a lightweight would have been spared the hardships of a defence-man, but that was not Clancy's good fortune.

More than forty years later, in his Maple Leaf Gardens' office, I asked "His Majesty" a question. "What made you think that 131 pounds fitted you for defence?"

King's answers are usually a delicious blend of humour and fact, and this time his explanation was, "There was nothing I could do about it. They wanted me on their team, and the only opening was on defence. I had to take it or leave it; and I took it." So the youngest and the lightest defenceman in National Hockey League history began a career that brought fun, colour and skill to hockey through more than two generations.

Clancy was professionally signed in 1921, and became an instant hit, dramatically and physically. To overcome his lack of poundage he adopted the art of crouching rather than crashing. He thus steered heavier opponents out of play, without hurting himself. While doing so, he acquired a guile that lured the "big fish" to their destruction. Some of his episodes have become hockey legends.

On one Stanley Cup night, Boston Bruins were leading Toronto Maple Leafs by a nice margin, when Eddie Shore, Boston's big man, received a minor penalty from the referee. Clancy skated slowly over to his opponent, expressed sympathy and confidentially told Shore that the call was quite unfair and that he had not deserved any penalty at all. This unexpected assurance convinced Shore that he was not receiving justice, so in an ugly mood he promptly fired the puck at the official. Equally agitated, the referee added ten minutes to the original penalty. While Shore was in the sin-bin, the Boston attack ceased, the tide of battle turned, Leafs recaptured the lead and won the game.

"The King" played in his first Stanley Cup series in the winter of 1922/23, when only nineteen years old. He began at a stipend of eight hundred dollars at a time when top salaries for players of Stanley Cup calibre was around fifteen hundred dollars. However no one moaned, and as Clancy recalls, "We were all close friends, both on and off the ice; and while we weren't crazy enough to tell the manager, the truth was we would have played for nothing if we had to. We really felt we were getting paid for having a lot of fun."

Clancy feels that players in the 1920s had a local pride to spur them on. They were not strangers, for most of them were native sons, playing for the city in which they were born and raised. Victory in later years may have been just as sweet, but it lacked that fierce personal desire.

Another factor contributing to the success of Ottawa hockey teams was that Governors General were all loyal fans. "The Byngs were the keenest," in King's opinion. "They attended every game and generally invited us to the big ballroom reception at Rideau Hall. In return, the players would send them greetings on big occasions and also keep them well supplied with autographed sticks. After the Byngs retired and returned to the Old Country, I accepted an invitation to visit them at their Scottish home. They were fine people, and I'm happy that Lady Byng's memory and name are retained in the Lady Byng Memorial Trophy." This trophy is annually awarded to the N.H.L. player who best combines sportsmanship and skill.

One Stanley Cup series that is still being pleasingly recalled by "King" was the 1922/23 battle with Vancouver. Any player, especially a teenager, is deeply impressed if he is privileged to play in a Stanley Cup game in any position, but this chance did not satisfy Clancy's ambition. In one game in his first series, he played not one but every position on the team. He started on left-defence, then moved to right-defence. When forwards were injured, he switched from centre, to left-wing and to right-wing. Finally when goalkeeper Benedict was penalized for two minutes (which then had to be served by the net-minder) the versatile Clancy, without even goalkeeper's pads, protected the goal. While briefly standing on guard, the kid aged a generation. "The way those Millionaires could shoot might have scarred me for life," King now recalls. "Fortunately, they didn't fire close enough to even singe me. So I retired with a perfect goalkeeping record."

That was King's first brush with Stanley Cup competition, but there were many more to follow. His playing career continued through nine seasons with Ottawa Senators and then seven more with Toronto Maple Leafs. Even his changing of clubs was headline news.

Conn Smythe had long been a Clancy admirer, and when the Leafs needed a star to match their new Gardens, the Toronto club paid thirty-five thousand dollars cash, plus two players valued at fifteen thousand dollars, for Clancy's hockey services. It was stated at the time of the deal, and later confirmed by figure-filberts, that based on the player's actual weight, the purchase price equalled Clancy's worth in gold. Yet, for all his value in nuggets, he was quite modest when he arrived in Toronto. Indeed, he was so humble and thrifty that, along with his suit case, he toted eight solid-hickory hockey sticks which he had salvaged from his Ottawa club. "King" now admits the story is true, and he chuckles as he boasts, "What's more, I had the same eight sticks at the end of the season. They sure were beauts."

In sixteen years with Ottawa and Toronto, Clancy thinks there were only about four in which he did not have some part in Stanley Cup playdowns. Following his retirement, he continued as referee, coach, manager and is currently assistant to "Punch" Imlach, Toronto Maple Leaf's general manager and coach. Even though Francis Michael Clancy's hockey skill earned him a place among the great in Hockey Hall of Fame, he has also earned the highest marks for the good-nature and humour he has given to the game he loves.

Sometimes the joke was on "King." One night, in Chicago, he was refereeing, and he skated close to the boards. As he leaned over, an irate feminine fan jabbed a large hat pin into the official seat. "King" quickly got the point. And when the rumpus ended, there were a couple of seat problems in the Stadium—one belonged to Clancy and the other to the fan who was forced to vacate.

Another night in which the Irishman came out on the wrong end occurred during a Stanley Cup game in Toronto. One of the Leafs was jovial "Babe" Pratt, who statured six feet four inches; and he was constantly needling the five foot seven inch referee. Clancy was willing to take the ribbing because the rules do not provide any penalty for indulging in a little joshing. However just before facing-off near the Toronto goal, "King" edged close enough to whisper to Pratt, "You big lug, I wish I was playing against you tonight." Before the puck dropped, the impish Pratt looked up at Clancy and retorted, "Who says you ain't?"

One time in Chicago—it seems things were always happening to Clancy in that city—a disgruntled spectator reached over the boards and swung a healthy right at the referee's face. Even though the blow missed its target, "King" climbed the railing to return the compliment. In the confusion it was difficult to know who was getting in the best licks. When the game ended, sportswriters dashed to the referee's room to get a blow-by-blow account of the battle of the century.

"Look!" exclaimed an exultant Clancy. "Take a good look at me. There isn't a mark on me".

"Not even a scratch?" asked a hungry newsman.

"Not a mark! Not a mark!" Clancy repeated.

The writer continued probing for some indication that the referee had suffered. When no evidence whatever was produced, the correspondent feigned disappointment and smilingly teased, "King! That's just too bad. You do look healthy. But you have just dashed the hopes of 19,842 Chicago fans."

Clancy also had admirers—thousands of them. One of the finest tributes ever given an active player was tendered on a St. Patrick's Day Night (if such an "Irishism" is allowed) in 1934, when "King" was playing for Toronto Maple Leafs.

Regardless of how it all ended, it began in good clean fun. In the centre face-off circle at the Gardens, there was painted a vivid green shamrock with the words "King Clancy." Prior to game time, a procession of decorated floats, each drawn by a hockey player, proceeded along the ice. "Ching" Johnson, New York Rangers defenceman, pulled a potato-shaped float, and out from the "Murphy" stepped four members of the St. Michael's Junior B team. Out of a high hat appeared Harold Cotton, wearing a silk topper. From a pipe smallish "Ken" Doraty escaped. George Hainsworth appeared in the opening of a huge boot, and he was followed by trainer "Tim" Daly who had been encased in an immense bottle. From an enormous boxing glove, Red Horner, the league's most penalized player, emerged. New York's Bill Cook stepped out of a shamrock; while Leafs' Joe Primeau was revealed in a huge harp, drawn by defenceman Alex Levinsky. Then Old King Cole, a grand white-bearded monarch, garbed in his robes and wearing his crown, was drawn along the ice by "Hap" Day. The gorgeous float stopped in mid-ice, while team-mates Day and Charlie Conacher politely offered to help the old ruler descend from his throne.

Then, as recalled by Ed Fitkin, "When the King extended his arm, the Gardens' lights were extinguished. Moments later, when they came on, Old King Cole had been shorn of his robes, crown and beard." In the bright light stood "King" Clancy, dressed from head to foot in a pool-table-green uniform. But somehow the personage did not seem to be the true Clancy. The reason for this doubt was later revealed, for when the lights went out, the fun-loving Day and his associate, Conacher, had smeared one side of Clancy's face with black shoe polish! Instantly the band saluted with "When Irish Eyes Are Smiling," and the crowd cheered. "'King" was joined at mid-ice by his wife and his father Thomas Clancy, who had been the original "King." Then the guest of the occasion was presented with a cabinet of silver, a silver tea-service and tray, a radio and a grandfather's clock.

Even then the celebration did not end, although the rest of it was not as pleasant. Clancy played the first period in his green uniform; but he proved too visible to his opponents. They gave him such a rough ride that, after playing poorly, he donned his blue and white Maple Leafs' uniform for the remainder of the game. Appropriately, for a true Irish honouring, the New York and the Toronto players turned the game into a roistering Donnybrook, in which only the guest of the evening behaved like a gentleman.

Out of his many hockey experiences, "King" Clancy has accumulated a wealth of inside knowledge in the profession he loves. We asked him if Stanley Cup matches were much different from regular league games. In the opinion of the veteran authority, there is a tremendous difference. "In Stanley Cup playoffs," Clancy tells us, "the games are played more frequently; there is more talk and publicity on the air and in the papers; fans get more excited and partisan; coaches are on the hot-seat. All this gets through to the player and he tightens up. Apart altogether from the extra money to be earned, and it could be some thousands of dollars, every player wants to brag that he played on a Stanley Cup winner. It seems to represent the peak of his ambitions; and it is one way he can later prove to his kids that he was really as good as he says he was."

"King" continued, "Another thing that makes Stanley Cup games stand out is that each of them is so decisive. In a seventy game schedule, you can say after a game, "Well! We sure blew that one; but we'll get them next time! But in a Stanley Cup series, your coach keeps telling you, 'There is no tomorrow; this is the big one'."

"King" thinks there are more surprises in Stanley Cup competition today. "It happens so often that the hero of a series is not the star who stands out all year. Instead the one who makes the headlines is frequently an average player who suddenly becomes hot. 'Ken' Doraty did that in the long Boston-Toronto overtime game. All season, he scored a total of about five goals. Then, after more than one hundred and sixty minutes of play, he fired the shot that ended it all.

"'Mel' Hill," I recall, "would frequently come up with the clincher in Stanley Cup games in the 1940s. During the regular season he was just an average scorer. But once he got on the ice in overtime in a Stanley Cup game, he was so effective that he became known as 'Sudden-Death Hill'." Clancy has an explanation for this paradox. "In my playing years, there were always key players who, on their seasonal record, could bust a game wide open. They might have been 'Babe' Dye, 'Nels' Stewart, 'Charlie' Conacher, 'Howie' Morenz. Later they would have to be Richard, Howe, Hull and players of that class. They were fellows who could score goals, and because it's goals that win the game, they had to be closely checked. That double-watch on one player made it easier for the lesser ones to do more roaming and shooting on their own."

During his playing years, "King" Clancy usually combined pleasure with business. One morning while Toronto Maple Leafs were practising, I was watching him tuning up for a Stanley Cup game the next night. He stood beside his own goal, with puck on the blade of his stick until he shouted in his shrill penetrating voice: "Nobody can even lay a hand on me." Then, with sharp jaw protruding, he dashed down the ice, dodging and stick-handling through the opposing maze and daring anyone to stop him. Just as he was about to shoot, he was spilled.

Clancy carried that impish love of fun into his refereeing days. "In Stanley Cup games, I knew from my own experiences that players were tense, and I tried to make allowances. If at all possible, I avoided giving misconduct penalties. If a youngster blew his top, I quietly told him to keep cool or he would hurt his team. If an older player became abusive I found that it helped to give him a second chance. So I would look tough and say, 'Just repeat what you said.' Usually they took the warning and skated away. Calling me names never hurt me. I never wanted to be a showboater and I didn't mind them having a little fun."

"King" played professional hockey for sixteen seasons, and from 1921 until 1936 he "bumped into" some great players. We asked him to recall those he had played with or against in Stanley Cup competition, and to name a mythical all-star team of his National Hockey League years.

In retrospect, "King" thinks that "Charlie" Gardiner was the best goalkeeper of his era. His career did not last very long, for he died when only thirty years old, following a brilliant season when Chicago Black Hawks won the Stanley Cup. "Charlie had everything," Clancy recalls, "sure hands, good eye, quick reflexes, no weak spots and a fine team spirit. In his last season of forty-eight games, ten of them were shutouts and in fourteen others he allowed only one goal. He also had a lot of fun in him. I remember the night someone threw a Derby hat on the ice. 'Charlie' skated over, picked up the lid, slapped it on his head as though it was a helmet and wore it while playing."

For one of his favourite defencemen, "King" would certainly name Eddie Gerard. "Eddie was a grand guy to have on your side when we both played defence for Ottawa Senators. He was big, strong and feared nobody. He was a fast skater, good puck-carrier and could play for the full sixty minutes without relief if he had to. Eddie began as a forward but later teamed up on defence with Sprague Cleghorn; and—boy!—they could really rough you up. After playing on three Stanley Cup winners, Gerard became a coach and also manager of the Montreal Maroons when they won the Cup.

"Eddie was both a great player and a nice fellow to know. In both respects he had a lot in common with 'Hap' Day, whom I would name as my other defenceman. 'Hap' learned his hockey the hard way, for when he was a teenage kid playing for Midland juniors, he had to walk five miles before and after each game from his home to the rink and back, and the return trip was made in his playing uniform. Later he was given the chance to play with Hamilton seniors, where he earned money to assist in paying his education at the University of Toronto, where he graduated as a pharmacist.

"In intercollegiate hockey he looked so good that 'Charlie' Querrie, St. Patrick's manager, offered him a professional hockey contract. At first Day turned it down because he did not want to think the time and money he spent on his education would be wasted. But Querrie was never a person to accept a first refusal as final. 'Look! "Hap",' he argued, 'you're an outdoor man. You'd die if you had to be cooped up all day in a stuffy old drug store. Besides, you could easily earn fifty thousand dollars from hockey in ten years. Then you could buy yourself a store and hire someone to run it for you while you were on the road during the hockey season.' "Hap" thought it over. The idea seemed good, and in 1924 he signed his first professional hockey contract.

"I didn't team up with 'Hap' until I joined Toronto Maple Leafs in 1930, and a couple of years later we were mates on the Stanley Cup champions. 'Hap' was more than just a fine player, for he was also one of those leaders whose loyalty and inspiration could fire up a whole club. He later became a smart coach, and his teams won the Stanley Cup five times. Right now I'm speaking of him only as a player. In that capacity, I'd like to have him on my mythical team."

Although Clancy was a defenceman, he thinks he is a better authority on forwards, for from his position he had to meet more attackers than he did defenders. "No forward in my day impressed me more than did 'Howie' Morenz," the "King" told me. "People often ask, 'Was Morenz really as good as oldtimers claim?' I have to say, 'You bet he was.' He could adjust to any situation. He could barge between a defence, or he could poke a puck between your legs, then wheel around you and pick it up. His shot was just like a bullet; and he didn't fool around looking for an opening, he just let it go. One year he scored forty goals in forty-four games, which would compare with more than sixty in our seventy game schedule. So I'd be content with Morenz at centre of my all-star Stanley Cuppers.

"For left-wing I'd like to have Aurel Joliat. I may be prejudiced about Joliat, for we both were born in Ottawa and were about the same size. But I stayed at home to play professional hockey, while Aurel went to Montreal Canadiens and played with the Habs. for sixteen years. Despite his lack of weight, he took on all-comers who outweighed him by forty or fifty pounds and never 'threw snow'. He was a good checker, could turn as quickly as any player I ever saw and had a fast accurate shot. On his play alone, Joliat could usually attract attention. But the fact that he always wore a black cap with a peak, something like a baseball player's hat, made him even more noticeable.

"For right-wing on a team composed of players I played with or against in Stanley Cup competition, I would like to have 'Charlie' Conacher. 'Charlie' was big, strong, aggressive and shared, with 'Babe' Dye, a reputation for owning hockey's hardest shot. Boy! He loved to let that puck spin. One day Conn Smythe commented: " 'Charlie' would rather hear the smack of the puck on the end-boards than the soft sigh as it nestled in the net.' He was also, like 'Hap' Day, a great fellow on or off the ice. We were often mixed up in high jinx; but invariably I got all the blame especially while Conacher went scot-free. However, I got even with him later when I was a referee and he was still playing. As a fellow-prankster he just got me into trouble. But, as a player, 'Charlie' was 'great'."

So, as "King" Clancy's first choices along the Stanley Cup trail, he would choose goalkeeper "Chuck" Gardiner; Defencemen Gerard and Day; Forwards Conacher, Morenz and Joliat. What a team that would be, coming or going. It is no surprise that each member is honoured in the Hockey Hall of Fame.

CHAPTER EIGHTEEN

HELLO CANADA AND HOCKEY FANS!

Foster Hewitt is much more than a voice, a public figure and a prominent sportsman, for he is also a tradition. He pioneered in Canadian broadcasting in 1922 and has been continuously on the air through nearly five decades. No one, in any phase of radio activity anywhere in the world, has matched this record.

Foster Hewitt's introduction to hockey broadcasting was not planned. Indeed, it came quite unexpectedly. One night, in the spring of 1923, the young *Toronto Star* reporter was walking down the hall on his way to the exit after a tiring day. Without a previous warning, he heard the loud voice of his editor calling him back. He returned, and his boss said rather commandingly, "Foster! I have a job for you tonight. You're to go to Mutual Street Arena and broadcast a hockey game. Parkdale and Kitchener Seniors are playing."

The reporter did not think very much of the idea. He had been operating the radio unit and doing some announcing. But describing a hockey game was something else. No one had tackled such a chore before, and the general opinion was that the play was too fast for words. However the boss insisted, and there was no reasonable way to evade the pioneering.

Foster arrived at the arena about half-an-hour before the start of the game. He picked up a program that gave the names and numbers of the players and walked slowly to the broadcasting booth. Booth? Well! That word was very flattering, for it was merely an air-tight glass box, three feet square by four feet high. Its only furniture was a telephone and a milking stool with sawed-off legs.

Foster acutely remembers that night when hockey broadcasting was born. "About ten minutes before 8:30, I took the telephone receiver off the hook, got the central operator and asked for CFCA's radio engineer. We compared our watches. I let the receiver hang down, so the line wouldn't close; and then I waited for the game to begin.

"When the referee dropped the puck, I began talking into the mouthpiece. At first the conditions weren't too uncomfortable, but gradually the box became stuffy, for it was completely enclosed to prevent any crowd noises. Then, as the play progressed, a vapour clouded the glass and the players appeared to be skating in a fog. I could discern the moving figures but had difficulty identifying the players. However, with eyes bulging and with my chin almost resting on my knees, I continued rather bravely, I thought. But all the while I was subconsciously saying to myself: "Stick it out, kid! it only lasts sixty minutes."

"At long last, the sixty minutes ended. But the game didn't. The two teams were tied; and I was fit to be. The struggle went on, and on, and on, through three ten-minute overtime periods. In all, including regular play, intermissions and overtimes, I talked more than three hours. At its end—if I had been permitted free choice—that would have been my first, last and only hockey broadcast."

Fortunately both for the game of hockey and for the millions who have thrilled with "He Shoots! He Scores"—the best-known phrase in all sport—Foster Hewitt did not retire after his initial performance. Instead, in his professional chore of telling the folks at home what was happening on the ice below, he has travelled across Canada and United States and over oceans into England, Norway, Sweden, Germany, Austria and Italy.

Inevitably during all those journeys he saw strange sights and met unusual persons. Some of his most impressionable occurrences have been related to Stanley Cup games where stakes are high and emotions at snapping-point.

One of Foster's most vivid Stanley Cup recollections relates to that long overtime game between Boston Bruins and Toronto

Maple Leafs in the spring of 1933. Many thousands of words have been written about that titanic and enduring struggle. But Foster's reaction is more personal. He remembers, "When the third period started, neither team had scored, but everybody in the broadcasting gondola was certain there would shortly be a goal. We were so sure that at 10:15, Gordon Castle went down to the rinkside to interview the players just as soon as the game ended.

"But the game didn't conclude as we had anticipated. At 1:30 the next morning, I was still on the air. My speech was getting thicker; the scene on the ice far below was blurring; my pauses were more frequent and getting longer. Observers in the gondola told me later that my eyes were half-closed, and that I was teetering on the chair. I've always disputed these comments, but it was definite that engineers were ready to cut me off the moment I became incoherent. However, the show had to go on, and I managed to survive until I could at last murmur an awfully feeble 'He Shoots! He Scores!'"

There were many other Stanley Cup nights when all was not well. During one series, Foster was broadcasting from Madison Square Garden in New York. Facilities at the time were comparatively crude, and it was necessary for him to climb over the balcony into a swaying, steel basket, which was suspended about thirty feet above the ice, just opposite one of the blue lines.

There was no difficulty until half-way through the second period, when Foster felt sharp pains in both ankles, as though he was being lashed by a long, blacksnake whip. He squirmed and kicked and rubbed. Then he began to feel cold. He did not know the cause and could not talk about it to anyone. So he continued with the torment until the game ended. Then he learned that the Garden management had just installed a new air-conditioning system, and unfortunately the sharp cold blasts were being forced in the direction of the broadcasting basket. Their full effect hit Foster just around his ankles.

This New York incident was at least unpleasant, but it was not nearly so painful as one that Foster experienced during a Stanley Cup game in Chicago. At the time Toronto Maple Leafs were playing the final game of their series against Chicago Black Hawks. It had been a mild afternoon, and Foster had sailed on

Lake Michigan with some American friends. After the sail, while helping to pull up the boat, he slipped and had torn a ligament in his hip. The pain became so severe that he was advised to forget the evening broadcast. But no one else was immediately available, so when Foster insisted, the doctor warned, "You're crazy to go on the air, and I don't want to be blamed for what happens. I'll give you a couple of pills to deaden the pain; but after that you're on your own."

It was a tough night for Foster, and he was really worried, not alone for himself, but also for the many hundreds of thousands who would be listening to the broadcast. With aid, he staggered up to his loft. By then he had lost all feeling in his leg. His tongue was dry and stiff, and his throat parched. He felt miserable from head to toe and could scarcely hold a pencil. Somehow, still in a semi-stupor, he stumbled through the broadcast.

Even the final whistle did not end Foster's distress. Right after the game he was ordered to bed. And when the effects of the pills wore off, the old pain returned, and his head throbbed like the beat of a jungle drum. Later he was taken to the train and deposited in the conductor's custody. When the pain increased, it was agreed he would be removed at Detroit for hospitalization. However the conductor heard that a carload of doctors en route to a convention was to be picked up at Detroit, and the train-man promised to get prompt attention for his patient. That idea seemed fine, but the travelling delegates had other things on their minds. Relief never arrived, and Foster squirmed in anguish all the way to Toronto. So there is much more to Stanley Cup hockey broadcasting than meets the eye.

While each and every game that Foster Hewitt broadcasts is important by itself, a Stanley Cup series is always something beyond the ordinary. Players are more tense; fans more explosive; listeners and viewers are more numerous and critical. This excitement extends into broadcasting gondolas and makes Foster more conscious of his responsibilities. He becomes the eyes for millions of unseen fans, and he is anxious to do a good job for them. Strangely this is the time of the year when trouble strikes.

Usually Foster can go through a season without any undue voice trouble, but occasionally, when the playoffs to decide the holder of Lord Stanley's bowl begin, the throat plays tricks. One year, in the midst of shouting "He Shoots! He Scores!" his voice broke and the piercing high note suddenly dropped to a husky bass. Foster managed to clear his throat and to jest "I sure blew a fuse on that one." In sympathetic response, a score of listeners jocularly mailed him every variety of electrical fuse to assist in restoring his stock. Their attitude convinced the broadcaster that sports fans do listen, and that they enjoy a healthy laugh.

Foster Hewitt's music box gave him concern during another Stanley Cup series, for he suddenly acquired that dread of all public speakers: laryngitis. On the morning of the final game he did not feel ill, and he could open his mouth, but he could not even whisper. He was away from home, and that is where misfortune has usually attacked. He promptly used the gesture language to indicate he wanted a doctor. The latter examined the patient and jocularly assured him that in a few days he would be talking as well as ever. Foster was almost shocked into speech by the announcement, for he knew that "in a few days" the series would be history. So between squawks and signs he let it be known that, in his profession, there was no tomorrow, and that he had to be at his shouting best that very night.

The doctor accepted the challenge. He arranged for the steaming water and balsam, covered the Hewitt head and shoulders with a large towel and prescribed: "Stop talking. Stay here all day. Keep the water piping hot and begin inhaling." He did as he was instructed, even though the temperature of his anxiety was steadily rising. As game time drew hourly nearer, Foster was still uncertain of his future. No replacement was found and the show had to go on. Still weakened by the heat of the cure, he gamely went to the arena and awaited the starting signal. It came. He opened his mouth. He began his often-repeated greeting to the fans in Canada, Newfoundland and United States. The early voice was rather muffled, but as the game continued, it improved. And the broadcaster's enviable record of never missing a game continued unbroken.

Most of Foster Hewitt's Stanley Cup memories have, of course, concerned participants rather than himself. One night he was broadcasting from high-up in the Detroit organ loft, eighty-five feet above ice level. It was a tougher than usual game, featuring up-raised sticks, high elbows and bouncing bodies. During one *mêlée* along the boards, "King" Clancy was badly cut around the eye and knocked to the ice. It was apparent that the player had been badly hurt, and he was removed from the ice for immediate medical examination. The extent of the injury was not immediately revealed. The rumour freely circulated, even up to Foster's lofty perch, that Clancy would likely lose his vision.

During the broadcast, while Foster did not make any announcement of what he heard, the thought was constantly on his mind that it was a terrible way for the courageous and likeable, almost lovable, little Irishman to end his long career. The tragedy bothered Foster, especially during the intermission, when he had a chance to contemplate. Without obtaining a definite report, the broadcaster continued describing the play on the ice far below. Late in the final period, without actually seeing anyone approaching, Foster sensed he was not alone. He half-turned from his microphone and what he observed was a ghastly almost ghostly Clancy—patched, weak and nearly breathless from the steep climb. While Foster concentrated on the play, he alternately glanced at the apparition beside him and wondered why the player had approached the booth.

Certainly, Clancy had not come so far to see how Foster was getting along, and it definitely was not his desire to play the big organ. Instead "King" had been told about the report that he might lose his sight. He staggered up to the loft to leave Foster a note requesting him to reassure his family at home that he was walking around and that his eye would be all right. The Voice of Hockey was more than pleased to convey the good tidings to Clancy's folks and friends.

During wartime years, most hockey games, and especially Stanley Cup matches, were broadcast overseas. They were so highly esteemed that during one interval, when their desirability was being reviewed, the Armed Forces pleaded for their continuance. One commanding officer stressed that nothing contributed more greatly to the morale of the troops than hockey broadcasts.

The procedure for overseas broadcasts involved long hours for Foster. It was necessary for him, after the ending of the regular coast-to-coast program, to hustle to the broadcasting station and listen to the recording of his descriptions. Then he selected the highlights, and especially the plays that led to goals. This condensed version was taped into a continuous half-hour story and short-waved to England, and thence to wherever Canadian forces were located.

The broadcasts got around all right, for Foster received wartime letters from China, India, Australia, Guadalcanal, New Guinea, Gibraltar, even from Tobruk when under siege, and one from a small force close to the North Pole that posted the letter on the first leg of its journey by dog-sled.

There was one small defect in the overseas wartime program, and certainly the broadcaster was not an accomplice to the conspiracy. It happened during several games, and particularly through the Stanley Cup playdowns and finals, that a small group of Canadian soldiers in England had access to a powerful receiving set. It was so effective that it picked up Foster's original broadcasts direct from Maple Leaf Gardens in Toronto. As soon as the insiders received the details of the game, they circulated among their unenlightened buddies and made wagers on who would win the games and who would score the goals. The condensed version, which was heard some hours later in England, confirmed the results and the defrauded losers were compelled to make good. Eventually the victims became suspicious. The trickery was revealed and the racket ended.

Through some hundreds of Stanley Cup games, Foster Hewitt has conveyed the story to many millions of listeners. These have included lonely trappers in the icy north and residents in crowded city tenements; youngsters who have coaxed their parents to stay up and quite elderly folks in homes for the aged. The broadcasts bring hockey's excitement to those who cannot see, and those who cannot speak, as well as to the more fortunate. Through nearly fifty seasons, his explosive "He Shoots! He Scores!" has thrilled many millions of hockey fans across the entire continent.

CHAPTER NINETEEN

THE ROAD AHEAD

The Stanley Cup is nearly twenty-five years older than the National Hockey League. Originally it was a challenge cup and defenders were expected to meet almost any claimants. Later the challengers had to be named by recognized leagues or associations. During the 1920s there were three contending groups, with two of them located in western Canada. Finally in 1926, when the western leagues disbanded, the National Hockey League became the sole custodian of the Stanley Cup; and so it has remained. Thus the story of the Stanley Cup would be incomplete without reference to the National Hockey League.

The N.H.L. was formed on November 22, 1917, under the presidency of Frank Calder, who never played the game he loved and for which he eventually died. He was born in England, was interested in cricket and soccer, but he never even saw a game of hockey until he later became a teacher in a Canadian private school. While he was involved in many sports, hockey soon became his favourite. Because he was a true sportsman himself, he hit hard at chicanery and was both feared and respected by sports-promoters. Yet it was one promoter who sponsored his election as secretary, treasurer and President of the new National Hockey League.

Through more than a quarter of a century, Frank Calder gave dignity, vision and energy to his offices; and if he had a weakness, it was his hesitancy in shifting some of his work-load to associates. He played no favourites. He condemned what he deemed to be injustices, and he continually defended his officials. His devotion to duty and concern over details prompted him to work long hours, travel great distances and ultimately lead to his sudden death induced by the stress of hockey in wartime. He was succeeded by Mervyn "Red" Dutton.

Dutton's background was quite different from Frank Calder's. There was little indication in Dutton's youth that he might become head-man in anybody's hockey league. "Red" was born in Russell, Manitoba. When only sixteen years old, he enlisted with Princess Pat's in World War I. In an early engagement he was so seriously wounded it was feared that unless his leg was amputated he might lose his life. "Red" pleaded with the doctors to spare his leg, so that if and when he returned to Canada he could again play hockey. The patient improved, but spent a year flat on his back with a leg suspended by pulleys. It was worth the ordeal, for recovery was complete, and the youth came back to play amateur hockey until he signed professionally with Calgary in the Western Canadian Hockey League.

When that league expired, Eddie Gerard signed him to a Montreal Maroons' contract and he played with them in the National Hockey League four years; then he enjoyed six more seasons with New York Americans. They were happy years, for "Red" was a rollicking defenceman who bashed opponents so vigorously that one year he led the N.H.L. in penalties. Americans never won Stanley Cup honours, but they were a fighting, fun-loving team. When "Red" retired as a player, he continued to manage the club. It was his aggressive leadership and his ability to make friends that later helped him found and develop one of western Canada's leading construction enterprises.

During World War II, Mr. Dutton's three sons were in uniform and two of them had given their lives. When Frank Calder died in February 1943, "Red" consented to become president of the league in which he had once earned the dubious distinction of being a "bad man." "Red" accepted the position with the understanding that it would be only a temporary appointment. Three years later, when his business demanded more time, he resigned and later became an associate of Cooper Smeaton as Stanley Cup trustee. He was succeeded in the presidency by Clarence S. Campbell in 1946.

Clarence Campbell, who has occupied the position for over twenty-five years had many qualifications for the office, yet much of his background is not generally known. He attended University of Alberta, where he played hockey and also earned the distinction of being a Rhodes Scholar. In his undergraduate years he refereed amateur hockey games and was one of the officials in the 1928 Winter Olympics held at St. Moritz, Switzerland. In the 1930s he practised law in Edmonton, and because the years were lean, he added to his income by refereeing in the Western Hockey League and the American Hockey League. His work attracted the praise of President Calder, and he was invited to become an N.H.L. official. He accepted, but after three years he returned to his improving law-practice in Edmonton.

When World War II commenced, Campbell enlisted as an infantry private, but he soon qualified as a lieutenant and received his commission. In May of 1944, as a major, he was appointed to command the 4th Canadian Armoured Division, went to France and served the entire campaign in North-West Europe. In 1945, he was promoted to lieutenant-colonel and transferred to War Crimes Unit, where he acted as Counsel in the trials of many important war criminals, including General Kurt Meyer. During the war he was decorated twice for gallantry, received the Oak Leaf for mention in despatches, and later became a Member of the British Empire (M.B.E.) in recognition of meritorious service.

These wartime honours for courage and leadership—plus many years' legal experience, together with an ice-level knowledge of hockey—earned Clarence Campbell the invitation of becoming the third president of the National Hockey League. His position is unusually difficult, for he has to deal justly with governors, players, officials, newsgatherers and fans. At times all five functions are involved in the one problem.

This was especially true in 1955, when he suspended "Rocket" Richard for the remainder of the season, including the playoffs. Later he was insulted by angry hoodlums while attending a game in the Montreal Forum. The N.H.L. presidency is no position for one who lacks courage and fears criticism. He is censured if he says too much and abused when he says too little. It is a job in which you are "damned if you do and damned if you don't." After every crucial game, someone—executive, commentator, writer or fan—is certain to use as the lead line: "Why doesn't Campbell—!"

Despite the tumult and the shouting, N.H.L. progress under President Campbell's direction has been remarkable. Attendance figures, which correspond to sales in most commercial enterprises, are a good indicator of prosperity; and in this respect few undertakings match the N.H.L. record. For instance, during 1966/67, the last year of the six-club league, the total attendance for the regular games was almost three millions, representing nearly 95 per cent of the available seating capacity. In Toronto and Montreal there has not been an unsold seat in twenty years and subscribers' tickets pass from generation to generation.

Fan enthusiasm is another barometer of success. In Canada, during Stanley Cup time, organizations plan their meetings to avoid conflict with the games. Theatre-goers sit with ear-plugs attached to transistor radios and tuned-in to the broadcasts. Once when a party leader arose to speak in the Ontario Legislature, the motion caused a pocket-radio to blare the broadcast of a Toronto-Detroit game, and many members would interrupt to shout: "What's the score? What's the score?" When a coroner's inquest ended, the presiding officer gave the latest hockey score to jury and witnesses. In Montreal, when a police officer was asked when certain evidence was received from a suspect, he reported it was during the second intermission of the Stanley Cup game played that night.

In addition to the fan-fever, which becomes so virulent during the Stanley Cup playoffs, the players also have reason to whoop and holler. In earlier years there were times when clubs actually lost money while challenging for the cup. On one occasion, Hamilton players were denied a modest two hundred dollars each for their share of Stanley Cup participation. Those days have gone forever.

The reward money now allocated by the N.H.L. to teams and players is generous. At the end of the 1970/71 season, the first four clubs in each division split $210,000. Additionally, all eight clubs competing in Stanley Cup playdowns divided $567,000, depending upon how far they advanced. It was possible for a player on a team winning both its division and the Stanley Cup to earn a bonus of $10,000. In all, the N.H.L. offered $827,000 in awards at the end of the season. Beyond that bounty, all players enjoy a pension fund which provides much security for non-playing years.

All this financial prosperity has intrigued American sportsmen and financiers. In one sense this is not exactly a modern trend for actually hockey in the United States is almost as old as the Stanley Cup itself. Even in the 1890's, Canada's better teams, following their regular seasons, tripped to New York and Boston to play exhibition series with as much as $2500 being awarded to the winners.

It is also true that early this century there were hockey teams in St. Paul, St. Louis, Pittsburg and American Soo—all manned by Canadians. In the winters of 1903/4/5, a small mining town in Michigan operated the Portage Lake Hockey Club, comprised of the best Canadian players. They were so good they twice defeated the famed Montreal Wanderers; and six of the Lakers were eventually members of Stanley Cup winning teams. That was early evidence that Canadian hockey players were willing to chase American dollars.

In 1912, Lester and Frank Patrick organized the Pacific Coast League with teams in Vancouver, New Westminster and Victoria. But even such a venture didn't remain Canadian; and four years later Seattle, Spokane and Portland came in to join Vancouver, the lone Canadian survivor. In 1917, Seattle Metropolitans were good enough to become the first American-owned but Canadian-manned hockey team to win the Stanley Cup.

The first massive expansion of the National Hockey League occurred during the 1920's. There were two reasons for the explosion; and one of them was the development of artificial-ice; which made it possible for hockey to be played anywhere in the United States. The second cause was that Canadian sponsors were losing so much money that the entire Western Canadian Hockey League, with over 100 good players, became available for distribution. The immediate result was that during the 1920's, new clubs were founded in Boston, Detroit, Chicago, New York, Pittsburgh; and later, in St. Louis and Philadelphia. In 1926, there were ten N.H.L. clubs, playing in two divisions; but gradually only the strong survived and, in 1942, only

Montreal Canadiens, Toronto Maple Leafs, Boston Bruins, New York Rangers, Detroit Red Wings and Chicago Black Hawks remained. For 25 years, those same six clubs comprised the National Hockey League; but suddenly the size of the group was doubled.

Through many years expansion of the N.H.L. had been mooted. Shrewd American sportsmen and financiers had noted that, through admissions and television rights, hockey could become a profitable enterprise. The game is ideally appropriate for cameras. It is fast, exciting, easily understood and has a touch of mayhem; it is also colourful in both surroundings and personalities. Moreover, it is weatherproof, for it is played indoors, under good lighting, on keen ice, with plenty of crowd reaction —and no postponements.

However, there was one big IF and that related to the availability of suitable playing personnel. Some of the cities seeking franchises had long been associated with minor hockey; but, it was recognized that if hockey was to fill huge arenas in new territory, it had to be major league in all respects.

The six older clubs realized this need for quality and agreed to retain only eleven members of their 1966/67 teams and permit the others to be drafted by the new clubs. The results were interesting. For example, Minnesota North Stars were enabled to sign new players from such varied sources as Montreal Canadiens, New York Rangers, Boston Bruins, Detroit Red Wings and from lesser teams in Buffalo, Houston, Omaha, Cleveland, Quebec, Regina, Fort William and Peterborough. Other new clubs had similar diversified origins and all six—Philadelphia, Los Angeles, St. Louis, Pittsburg, Minnesota (Minneapolis) and Oakland; some of them in magnificent new arenas were ready for the drop of the puck when the 1967/68 season opened.

How was the competition? Many forecasters had predicted that the "original six" would be so sound and mature that they would overwhelm the "newer six"; indeed some of the more pessimistic forecasters thought it would take five years for the twelve to be properly matched. However, it didn't work out that way for it soon became evident that many players who had long been rooted in minor clubs needed only the opportunity provided by expansion to prove they were really big leaguers.

Indeed the first extension was so satisfactory that, after three years' trial, two more clubs were added. While this growth may strain the quality of play, there is still an adequate supply of material in minor leagues, American colleges and especially in Canada, where over 300,000 lads are now registered in organized hockey groups.

Under President Clarence Campbell's direction, N.H.L. governors have worked harmoniously and every reasonable opportunity has been given the new clubs to prepare good foundations and build lasting institutions. One example was evidenced in arrangements for Stanley Cup competition. Originally it was feared that if four new clubs were pitted against four older clubs, the latter might so dominate that overall interest would flop. So, it was agreed that the four top teams in the older eastern division and the four leading teams in the newer western division would have separate playdowns; then the ultimate winner of each would meet in the Stanley Cup final round.

So far, expansion has exceeded expectations — competitively, financially and in public support. It was so astutely planned and capably executed that already there is talk of — extension to expansion.

CHAPTER TWENTY HOCKEY HALL OF FAME

It is unlikely that the Stanley Cup will ever again be subjected to the indignities once visited upon it. No more will it be booted into canals, deserted on street-corners, employed for commercial displays or stolen from show-cases. After nearly eighty years, redesigned and glistening, it has a permanent home in a setting that affords the dignity, respect and protection its age and prestige command. When the Stanley Cup is not immediately required for presentation and celebration, it has become the principal attraction in the Hockey Hall of Fame.

This hockey temple is centrally located in the Canadian National Exhibition Grounds in Toronto. There, preserved in picture, plaque and collections, is the memorable record of notable clubs, honoured players, outstanding officials and worthy builders. It is unique that the National Hockey League provided the funds for its construction, the City of Toronto donated the site, and the Canadian National Exhibition finances its maintenance and operation.

Within the Hockey Hall of Fame there are many souvenirs of hockey, including the skates, sticks and uniforms of great players. There are also the trophies of the game, those silver symbols annually presented to the champion teams and individual stars. However, the Hall is more than a showplace and museum, for it includes exhibition rooms, a motion picture theatre, a library containing valuable hockey history, together with a conference place and executive offices.

Outside the Hall, during the summer season, there are bubbling fountains and attractive floral displays. On a long outdoor platform there are aluminum flag-poles from which, on special occasions, the colourful pennants of all National Hockey League teams fly in the breeze.

On September 9, 1960, Fred "Cyclone" Taylor, O.B.E., a hockey immortal, earlier-famed for his speed and skill, was invited to turn the first sod on the Hall site. On Saturday, August 26, 1961, in the presence of a large throng, Right Honourable John G. Diefenbaker, then Canada's Prime Minister, officially opened the building.

One of the principal purposes of the edifice is to include an Honour Roll of famous hockey players and others associated with the game. The players are annually elected by a committee headed by Frank J. Selke, and it is required that candidates for election shall be chosen on the basis of playing ability, integrity, character, and their contribution to their team and the game of hockey in general! In 1971, there were 175 Honoured Members, including 127 players, 41 builders, and seven referees.

Included in the archives of Hockey Hall of Fame are the records of Stanley Cup winners, the names of members of Stanley Cup champion teams, and facts relating to outstanding performances of teams and individuals during Stanley Cup competition.

CHAPTER TWENTY-ONE RECORDS

Stanley Cup Winners

SEASON	CHAMPIONS	MANAGER	COACH
1893/94	Montreal A.A.A.	———	———
1894/95	Montreal Victorias	———	Mike Grant
1895/96	Winnipeg Victorias	———	———
1896/97	Montreal Victorias	———	Mike Grant
1897/98	Montreal Victorias	———	F. Richardson
1898/99	Montreal Shamrocks (March)	———	———
1898/99	Montreal Victorias (February)	———	G. Drinkwater
1899/1900	Montreal Shamrocks	———	H. J. Trihey
1900/01	Winnipeg Victorias	———	———
1901/02	Montreal A.A.A.	———	———
1902/03	Ottawa Silver Seven	———	A. T. Smith
1903/04	Ottawa Silver Seven	———	A. T. Smith
1904/05	Ottawa Silver Seven	———	A. T. Smith
1905/06	Montreal Wanderers	———	———
1906/07	Montreal Wanderers (March)	R. R. Boon	Cecil Blachford
1906/07	Kenora Thistles (January)	F. A. Hudson	Tommy Phillips
1907/08	Montreal Wanderers	R. R. Boon	Cecil Blachford
1908/09	Ottawa Senators	———	Bruce Stuart
1909/10	Montreal Wanderers	R. R. Boon	———
1910/11	Ottawa Senators	———	Pud Glass
1911/12	Quebec Bulldogs	M. J. Quinn	C. Nolan
1912/13	Quebec Bulldogs	M. J. Quinn	———
1913/14	Toronto Ontarios	Jack Marshall	Scotty Davidson
1914/15	Vancouver Millionaires	Frank Patrick	Frank Patrick
1915/16	Montreal Canadiens	George Kennedy	George Kennedy
1916/17	Seattle Metropolitans	Pete Muldoon	Pete Muldoon
1917/18	Toronto Arenas	Charlie Querrie	Dick Carroll
1918/19	No decision		
1919/20	Ottawa Senators	Tommy Gorman	Pete Green
1920/21	Ottawa Senators	Tommy Gorman	Pete Green

SEASON	CHAMPIONS	MANAGER	COACH
1921/22	Toronto St. Pats	Charlie Querrie	Eddie Powers
1922/23	Ottawa Senators	Tommy Gorman	Pete Green
1923/24	Montreal Canadiens	Leo Dandurand	Leo Dandurand
1924/25	Victoria Cougars	Lester Patrick	Lester Patrick
1925/26	Montreal Maroons	Eddie Gerard	Eddie Gerard
1926/27	Ottawa Senators	Dave Gill	Dave Gill
1927/28	New York Rangers	Lester Patrick	Lester Patrick
1928/29	Boston Bruins	Art Ross	Cy Dennenny
1929/30	Montreal Canadiens	Cecil Hart	Cecil Hart
1930/31	Montreal Canadiens	Cecil Hart	Cecil Hart
1931/32	Toronto Maple Leafs	Conn Smythe	Dick Irvin
1932/33	New York Rangers	Lester Patrick	Lester Patrick
1933/34	Chicago Black Hawks	Tommy Gorman	Tommy Gorman
1934/35	Montreal Maroons	Tommy Gorman	Tommy Gorman
1935/36	Detroit Red Wings	Jack Adams	Jack Adams
1936/37	Detroit Red Wings	Jack Adams	Jack Adams
1937/38	Chicago Black Hawks	Bill Stewart	Bill Stewart
1938/39	Boston Bruins	Art Ross	Art Ross
1939/40	New York Rangers	Lester Patrick	Frank Boucher
1940/41	Boston Bruins	Art Ross	Conney Weiland
1941/42	Toronto Maple Leafs	Conn Smythe	Hap Day
1942/43	Detroit Red Wings	Jack Adams	Jack Adams
1943/44	Montreal Canadiens	Tommy Gorman	Dick Irvin
1944/45	Toronto Maple Leafs	Conn Smythe	Hap Day
1945/46	Montreal Canadiens	Tommy Gorman	Dick Irvin
1946/47	Toronto Maple Leafs	Conn Smythe	Hap Day
1947/48	Toronto Maple Leafs	Conn Smythe	Hap Day
1948/49	Toronto Maple Leafs	Conn Smythe	Hap Day
1949/50	Detroit Red Wings	Jack Adams	Tommy Ivan
1950/51	Toronto Maple Leafs	Conn Smythe	Joe Primeau
1951/52	Detroit Red Wings	Jack Adams	Tommy Ivan
1952/53	Montreal Canadiens	Frank Selke	Dick Irvin
1953/54	Detroit Red Wings	Jack Adams	Tommy Ivan
1954/55	Detroit Red Wings	Jack Adams	Jimmy Skinner
1955/56	Montreal Canadiens	Frank Selke	Toe Blake
1956/57	Montreal Canadiens	Frank Selke	Toe Blake
1957/58	Montreal Canadiens	Frank Selke	Toe Blake
1958/59	Montreal Canadiens	Frank Selke	Toe Blake
1959/60	Montreal Canadiens	Frank Selke	Toe Blake
1960/61	Chicago Black Hawks	Tommy Ivan	Rudy Pilous
1961/62	Toronto Maple Leafs	Punch Imlach	Punch Imlach
1962/63	Toronto Maple Leafs	Punch Imlach	Punch Imlach
1963/64	Toronto Maple Leafs	Punch Imlach	Punch Imlach
1964/65	Montreal Canadiens	Sam Pollock	Toe Blake
1965/66	Montreal Canadiens	Sam Pollock	Toe Blake
1966/67	Toronto Maple Leafs	Punch Imlach	Punch Imlach
1967/68	Montreal Canadiens	Sam Pollock	Toe Blake
1968/69	Montreal Canadiens	Sam Pollock	Claude Ruel
1969/70	Boston Bruins	Milt Schmidt	Harry Sinden
1970/71	Montreal Canadiens	Sam Pollock	Al MacNeil

Stanley Cup Playoff Records (1927-1971)

TEAMS

MOST TIMES STANLEY CUP CHAMPIONS 15

Montreal Canadiens have won the Stanley Cup 15 times.

MOST CONSECUTIVE YEARS STANLEY CUP FINALISTS 10

Montreal Canadiens played in 10 consecutive Cup finals, 1950/51 to 1959/60.

LONGEST HOCKEY GAME 176 minutes, 30 seconds

Detroit Red Wings defeated Montreal Maroons, 1-0 at Montreal on March 24 and 25, 1936, with the winning goal being scored after 116 minutes and 30 seconds of overtime play. The winning goal was scored by Mud Bruneteau on a pass from Hec Kilrea at 16.30 of the sixth overtime period. It was 2.25 a.m. when the game ended.

SHORTEST OVERTIME GAME 25 seconds

Syd Howe scored for Detroit after 25 seconds of 1st overtime period to give Detroit a 2-1 win over New York Americans, on March 19, 1940, at Detroit.

FASTEST 5 GOALS 3 minutes 36 seconds

5 goals were scored in 3rd period in 3 minutes and 36 seconds on March 30, 1944, by Montreal Canadiens, as Canadiens defeated Toronto Maple Leafs, 11-0, at Montreal.

HIGHEST SHUTOUT GAME 11

Montreal Canadiens defeated Toronto Maple Leafs 11-0 in fifth game of semi-final round at Montreal on March 30, 1944.

MOST GOALS IN A STANLEY CUP FINAL GAME 12

Toronto Maple Leafs defeated Chicago Black Hawks, 8-4, in fifth game of finals, at Toronto, on April 19, 1962.

MOST GOALS IN A PLAYOFF GAME 13

Montreal Canadiens defeated Toronto Maple Leafs, 10-3, in semi-finals at Montreal, on March 29, 1945.

CONSECUTIVE GAME RECORD FOR WINS 8

Detroit Red Wings and Montreal Canadiens each won the Stanley Cup in 8 straight games. Detroit defeated Toronto and Canadiens in 1951/52; while Montreal defeated Chicago and Toronto in 1959/60.

MOST GOALS IN A FINAL SERIES 47

Detroit scored 27 goals and Canadiens 20 in a seven-game final series in 1955.

NUMBER OF GAMES HOME TEAM WINLESS 9

The home team failed to win one game in the first 9 games played in the 1950/51 Stanley Cup playoffs. 5 games in Montreal-Detroit series were won by visitors, while 4 games in Toronto-Boston series were played before home team skated off ice as winners.

MOST PENALTIES, ONE TEAM, ONE SERIES 72

72 penalties were given to Montreal Canadiens, for a total of 185 minutes, in the seven-game final series against Chicago Black Hawks, during 1965 playoffs.

MOST PENALTIES IN ONE GAME 35

35 penalties were called by Referee Art Skov in the fourth game of the Montreal-Toronto semi-final series played at Toronto, April 14, 1966. The penalties totalled 154 minutes.

MOST PENALTIES IN ONE PERIOD 23

23 penalties were called by Referee Art Skov in first period of fourth game of Montreal-Toronto semi-final series played at Toronto, April 14, 1966. It required 65 minutes to complete the one period.

Individual Records (1927-1971)

MOST POINTS IN PLAYOFF SERIES 27

In 1970, Phil Esposito, Boston Bruins, earned 13 goals and 14 assists, totalling 27 points. In 1971, Frank Mahovlich, Montreal Canadiens, earned 14 goals and 13 assists, totalling 27 points.

MOST GOALS IN PLAYOFF SERIES 14

Frank Mahovlich, Montreal Canadiens, in 20 games in 1971 series, scored 14 goals.

MOST ASSISTS IN PLAYOFF SERIES 16

Jean Beliveau, Montreal Canadiens, in 20 games in 1971 series, earned 16 assists.

MOST WINNING GOALS SCORED 18

Maurice Richard, of Montreal Canadiens, scored 18 winning goals in 15 playoff series. Six of the 18 were scored in overtime play.

MOST "HAT TRICKS" 7

Maurice Richard scored 3 or more goals in a game seven times during 15 playoff series.

MOST POINTS IN A GAME BY A DEFENCEMAN 5

Eddie Bush, of Detroit Red Wings, scored 1 goal and had 4 assists for 5 points, against the Maple Leafs, in Toronto, on April 9, 1942. Score was Detroit 5, Toronto 2.

MOST GAMES IN PLAYOFFS 164

Leonard "Red" Kelly, Detroit and Toronto, played 164 games during 19 playoff series.

HIGHEST SCORING LINE IN PLAYOFF SERIES 51 points

Detroit Red Wings' line of Centre Earl Reibel, Right Wing Gordie Howe and Left Wing Ted Lindsay in 1954/55 in 11 playoff games against Toronto and Canadiens, accumulated a total of 51 scoring points. Howe had 20 points; Lindsay 19; and Reibel 12.

MOST SHUTOUTS RECORDED IN PLAYOFF SERIES 4

Terry Sawchuk, of Detroit Red Wings, had four shutouts in 1951/52 playoff series against Toronto and Canadiens. He blanked Toronto in first 2 games of semi-finals and Canadiens in last 2 games of finals.

Frank McCool, of Toronto Maple Leafs, had four shutouts in 13 games in 1944/45 playoff series against Montreal Canadiens and Detroit Red Wings. Three of the shutouts were in succession against Detroit.

Dave Kerr, of New York Rangers, had four shutouts in 9 games in 1936/37 playoff series against Montreal Maroons and Detroit Red Wings.

Clint Benedict, of Montreal Maroons, had 4 shutouts in 9 games in 1927/28 against Ottawa, Canadiens and Rangers.

MOST POINTS BY A DEFENCEMAN 20

Bobby Orr, Boston Bruins, in 1970, earned 9 goals and 11 assists, in 14 games.

MOST GOALS SCORED IN SINGLE PLAYOFF GAME 5

Maurice Richard, of Montreal Canadiens, scored 5 goals in second game of semi-final series against Toronto Maple Leafs on March 23, 1944. Canadiens won game 5-1 with Richard scoring all of team's goals. Game was played in Montreal.

MOST ASSISTS IN SINGLE PLAYOFF GAME 5

Toe Blake, Maurice Richard, Bert Olmstead, of Canadiens, and Don McKenney, of Boston, all had 5 assists in one game. Blake on March 23, 1944, against Toronto; Richard on March 27, 1956, against Rangers; Olmstead on March 30, 1957, against Rangers; and McKenney, on April 5, 1958, against Rangers.

MOST POINTS IN SINGLE PLAYOFF GAME 6

Dickie Moore, of Montreal Canadiens, scored 2 goals and had 4 assists for 6 points, against Boston Bruins, on March 25, 1954, at Montreal, Score Canadiens 8, Boston 1.

FASTEST GOAL IN A PLAYOFF GAME 9 seconds

Gordie Howe, of Detroit Red Wings, scored 9 seconds after start of game on April 1, 1954, at Detroit, Detroit defeated Toronto Maple Leafs in overtime, 4-3.

MOST SHUTOUTS BY A GOALKEEPER 13

Turk Broda, of Toronto Maple Leafs, had 13 shutouts in 13 playoff series.

MOST POINTS IN PLAYOFF COMPETITION 176

Jean Beliveau, Montreal Canadiens, has earned 79 goals and 97 assists, totalling 176 points.

MOST GOALS IN PLAYOFF COMPETITION 82

Set by Maurice Richard, of Montreal Canadiens, in 15 playoff series.

MOST ASSISTS IN PLAYOFF COMPETITION 97

Jean Beliveau, Montreal Canadiens, earned 97 assists during 17 playoff series.

Members of Stanley Cup Winning Teams

1893/94 *Montreal AAA*—E. M. O'Brien, A. A. Hodgson, H. Routh, A. C. Ward, G. R. James, H. G. Collins, A. Cameron, W. M. Barlow, A. T. Mussen, A. B. Kingan.

1894/95 *Montreal Victorias*—G. Drinkwater, H. Henderson, R. W. Jones, N. S. Rankin, R. L. MacDougal, S. Davidson, Mike Grant (captain).

1895/96 *Winnipeg Victorias*—Flett, Campbell, Higginbotham, Howard, Merritt, Armytage, Bain.

1896/97 *Montreal Victorias*—D. T. Gillelan, D. H. Henderson, E. McLea, G. Drinkwater, S. Davidson, R. L. MacDougal, G. G. Lewis, Mike Grant (captain).

1897/98 *Montreal Victorias*—F. Richardson (captain), G. G. Lewis, E. McLea, H. B. Macdougal, R. L. MacDougal, Mike Grant, G. Drinkwater, Dr. C. Davidson.

1898/99 *Montreal Victorias*—(February)—W. Ewing, F. McRobie, Mike Grant, F. Richardson, R. Bowie, Dr. C. Davidson, G. G. Lewis, E. McLea, R. L. MacDougal, G. Drinkwater (captain).

1898/99 *Montreal Shamrocks*—(March)—J. H. McKenna, F. C. Tansey, F. Wall, H. J. Trihey, A. F. Farrell, F. Scanlon, J. P. Brennan.

1899/1900 *Montreal Shamrocks*—F. C. Tansey, F. Scanlan, A. F. Farrell, J. H. McKenna, F. Wall, J. P. Brennan, C. Hoerner, H. J. Trihey (captain), J. Brennan.

1900/01 *Winnipeg Victorias*—E. B. Wood, J. Marshall, A. B. Gingras, F. T. Cadham, G. W. Johnstone, R. M. Flett, M. L. Flett, D. Bain, A. Brown.

1901/02 *Montreal AAA*—T. G. Hodge, G. Smith, R. R. Boon, W. C. Nicholson, A. Hooper, W. J. Billingham, C. A. Liffiton, J. Marshall, J. Gardiner.

1902/03 *Ottawa*—S. C. Gilmour, A. Moore, P. T. Sims, J. B. Hutton, D. J. Gilmour, H. L. Gilmour, H. Westwick, Frank McGee, F. H. Wood, A. A. Fraser, C. D. Spittall, E. H. Pulford (captain), A. T. Smith (coach), Pete Green (trainer).

1903/04 *Ottawa*—S. C. Gilmour, A. Moore, P. T. Sims, F. McGee, J. B. Hutton, D. J. Gilmour, H. L. Gilmour, H. Westwick, A. A. Fraser, F. H. Wood, E. H. Pulford (captain), A. T. Smith (coach), Pete Green (trainer), M. H. McGilton (trainer).

1904/05 *Ottawa*—D. N. Finnie, A. E. Moore, H. Westwick, H. L. Gilmour, Frank McGee, M. H. McGilton (trainer), E. H. Pulford (captain), A. T. Smith (playing coach).

1905/06 *Montreal Wanderers*—Doc Menard, Lester Patrick, Billy Strachan, Rod Kennedy, Pud Glass, Ernie Russell, Ernie (Moose) Johnson.

1906/07 *Kenora Thistles*—(January)—F. A. Hudson (manager), Joe Hall, T. Hooper, W. McGinsie, Si Griffis, E. Giroux, Art Ross, R. Phillips, Tommy Phillips (captain), D. R. Beaudro.

1906/07 *Montreal Wanderers*—(March)—R. R. Boon (manager), W. S. Strachan, Pud Glass, C. W. Blachford (captain), Hod Stuart, Ernie (Moose) Johnson, H. C. Strachan, W. M. Hern, Bruce Stuart, Art Ross, Lester Patrick, Walter Smaill, Ernie Russell, Jack Marshall, E. Liffiton, T. R. Kennedy, Paul Lefebvre (trainer).

1907/08 *Montreal Wanderers*—W. S. Strachan, Pud Glass, Ernie (Moose) Johnson, H. C. Strachan, W. M. Hern, Bruce Stuart, Art Ross, Lester Patrick, Walter Smaill, Ernie Russell, Jack Marshall, E. Liffiton, C. W. Blachford (captain), R. R. Boon (manager).

1908/09 *Ottawa*—Fred Lake, Percy Lesueur, Fred (Cyclone) Taylor, W. Gilmour, Alex Kerr, E. Day, Marty Walsh, Bruce Stuart (captain).

1909/10 *Montreal Wanderers*—C. W. Blachford, Ernie (Moose) Johnson, Ernie Russell, Riley Hern, Harry Hyland, Jack Marshall, W. Chipchase, Pud Glass (captain), R. R. Boon (manager).

1910/11 *Ottawa*—Hamby Shore, Percy Lesueur, Jack Darragh, Bruce Stuart, Marty Walsh, Bruce Ridpath, Fred Lake, Alex Kerr, Currie.

1911/12 *Quebec Bull Dogs*—Goldie Prodgers, Joe Hall, W. Rooney, Paddy Moran, J. Marks, J. MacDonald, Eddie Oatman, Joe Malone (captain), C. Nolan (coach), M. J. Quinn (manager), D. Beland (trainer).

1912/13 *Quebec Bull Dogs*—Joe Malone, Joe Hall, W. Rooney, Paddy Moran, J. Marks, Billy Creighton, Jeff Malone, T. Smith, Rusty Crawford, Harry Mummery, M. J. Quinn (manager), D. Beland (trainer).
(This marked the first meeting between the champions of the East and the champions of the West. The series was an unofficial one and Quebec refused to place the Cup in competition. Victoria, led by the playing-coach Lester Patrick, therefore did not receive the Cup although they defeated Quebec.)

1913/14 *Toronto*—Con Corbeau, F. R. McGiffen, Jack Walker, G. McNamara, Cully Wilson, Frank Foyston, Harry Cameron, Happy Holmes, A. M. Davidson (captain), Jack Marshall (manager), Frank and Dick Carroll (trainers).

1914/15 *Vancouver Millionaires*—Kenny Mallen, Frank Nighbor, Fred (Cyclone) Taylor, Hughie Lehman, Lloyd Cook, Mickey MacKay, Barney Stanley, Jim Seaborn, Si Griffis (captain), Frank Patrick (playing manager).

1915/16 *Montreal Canadiens*—Georges Vezina, Bert Corbeau, Jack Laviolette, Newsy Lalonde, Louis Berlinquette, Goldie Prodgers, George McNamara, Didier Pitre, S. Ronan, J. Arbour, S. Poulin, George Kennedy (manager).

1916/17 *Seattle Metropolitans*—Happy Holmes, Ed Carpenter, Cully Wilson, Jack Walker, Bernie Morris, Frank Foyston, Roy Rickey, Jim Riley, Bobby Rowe (captain), Pete Muldoon (manager).

1917/18 *Toronto Arenas*—Rusty Crawford, Harry Meeking, Ken Randall, Corb Denneny, Harry Cameron, Jack Adams, Alf Skinner, Harry Mummery, Happy Holmes, Reg Noble, Charlie Querrie (manager), Dick Carroll (coach), Frank Carroll (trainer).

1918/19 *No decision.* Series halted by Spanish influenza epidemic, illness of several players and death of Joe Hall of Canadiens from 'flu. Five games had been played, when the series was halted, each team having won two and tied one.

1919/20 *Ottawa Senators*—Jack McKell, Jack Darragh, Morley Bruce, Horace Merrill, George (Buck) Boucher, Eddie Gerard, Clint Benedict, Sprague Cleghorn, Frank Nighbor, Harry Broadbent, Cy Denneny, Tommy Gorman (manager), Pete Green (coach).

1920/21 *Ottawa Senators*—Jack McKell, Jack Darragh, Morley Bruce, Horace Merrill, George (Buck) Boucher, Eddie Gerard, Clint Benedict, Sprague Cleghorn, Frank Nighbor, Harry Broadbent, Cy Denneny, Tommy Gorman (manager), Pete Green (coach), C. Dolan (trainer).

1921/22 *Toronto St. Pats*—Ted Stackhouse, Glenn Smith, Corb Denneny, Rod Smylie, Lloyd Andrews, John Ross Roach, Harry Cameron, Red Stuart, Cecil (Babe) Dye, Ken Randall, Reg. Noble, Eddie Gerard (borrowed for the series from Ottawa), Charlie Querrie (manager), Eddie Powers (coach).

1922/23 *Ottawa Senators*—George (Buck) Boucher, Lionel Hitchman, Frank Nighbor, Frank (King) Clancy, Harry Helman, Clint Benedict, Jack Darragh, Eddie Gerard, Cy Denneny, Harry Broadbent, Tommy Gorman (manager), Pete Green (coach), C. Dolan (trainer).

1923/24 *Montreal Canadiens*—Georges Vezina, Sprague Cleghorn, Billy Coutu, Howie Morenz, Aurel Joliat, Billy Bell, Billy Boucher, Robert Boucher, Odie Cleghorn, Sylvio Mantha, J. (Curley) Hedley, Leo Dandurand (manager-coach).

1924/25 *Victoria Cougars*—Happy Holmes, Clem Loughlin, Gordie Fraser, Frank Frederickson, Jack Walker, Gizzy Hart, Slim Halderson, Frank Foyston, Harry Meeking, Jocko Anderson, Lester Patrick (manager-coach).

1925/26 *Montreal Maroons*—Clint Benedict, Reg Noble, Frank Carson, Dunc Munro, Nels Stewart, Harry Broadbent, Babe Siebert, Dinny Dinsmore, Bill Phillips, Hobie Kitchen, Sammy Rothschild, Frank Lowerry, Yoots Holway, Shorty Horne, Eddie Gerard (manager-coach), Bill O'Brien (trainer).

1926/27 *Ottawa Senators*—Alex Connell, Frank (King) Clancy, George (Buck) Boucher, Ed Gorman, Frank Finnigan, Alex Smith, Hec Kilrea, Hooley Smith, Cy Denneny, Frank Nighbor, Jack Adams, Stan Jackson, Milt Halliday, Dave Gill (manager-coach).

1927/28 *New York Rangers*—Lorne Chabot, Taffy Abel, Leo Bourgault, Ching Johnson, Bill Cook, Bun Cook, Frank Boucher, Billy Boyd, Murray Murdoch, Paul Thompson, Alex Gray, Laurie Scott, Les Patrick (sub goaltender), Joe Miller (sub goaltender), Lester Patrick (manager-coach), Harry Westerby (trainer), Patsy Gallighen.

1928/29 *Boston Bruins*—Cecil (Tiny) Thompson, Hal Winkler (sub goaltender), Eddie Shore, Lionel Hitchman, Perk Galbraith, Eric Pettinger, Frank Frederickson, Mickey MacKay, Red Green, Dutch Gainor, Harry Oliver, Eddie Rodden, Dit Clapper, Cooney Weiland, Lloyd Klein, Cy Denneny, Bill Carson, George Owen, Myles Lane, Art Ross (manager-coach), Win Green (trainer).

1929/30 *Montreal Canadiens*—George Hainsworth, Marty Burke, Sylvio Mantha, Howie Morenz, Bert McCaffrey, Auriel Joliat, Albert Leduc, Pit Lepine, Wildor Larochelle, Nick Wasnie, Gerald Carson, Armand Mondou, Georges Mantha, Gus Rivers, Leo Dandurand (manager), Cecil Hart (coach), Ed Dufour (trainer).

1930/31 *Montreal Canadiens*—George Hainsworth, W. Larochelle, Marty Burke, Sylvio Mantha, Howie Morenz, Johnny Gagnon, Aurel Joliat, Armand Mondou, Pit Lepine, Albert Leduc, Georges Mantha, Art Lesieur, Nick Wasnie, Bert McCaffrey, Gus Rivers, Leo Dandurand (manager), Cecil Hart (coach), Ed Dufour (trainer).

1931/32 *Toronto Maple Leafs*—Chuck Conacher, Harvey Jackson, King Clancy, Andy Blair, Red Horner, Lorne Chabot, Alex Levinsky, Joe Primeau, Hal Darragh, Hal Cotton, Frank Finnigan, Hap Day, Ace Bailey, Bob Gracie, Fred Robertson, Conn Smythe (manager), Dick Irvin (coach), Tim Daly (trainer).

1932/33 *New York Rangers*—Ching Johnson, Butch Keeling, Frank Boucher, Art Somers, Babe Siebert, Bun Cook, Andy Aitkinhead, Ott Heller, Ozzie Asmundson, Gord Pettinger, Doug Brennan, Cecil Dillon, Bill Cook (captain), Murray Murdoch, Earl Seibert, Lester Patrick (manager-coach), Harry Westerby (trainer).

1933/34 *Chicago Black Hawks*—Taffy Abel, Lolo Couture, Lou Trudel, Lionel Conacher, Paul Thompson, Leroy Goldsworthy, Art Coulter, Roger Jenkins, Don McFadyen, Tommy Cook, Doc Romnes, Johnny Gottselig, Mush March, Johnny Sheppard, Chuck Gardiner (captain), Jack Leswick, Bill Kendall, Tommy Gorman (manager-coach), Eddie Froelich (trainer).

1934/35 *Montreal Maroons*—Marvin (Cy) Wentworth, Dutch Gainor, Alex Connell, Toe Blake, Stew Evans, Earl Robinson, Bill Miller, Dave Trottier, Jimmy Ward, Larry Northcott, Hooley Smith, Russ Blinco, Allan Shields, Sammy McManus, Gus Marker, Dutch Gainor, Bob Gracie, Herb Cain, Bill MacKenzie, Tommy Gorman (manager), Lionel Conacher (coach), Bill O'Brien (trainer).

1935/36 *Detroit Red Wings*—Johnny Sorrell, Sid Howe, Marty Barry, Herbie Lewis, Mud Bruneteau, Wally Kilrea, Hec Kilrea, Gordon Pettinger, Bucko McDonald, Scotty Bowman, Larry Aurie, Pete Kelly, Doug Young, Ebbie Goodfellow, Normie Smith, Tooke (sub goaltender), Jack Adams (manager-coach), Honey Walker (trainer).

1936/37 *Detroit Red Wings*—Normie Smith, Pete Kelly, Larry Aurie, Herbie Lewis, Hec Kilrea, Mud Bruneteau, Sid Howe, Wally Kilrea, Jimmy Franks (sub goaltender), Doug Young, Bucko McDonald, Gordon Pettinger, Orville Roulston, Ebbie Goodfellow, Johnny Gallagher, Scotty Bowman, Johnny Sorrell, Marty Barry, Earl Robertson (sub goaltender), Johnny Sherf, Howard Mackie, Jack Adams (manager-coach), Honey Walker (trainer).

1937/38 *Chicago Black Hawks*—Art Wiebe, Carl Voss, Hal Jackson, Mike Karakas, Mush March, Jack Shill, Earl Seibert, Cully Dahlstrom, Alex Levinsky, Johnny Gottselig, Lou Trudel, Pete Palangio, Bill MacKenzie, Roc Romnes, Paul Thompson, Roger Jenkins, Virgil Johnson, Alf Moore (sub goaltender), Bert Connolly, Paul Goodman (sub goaltender), Bill Stewart (manager-coach), Eddie Froelich (trainer).

1938/39 *Boston Bruins*—Bobby Bauer, Mel Hill, Flash Hollett, Roy Conacher, Gord Pettinger, Milt Schmidt, Woody Dumart, Jack Crawford, Ray Getliffe, Frank Brimsek, Eddie Shore, Dit Clapper, Charlie Sands, Bill Cowley, Jack Portland, Red Hamill, Art Ross (manager-coach), Win Green (trainer).

1939/40 *New York Rangers*—Dave Kerr, Art Coulter, Ott Heller, Alex Shibicky, Mac Colville, Neil Colville, Phil Watson, Lynn Patrick, Clint Smith, Muzz Patrick, Babe Pratt, Bryan Hextall, Kilby Macdonald, Dutch Hiller, Alf Pike, Lester Patrick (manager), Frank Boucher (coach), Harry Westerby (trainer).

1940/41 *Boston Bruins*—Bill Cowley, Des Smith, Dit Clapper, Frank Brimsek, Flash Hollett, John Crawford, Bobby Bauer, Pat McCreavy, Herb Cain, Mel Hill, Milt Schmidt, Woody Dumart, Roy Conacher, Terry Reardon, Art Jackson, Eddie Wiseman, Jack Shewchuk, Art Ross (manager). Cooney Weiland (coach), Win Green (trainer).

1941/42 *Toronto Maple Leafs*—Reg Hamilton, Wally Stanowski, Syl Apps, Bob Goldham, Gord Drillon, Hank Goldup, Ernie Dickens, Dave Schriner, Bucko McDonald, Bob Davidson, Nick Metz, Bingo Kampman, Don Metz, Gaye Stewart, Turk Broda, Johnny McCreedy, Lorne Carr, Pete Langelle, Billy Taylor, Conn Smythe (manager), Hap Day (coach), Frank Selke (business manager), Tim Daly (trainer).

1942/43 *Detroit Red Wings*—Jack Stewart, Jimmy Orlando, Sid Abel, Alex Motter, Harry Watson, Joe Carveth, Joe Turner (sub goaltender), Mud Bruneteau, Eddie Wares, Ralph Almas (sub goaltender), Johnny Mowers, Cully Simon, Don Grosso, Carl Liscombe, Connie Brown, Johnny Holota, Sid Howe, Jack Adams (manager), Ebbie Goodfellow (playing-coach), Honey Walker (trainer), Les Douglas, Hal Jackson, Joe Fisher.

1943/44 *Montreal Canadiens*—Toe Blake, Maurice Richard, Elmer Lach, Ray Getliffe, Murph Chamberlain, Phil Watson, Emile Bouchard, Glen Harmon, Buddy O'Connor, Jerry Heffernan, Mike McMahon, Leo Lamoreux, Fernand Majeau, Bob Fillion, Bill Durnan, Tommy Gorman (manager), Dick Irvin (coach), Ernie Cook (trainer).

1944/45 *Toronto Maple Leafs*—Don Metz, Frank McCool, Wally Stanowski, Reg Hamilton, Elwyn Morris, Johnny McCreedy, Tommy O'Neil, Ted Kennedy, Babe Pratt, Gus Bodnar, Art Jackson, Jack McLean, Mel Hill, Nick Metz, Bob Davidson, Dave Schriner, Lorne Carr, Conn Smythe (manager), Frank Selke (business manager), Hap Day (coach), Tim Daly (trainer).

1945/46 *Montreal Canadiens*—Elmer Lach, Toe Blake, Maurice Richard, Bob Fillion, Dutch Hiller, Murph Chamberlain, Ken Mosdell, Buddy O'Connor, Glen Harmon, Jim Peters, Emile Bouchard, Bill Reay, Ken Reardon, Leo Lamoureux, Frank Eddolls, Jerry Plamondon, Bill Durnan, Tommy Gorman, (manager), Dick Irvin (coach), Ernie Cook (trainer).

1946/47 *Toronto Maple Leafs*—Turk Broda, Garth Boesch, Gus Mortson, Jim Thomson, Wally Stanowski, Bill Barilko, Harry Watson, Bud Poile, Ted Kennedy, Syl Apps, Don Metz, Nick Metz, Bill Ezinicki, Vic Lynn, Howie Meeker, Gaye Stewart, Joe Klukay, Gus Bodnar, Bob Goldham, Conn Smythe (manager), Happy Day (coach), Tim Daly (trainer).

1947/48 *Toronto Maple Leafs*—Turk Broda, Jim Thomson, Wally Stanowski, Garth Boesch, Bill Barilko, Gus Mortson, Phil Samis, Syl Apps, Bill Ezinicki, Harry Watson, Ted Kennedy, Howie Meeker, Vic Lynn, Nick Metz, Max Bentley, Joe Klukay, Les Costello, Don Metz, Sid Smith, Conn Smythe (manager), Hap Day (coach), Tim Daly (trainer).

1948/49 *Toronto Maple Leafs*—Turk Broda, Jim Thomson, Gus Mortson, Bill Barilko, Garth Boesch, Bill Juzda, Ted Kennedy, Howie Meeker, Vic Lynn, Harry Watson, Bill Ezinicki, Cal Gardner, Max Bentley, Joe Klukay, Sid Smith, Don Metz, Ray Timgren, Fleming Mackell, Harry Taylor, Bob Dawes, Tod Sloan, Conn Smythe (manager), Hap Day (coach), Tim Daly (trainer).

1949/50 *Detroit Red Wings*—Harry Lumley, Jack Stewart, Leo Reise, Clare Martin, Al Dewsbury, Lee Fogolin, Marcel Pronovost, Red Kelly, Ted Lindsay, Sid Abel, Gordie Howe, George Gee, Jimmy Peters, Marty Pavelich, Jim McFadden, Pete Babando, Max McNab, Gerry Couture, Joe Carveth, Steve Black, John Wilson, Larry Wilson, Jack Adams (manager), Tommy Ivan (coach), Carl Mattson (trainer).

1950/51 *Toronto Maple Leafs*—Turk Broda, Al Rollins, Jim Thomson, Gus Mortson, Bill Barilko, Bill Juzda, Fern Flaman, Hugh Bolton, Ted Kennedy, Sid Smith, Tod Sloan, Cal Gardner, Howie Meeker, Harry Watson, Max Bentley, Joe Klukay, Danny Lewicki, Ray Timgren, Fleming Mackell, Johnny McCormack, Bob Hassard, Conn Smythe (manager), Joe Primeau (coach), Jim Daly (trainer).

1951/52 *Detroit Red Wings*—Terry Sawchuk, Bob Goldham, Ben Woit, Red Kelly, Leo Reise, Marcel Pronovost, Ted Lindsay, Tony Leswick, Gordie Howe, Metro Prystai, Marty Pavelich, Sid Abel, Glen Skov, Alex Delvecchio, Johnny Wilson, Vic Stasiuk, Larry Zeidel, Jack Adams (manager), Tommy Ivan (coach), Carl Mattson (trainer).

1952/53 *Montreal Canadiens*—Gerry McNeil, Jacques Plante, Doug Harvey, Butch Bouchard, Tom Johnson, Dollard St. Laurent, Bud MacPherson, Maurice Richard, Elmer Lach, Bert Olmstead, Bernie Geoffrion, Floyd Curry, Paul Masnick, Billy Reay, Dickie Moore, Ken Mosdell, Dick Gamble, Johnny McCormack, Lorne Davis, Calum MacKay, Eddie Mazur, Frank Selke (manager), Dick Irvin (coach), Hector Dubois (trainer).

1953/54 *Detroit Red Wings*—Terry Sawchuk, Red Kelly, Bob Goldham, Ben Woit, Marcel Pronovost, Al Arbour, Keith Allen, Ted Lindsay, Tony Leswick, Gordie Howe, Marty Pavelich, Alex Delvecchio, Metro Prystai, Glen Skov, John Wilson, Bill Dineen, Jim Peters, Earl Reibel, Vic Stasiuk, Jack Adams (manager), Tommy Ivan (coach), Carl Mattson (trainer).

1954/55 *Detroit Red Wings*—Terry Sawchuk, Red Kelly, Bob Goldham, Marcel Pronovost, Ben Woit, Jim Hay, Larry Hillman, Ted Lindsay, Tony Leswick, Gordie Howe, Alex Delvecchio,

Marty Pavelich, Glen Skov, Earl Reibel, John Wilson, Bill Dineen, Vic Stasiuk, Marcel Bonin, Jack Adams (manager), Jimmy Skinner (coach), Carl Mattson (trainer).

1955/56 *Montreal Canadiens*—Jacques Plante, Doug Harvey, Butch Bouchard, Bob Turner, Tom Johnson, Jean-Guy Talbot, Dollard St. Laurent, Jean Beliveau, Bernie Geoffrion, Bert Olmstead, Floyd Currie, Jackie Leclair, Maurice Richard, Dickie Moore, Henri Richard, Ken Mosdell, Don Marshall, Claude Provost, Frank Selke (manager), Toe Blake (coach), Hector Dubois (trainer).

1956/57 *Montreal Canadiens*—Jacques Plante, Gerry McNeil, Doug Harvey, Tom Johnson, Bob Turner, Dollard St. Laurent, Jean-Guy Talbot, Jean Beliveau, Bernie Geoffrion, Floyd Curry, Dickie Moore, Maurice Richard, Claude Provost, Bert Olmstead, Henri Richard, Phil Goyette, Don Marshall, Andre Pronovost, Connie Broden, Frank Selke (manager), Toe Blake (coach), Hector Dubois (trainer).

1957/58 *Montreal Canadiens*—Jacques Plante, Gerry McNeil, Doug Harvey, Tom Johnson, Bob Turner, Dollard St. Laurent, Jean-Guy Talbot, Albert Langlois, Jean Beliveau, Bernie Geoffrion, Maurice Richard, Dickie Moore, Claude Provost, Bert Olmstead, Henri Richard, Marcel Bonin, Phil Goyette, Don Marshall, Andre Pronovost, Connie Broden, Frank Selke (manager), Toe Blake (coach), Hector Dubois (trainer).

1958/59 *Montreal Canadiens*—Jacques Plante, Charlie Hodge, Doug Harvey, Tom Johnson, Bob Turner, Jean-Guy Talbot, Albert Langlois, Bernie Geoffrion, Ralph Backstrom, Bill Hicke, Maurice Richard, Dickie Moore, Claude Provost, Ab McDonald, Henri Richard, Marcel Bonin, Phil Goyette, Don Marshall, André Pronovost, Frank Selke (manager), Toe Blake (coach), Hector Dubois (trainer).

1959/60 *Montreal Canadiens*—Jacques Plante, Charlie Hodge, Doug Harvey, Tom Johnson, Bob Turner, Jean-Guy Talbot, Albert Langlois, Ralph Backstrom, Jean Beliveau, Marcel Bonin, Bernie Geoffrion, Phil Goyette, Bill Hicke, Don Marshall, Ab McDonald, Dickie Moore, Andre Pronovost, Claude Provost, Henri Richard, Maurice Richard, Frank Selke (manager), Toe Blake (coach), Hector Dubois, Larry Aubut (trainers).

1960/61 *Chicago Black Hawks*—Glenn Hall, Al Arbour, Pierre Pilote, Elmer Vasko, Jack Evans, Dollard St. Laurent, Reg Fleming, Tod Sloan, Ron Murphy, Eddie Litzenberger, Bill Hay, Bobby Hull, Ab McDonald, Eric Nesterenko, Ken Wharram, Earl Balfour, Stan Mikita, Murray Balfour, Tommy Ivan (manager), Rudy Pilous (coach), Nick Garen (trainer).

1961/62 *Toronto Maple Leafs*—Johnny Bower, Don Simmons, Carl Brewer, Tim Horton, Bob Baun, Allan Stanley, Al Arbour, Larry Hillman, Red Kelly, Dick Duff, George Armstrong, Frank Mahovlich, Bob Nevin, Ron Stewart, Billy Harris, Bert Olmstead, Bob Pulford, Eddie Shack, Dave Keon, Ed Litzenberger, John MacMillan, Punch Imlach (manager-coach), Bob Haggert (trainer).

1962/63 *Toronto Maple Leafs*—Johnny Bower, Don Simmons, Carl Brewer, Tim Horton, Kent Douglas, Allan Stanley, Bob Baun, Larry Hillman, Red Kelly, Dick Duff, George Armstrong, Bob Nevin, Ron Stewart, Dave Keon, Billy Harris, Bob Pulford, Eddie Shack, Ed Litzenberger, Frank Mahovlich, John MacMillan, Punch Imlach (manager-coach), Bob Haggert (trainer).

1963/64 *Toronto Maple Leafs*—Johnny Bower, Don Simmons, Carl Brewer, Tim Horton, Allan Stanley, Bob Baun, Larry Hillman, Red Kelly, George Armstrong, Ron Stewart, Dave Keon, Billy Harris, Bob Pulford, Eddie Shack, Frank Mahovlich, Don McKenney, Andy Bathgate, Gerry Ehman, Ed Litzenberger, Al Arbour, Punch Imlach (manager-coach), Bob Haggert (trainer).

1964/65 *Montreal Canadiens* — Charlie Hodge, Lorne Worsley, Jacques Laperriere, Terry Harper, Jean-Guy Talbot, Jean-Claude Tremblay, Ted Harris, Noel Picard, Jean Beliveau, John Ferguson, Henri Richard, Claude Provost, Ralph Backstrom, Jim Roberts, Red Berenson, Claude Larose, Gilles Tremblay, Dick Duff, Bobby Rousseau, Yvon Cournoyer, Bryan Watson, Dave Balon, Gary Peters, Jean Gauthier, Sam Pollock (manager), Toe Blake (coach), Andy Galley, Larry Aubut (trainers).

1965/66 *Montreal Canadiens*—Lorne Worsley, Charlie Hodge, Jean-Claude Tremblay, Ted Harris, Terry Harper, Jacques Laperriere, Jean-Guy Talbot, Noel Price, Jean Beliveau, Ralph Backstrom, Dick Duff, Claude Larose, Yvan Cournoyer, Claude Provost, Bobby Rousseau, Henri Richard, Dave Balon, John Ferguson, Gilles Tremblay, Jim Roberts, Leon Rochefort, Toe Blake (coach), Sam Pollock (general manager), Andy Galley (head trainer) and Larry Aubut.

1966/67 *Toronto Maple Leafs*—Johnny Bower, Terry Sawchuk, Tim Horton, Allan Stanley, Bob Baun, Red Kelly, Marcel Pronovost, Larry Hillman, George Armstrong, Dave Keon, Bob Pulford, Eddie Shack, Frank Mahovlich, Ron Ellis, Pete Stemkowski, Larry Jeffrey, Mike Walton, Jim Pappin, Brian Conacher, Miles Marcetta, Aut Erickson, Punch Imlach (manager-coach), King Clancy (assistant manager), Bob Haggert (trainer), Tom Naylor (assistant-trainer).

1967/68 *Montreal Canadiens*—Lorne Worsley, Rogatien Vachon, Jean-Claude Tremblay, Ted Harris, Terry Harper, Jacques Laperriere, Serge Savard, Jean Beliveau, Ralph Backstrom, Dick Duff, Claude Larose, Yvan Cournoyer, Claude Provost, Bobby Rousseau, Henri Richard, John Ferguson, Gilles Tremblay, Mickey Redmond, Jacques Lemaire, Danny Grant, Carol Vadnais, Sam Pollock (manager), Toe Blake (coach), Larry Aubut and Eddy Palchak (trainers).

1968/69 *Montreal Canadiens*—Lorne Worsley, Rogatien Vachon, Jacques Laperriere, Jean-Claude Tremblay, Ted Harris, Serge Savard, Terry Harper, Larry Hillman, Jean Beliveau, Ralph Backstrom, Dick Duff, Yvan Cournoyer, Claude Provost, Robert Rousseau, Henri Richard, John Ferguson, Christian Bordeleau, Mickey Redmond, Jacques Lemaire, Lucien Grenier, Tony Esposito (spare goaltender), Claude Ruel (coach), Sam Pollock (general manager), Larry Aubut, Eddy Palchak (trainers).

1969/70 *Boston Bruins*—Gerry Cheevers, Ed Johnston, Bobby Orr, Rick Smith, Dallas Smith, Bill Speer, Gary Doak, Don Awrey, Phil Esposito, Ken Hodge, John Bucyk, Wayne Carleton, Wayne Cashman, Derek Sanderson, Fred Stanfield, Ed Westfäll, John McKenzie, Jim Lorentz, Don Marcotte, Bill Lesuk, Dan Schock, Harry Sinden (coach), Milt Schmidt (general manager), Dan Canney, John Foristall (trainers).

1970/71 *Montreal Canadiens* — Ken Dryden, Rogatien Vachon, Phil Myre, Terry Harper, Guy Lapointe, Jacques Laperriere, Jean-Claude Tremblay, Pierre Bouchard, Serge Savard, Jean Beliveau, Henri Richard, Jacques Lemaire, John Ferguson, Yvan Cournoyer, Rejean Houle, Frank Mahovlich, Peter Mahovlich, Leon Rochefort, Phil Roberto, Marc Tardif, Claude Larose, Bob Sheehan, Larry Pleau, Al MacNeil (coach), Sam Pollock (general manager), Eddy Palchak (trainer) and Phil Langlois.